EROTIC LOVE

THROUGH THE AGES

EROTIC LOVE

THROUGH THE AGES

by
'SARDI'

●

DORSET PRESS

New York

This edition published by Dorset Press,
a division of Marboro Books Corp.

1992 Dorset Press

ISBN 0-88029-990-8

Printed and bound in the United States of America

M 9 8 7 6 5 4 3 2

To

WALTER TAYLOR
and
'BOBBY' HUDSON

who walked with me
awhile
after the fashion of
Simon of Cyrene

CONTENTS

Love rules the court, the camp, the grove,
And saints above and men below,
For love is heaven,
And Heaven is love.

—*Sir Walter Scott*

———

Yet, love, mere love, is beautiful indeed
And worthy of acceptation. Fire is bright,
Let temple burn, or flax; an equal light
Leaps in the flame from cedar-plank or weed:
And love is fire. And when I say at need
I *love thee* . . . mark ! . . . I *love thee*—in thy sight
I stand transfigured, glorified aright,
With conscience of the new rays that proceed
Out of my face toward thine. There's nothing low
In love, when love the lowest: meanest creatures
Who love God, God accepts while loving so.
And what I *feel*, across the inferior features
Of what I *am*, doth flash itself, and show
How that great work of Love enhances Nature's.

— From " Sonnets from the Portuguese "
by *Elizabeth Barrett Browning*.

CHAPTER 1

MATRIARCHY AND SEX TABOOS

The Stone Age and the Pastoral Period—Aurignacian, Magdalenian, and Ice Ages—Fertility, Phallic, and Mother Cults—Matriarchy or ' Jus Maternum '—Promiscuity, Polygamy, Polygyny, and Polyandry —Kaleidoscope of Matriarchal Societies—Husband plays Inferior Role—Wife's Brother controls Matrilineal Household—Inheritance through Mother's Line—Incest Taboo and Exogamy—Endogamy : Marriage within the Clan—Exogamy : Marriage outside the Clan— Women capture Husbands—Sexual Freedom and Sexual Taboos— Free Love in the ' Bukumatula '—Totemism and Exogamy—Totem : Common Clan-Ancestor—Horror of Incest among Savages analysed —Totemism and the Œdipus Complex—Prohibition on eating or killing the Totem-Animal—Feasting on the Totem-Animal—Incest Taboo as Atonement for Communal Guilt.

THE most powerful instinct that man shares with other inmates of the animal kingdom is the sexual urge. While in many respects, such as the wearing of clothes or the preparation of food, *homo sapiens* surpasses the lower forms of animal existence, his sexual life is, at times, less exemplary than theirs. Amongst animals, the sex instinct almost wholly serves the purpose of reproduction as animals mate only in the rutting season. Courtship among birds and beasts is customary, the male of the species assuming his showiest colours and lordliest mien as in the case of the peacock preening himself before the peahen. Forcing the partner into sexual union is physiologically impossible, so that rape remains man's doubtful privilege shared only with a single species of spider as N. I. Berrill points out in his **Sex and the Nature of Things**.

Certain sexual practices and anomalies, such as masturbation and homosexuality, also appear in animal life, but to an extremely limited extent. Man alone, with his imagination and lust for life, has put the sexual urge to various uses quite apart from procreation, in both his heterosexual or normal relations and his deflections from the norm, and mostly in the pursuit of sensual gratification. It is these erotic meanderings that make his sex-life, if not always meritorious, at least

1

interesting, though it must be admitted that certain of his practices tend to be nauseating, particularly when they wander into psychopathic bypaths.

The Stone Age and the Pastoral Period

Little is known of the prehistoric men of the Palæolithic or Stone Age; hence they are named after such places as betray traces of their origin. A study of fossil bones and their anatomy, the nature of their implements, and the geology of the places where their remains are first discovered, furnish but a shadowy silhouette. Naturally, little is known of their sex-lives. Did promiscuity reign supreme among them, or did they abide by horde-laws? Only bold hypotheses can furnish answers to such questions.

The discovery of pottery, statuettes, and cave paintings, provides some clue at least in respect of the place of woman in prehistoric society. In the last century, statuettes representing human figures, in size about the span of a hand, were found in the northern part of Spain and in the south of France. Most of them were reckoned to belong to the Aurignacian Age (of the Palæolithic Epoch). What is noteworthy is that the majority of the statuettes depict the female form generally with voluptuous features such as wide hips, buxom breasts, steatopygous thighs and buttocks, and, of course, with emphasis on the sexual organ and the stomach. In the first decade of the present century, at Willendorf on the Danube, was discovered the sandstone figure of a nude woman which is reckoned to be the oldest existing representation of her sex, dating back some 20,000 years, in a spot where the bones of palæolithic animals were also found. As with the earlier finds, the proportions are ample with the organs of reproduction over-emphasised. The breasts and hips are full, and the thighs heavy though not quite steatopygous. Adornments round the figure's arms and head suggest that then, as now, the lily required gilding.

Like her predecessors, the statuette was dubbed a Venus. Says Richard Lewinsohn* in his excellent and valuable work, **A History of Sexual Customs**: " It is not surprising that, though they named her Venus, man regarded this ancestress with consternation. Up to that date people had pictured prehistoric Eve as a fascinating beauty. Each age depicted her according to its own taste. The Eve of the Early Middle Ages, which were still influenced by the Roman ideal of beauty, was rather broad and heavy. In the Gothic period she was over-slender, with seductive eyes and theatrical poses. In the

---

* When an author is quoted for the first time in a chapter, the name of the work from which the quotation has been taken will be mentioned; if in the same chapter he is again quoted from the same work, the title will not be repeated, but if from a different work, the name of it will be given alongside the writer's own name, which, in either case, will always be mentioned.

Renaissance she was a generously-built, high-bosomed, symmetrically-proportioned woman, almost too noble to perform her mission . . . Whether created for the purpose of a religious cult or not, she was the work of an artist who was capable of observation, though concerned not with a portrait but with a female type. If this type bore even the remotest resemblance to her contemporaries' ideal of beauty, sex life in the palæolithic age must have been quite unerotic, for this Venus was no more than a lump of fat, and surely far from attractive to any man; no fertility symbol, but a matron deformed by child-bearing . . . " To this strange revulsion Lewinsohn displays, the only answer can be in the French idiom, *chacun a son goût*.

Palæolithic sculptures and bas-reliefs display an anatomical fidelity particularly by depicting the Mount of Venus by a triangular *cunus*. However, the emphasis is undoubtedly on the copulatory rather than the reproductive aspect, and the artists were, obviously, men; which leads Lewinsohn to declare: "This gives even humanity's earliest artistic manifestations the aspect of a woman-cult." He goes on to refute the nineteenth century theory that these representations bore a magical-religious significance and that the palæolithic Venuses were fertility cult symbols, on the ground that while the statuettes make the subjects appear to be pregnant, there is not a single mother-and-child representation amongst them. This is probably because the hunters of the Stone Age, for ever on the move, did not value children; one would imagine infanticide was common enough among them as too many children would have been an encumbrance during their wanderings.

In the Magdalenian Age which followed the Aurignacian, living conditions were harder and the men busy with the hunt. This period produced many paintings in caves, most of them showing hunting scenes. Then the Mesolithic or Middle Stone Age set in when men deserted the ice-bound and uninhabitable parts of northern Europe for warmer climes in the south. The Ice Age, which lasted approximately four thousand years, came to an end in about 12,000 B.C. The great monsters that had roamed the earth had not survived the intense cold, and the age of the huntsman gave way to the age of the tiller of the soil. Grain and fruit replaced, for a large part, animal fat as man's diet.

It is with the early beginnings of agriculture, or the Pastoral Period, that communities started to be formed and horde-laws came into being. As the life of the peasant depended on the fertility of the soil, and the latter on the elements, a parallel was obviously drawn between the productivity of the earth and human reproduction. Seed was necessary for planting so that it might yield grain. Hence seed and grain, wind and rain, everything conducive to fertility, became deified, and the rich earth that fed her children earned the name of Mother. These were the beginnings of Nature Worship which persisted even among the highly civilised Aryans of ancient India from whom is descended the modern Hindu, and also among the Greeks and the Romans. The Aryans of *Arya-varta* or Land of the Aryans as India was then called, had their Indra or god of thunder, Varuna or god of rain; the Scandinavians had Thor or god of thunder and agriculture; the Romans their Flora or goddess of flowers; and the Greeks, Persephone or goddess of Spring, to take but random examples of nature deities from the inexhaustible storehouse of world mythology.

Nature fertility cults led to analogous worship of the creative aspects of human life. The Phallic cult persisted even in civilised societies; the early Hindus started the worship of the *lingam* or phallus of the god Shiva, and the Greeks and Romans had their own ithyphallic gods. Erotic love came to be enthroned in the hearts of men right into the classical periods, and every civilised country had its god of love. In Greece, there was Eros; in India, Kama; in Rome, Cupid. In each of these countries, the god was represented as a boy with a bow and arrow aimed at the hearts of mortals. Similarly, there were the goddesses of love, the Venus of Rome, the Greek Aphrodite, and India's Prajapati. Then there were the goddesses identified as mother-figures: Ishtar of the Babylonians, Cybele of the Phrygians, Rhea of the Cretans, Anaïtis of the Persians, Ceres of the Romans, Astarte of the Phœnicians, and down to our own time, the Virgin Mary of the Christians.

But we are anticipating events, for these myths belong to the annals of classical times, whereas we are still dealing with the beginnings of human society. There is, alas, no safe bridge between prehistoric and historic times. However, certain ideas and concepts have percolated through and remain with us to this day. Hence it is vital to trace them to their source to comprehend the place of man and woman in society, the relative importance granted the two sexes, and, above all, the growth of the family.

Matriarchy or 'Jus Maternum'

In the Stone Age, it would appear, woman probably had greater equality with man than she has had since. It is very likely that her entire system, respiratory and muscular, was, in those primitive conditions, far hardier than in subsequent times. While the man went out hunting, she did productive work such as gardening and pottery, and even carried burdens while on the move in the nomadic existence that was the lot of primitive man in pre-pastoral times, while the man kept his hands free for tackling aggressors and wild animals.

One of the reasons why palæolithic pictures and bas-reliefs do not depict a mother-and-child device, is that in nomadic times, though perpetuation of the species was of primary importance, children were not greatly valued as they added to the tribulations of a wandering life. Hence, as already observed, infanticide and neglect of children were most probably rampant. Child-bearing must have hampered the woman considerably; even so, the importance of her economic role among the tribal hordes seems to have been recognised, and she appears to have enjoyed a great measure of equality with the man.

When the nomads eventually settled down to a pastoral existence, and primitive man found himself more or less free of the former intense struggle against hostile forces, he began to organise the community and to introduce codes of behaviour. Collective ownership of land having been established, the clan became aware of itself and its existence as a group; thus it felt deeply the need for posterity to carry on the inheritance of the land and the survival of the name of the clan whose totemic ancestor was highly revered. Children now came into their own, for, through them, the clan could achieve transcendence.

Opinions are divided as to whether general promiscuity constituted the common practice amongst these prehistoric clans, or whether polygamy* prevailed. Whichever the case, the need for children converted maternity into a sacred office, and woman—the vehicle of propagation of the species—was placed on a pedestal.

If promiscuity existed, then it is obvious that the paternity of the child could not be exactly ascertained. If even a form of monogamy was then the rule, paternity was not attributed to the human father but rather to ancestral spirits, for these tribes were ignorant of the role of the male in procreation and attributed fatherhood to external forces such as these, which, they imagined, entered the woman either through the vagina or even other orifices such as the mouth or ears. This accounts for virginity not being highly prized, but considered rather a hindrance, and for defloration not being normally effected by the chosen mate. Thus whilst paternity remained a dubious factor, maternity was a proven fact. Hence woman's position assumed tremendous importance. A kind of ' gynæcocracy ' came into being and matriarchy held sway. The mother was the hub around which revolved the family and the rights of inheritance. For this reason, the children belonged to the clan of the mother and bore her clan's name. Property, too, was handed down through her.

Pastoral man viewed with awe the fecundity of the soil and the shoots of grain that burgeoned under his furrow. Similarly, the woman's fertility was also a cause of marvel to him. Both the grain and the human mother's offspring seemed to him not products of creation, but rather the emanations of mysterious nature conjured as if by magic. Woman was the life and soul of the community. She participated in making the earth yield its riches of grain and corn; she did gardening; she tended to the children, and to the herd and

---

* *It should be carefully noted that the term* polygamy *applies, in general, to* both *plurality of wives or husbands. When the sense is restricted to a man having more than one wife, the proper term is* polygyny, *while the custom of a woman having more than one husband is called* polyandry. *Thus polygamy is a comprehensive term for both polygyny and polyandry. These terms will be used in their correct sense throughout this work.*

the flock; she made pottery, wove fabrics as domestic industry evolved, and even handled the bartering of goods. Man bowed to her apparent magical powers and raised her to the position of a mother-goddess. All fertility and mother-cults of future ages had their origins in this early worship of the woman.

In the Hindu epic, **The Ramayana,** Sita, the proverbial ideal of Hindu womanhood, is born miraculously of a field-furrow. When, after sharing her husband's vicissitudes in exile, and proving her chasity through ordeal by fire, he again calls upon her, in later years, to give renewed proof of her untarnished honour, she invokes her mother, the earth, to take her back to her bosom, and the earth, yawning, receives her child back into the womb whence she came. This myth, combining the fertility and mother cults of olden days, elaborates the role of Sita, who, in the **Rig Veda** or Hindu Book of Hymns, is the goddess of the field-furrow bearing crops for men, the equivalent of the Roman corn-goddess, Ceres. Similarly, other cults of the mother-goddess grew and flourished such as Egypt's cult of Isis, the Greek adoration of Cybele, and the Phœnician worship of Astarte. Greek mythology presents us with matriarchal mothers such as Medea and Niobe who enjoy a very exclusive relationship with their children. The Virgin Mary, as already mentioned, embodies the latest mother cult which is a modern relic of the ancient ones.

In the nineteenth century, an essentially patrist period, considerable controversy was aroused on the theory of *jus maternum* as propounded by a Swiss jurist, Johann Jakob Bachofen in his work **Das Mutterrecht.** He denied man's superiority over woman, and disclaimed any intention on the part of nature to appoint man as head of the family, which place, he claimed, was woman's natural right that man has usurped from her. He furnished instances of matrist societies such as that of the Lydians, among whom, as Herodotus has described, the men took the names of their mothers' families. He brought forward similar evidence regarding antiquity, as well as modern primitive tribes, amongst whom family names and inheritance are through the mother's line if the communities are matrilineal.

The transition from matriarchal rule to *jus paternum* or patrist society in which nomenclature and inheritance pass from father to son, was aptly described by Lewis N. Morgan, an American ethnologist, in his work, **The League of the Iroquois.** He assumed that the promiscuity of the primitive hordes had been replaced, among organised tribes of hunters, by group marriages in which exogamy, *i.e.,* marriage outside the parental group, was obligatory, but was strictly a collective and not an individual affair. Hence, as in a group marriage paternity could not be ascertained, the mother was the link with the future, and it was through her that inheritance was decided.

Morgan went on to explain that, with advanced production, when a man and a woman were able to set themselves up economically without depending on collective aid, monogamy became a reality and private property assumed primary importance. The man became the chief bread-winner, and with the increase of economic power concentrated in his hands, his wife became his chattel. Thus, while in a patrist society a man got off lightly with lapses from the established moral code, particularly the sexual mores, the woman was severely punished for such lapses, as in the case of adultery.

Socialists such as Karl Marx and Friedrich Engels welcomed Morgan's theory and used it to bolster their fight on behalf of the emancipation of women. " But while these theories became the commonplace of ' educated ' society," Lewinsohn tells us, " the specialists brought up heavier artillery, and made one breach after another in this artificial doctrinal structure. That traces of *jus maternum* are to be found among many primitive peoples, and also among peoples of antiquity, especially in Greece and Rome, is undeniable. But one must distinguish between ' matrilinear ' and ' matriarchal '. That origin is traced through the mother is no proof that the woman was the ruler of the family, and still less of the tribe. If one surveys the mass of archæological and ethnological material, pure matriarchy seems to be the exception rather than the rule. Where women were really recognised as rulers, there was generally a man behind them who exercised the effective power; if not the woman's husband, then her brother."

The customs of matrilineal societies among modern primitive tribes support the foregoing statement. The novelist, Simone de Beauvoir, in her instructive and essentially poetic work, **A History of Sex,** says much the same thing:

" . . . in truth, the Golden Age of Woman is only a myth . . . Earth, Mother, Goddess—she was no fellow creature in man's eyes; it was *beyond* the human realm that her power was affirmed, and she was therefore *outside* of that realm. Society has always been male; political power has always been in the hands of men . . .

" For the male it is always another male who is a fellow being . . . ' The reciprocal bond basic to marriage is not set up between men and women, but between men and men by means of women, who are only the principal occasion for it,' says Lévi-Strauss. The actual condition of women has not been affected by the type of filiation (mode of tracing descent) that prevails in the society to which she belongs; whether the system be patrilineal, matrilineal, bilateral, or non-differentiated . . . she is always under the guardianship of the males. The only question is whether the woman after marriage will remain subject to the authority of her father or of her elder brother —an authority that will extend also to her children—or whether she will become subject to that of her husband . . . The fact is that the relations of two groups of men are defined by the system of filiation, and not the relation between the sexes . . . "

With the dethronement of woman, the female deities that had reigned supreme in various lands toppled, giving way to male deities.

Thus Isis, though not losing her place in the Egyptian hierarchy of gods and goddesses, is yet outshone by Ra, the sun-god; Zeus ousted the divinity of Rhea, and in Babylonia, Ishtar became merely the spouse of the god Bel-Marduk who, of course, outdazzled her.

The patriarchate might have relinquished part of its rights to woman, from time to time; but, in the main, throughout mankind's known history, the reins have always been in male hands. The matrilineal regime is, of course, not entirely dead, but it exists among tribes that have remained almost as primitive as their ancestors, and where woman is feared for the magical qualities attributed to her rather than revered. It is such primitive societies that we shall now examine.

Kaleidoscope of Matri-archal Societies

In North America, among the Pueblo Indians of the South West, is a tribe called the Zuni that still adheres to the matrilineal system. The owners of the household are the female members of the family. When the women marry, they do not leave their home, but rather do their husbands come to live in their midst. These husbands, of course, have their rightful place in the homes of their mothers or their sisters, and it is their wives' brothers who, though married into other clans, owe fealty to the homes into which these men have married, and these brothers-in-law return frequently to perform the religious functions of the household. It is not the husbands but their brothers-in-law who act as advisers to the wives.

In a matrilineal society, men, of course, owe a double allegiance: Their wives, their mothers-in-law, and they themselves, form an economic unit to which they contribute their labour and its produce such as corn. But while their contribution is to the economy of the household into which they are married, they are outsiders in the ceremonial group, owing fealty to the household gods of their blood-relationship group on the female side, i.e., to the maternal home or that of their sisters. Their standing as husbands in their wives' homes is of small consequence till the children are grown up and pay respect to them, not as bread-winners, but as fathers; yet, as brothers in the home to which they are bound by blood ties, they have considerable prestige.

In her **Patterns of Culture,** Ruth Benedict gives us yet another glimpse of a matrilinear tribe, this time the Dobuans who live on Dobu Island in a group off New Guinea. Their matrilineal line is called the *susu,* and inheritance is through the female. Amongst these dangerous and warring people, the prospective husband is treated as a rank out-sider. He serves an apprenticeship of about a year during which he becomes a servant of his future wife's parents, and is put to work by his mother-in-law shoving a stick into his hand and commanding him to labour in the garden. He is not even permitted to share his meals with his in-laws, but must carry on working while they eat.

The apprentice husband also labours for his own family household. On marriage, he and his wife are provided with a common room where they enjoy strict privacy. They cultivate their own gardens, a separate one for each partner. However, they can labour together in them and pool the food. But as the husband owes labour allegiance to his female blood-relations as well, this common-room and garden are set up one year in the wife's village, and the next in the husband's, thus alternating right through their married lives. Among this aggressive tribe, each partner in marriage is an alien in the other's village and is not very welcome there. When marital quarrels occur, the outsider finds not merely the in-laws but practically the entire village in an organised opposition against him. Whenever there is a betrothal and gifts are exchanged, the alien spouse must not be on the scene, thus being treated perpetually as an Ishmaelite.

The most heartless custom of this matrilineal tribe we must leave Ruth Benedict to describe in her own words: " As soon as the marriage is dissolved by death, or whenever the father dies even though the father and mother have separated for years before, all food from the father's village, every bird, or fish or fruit, becomes strictly tabu to his children. Only during his lifetime they eat it without hurt . . . In similar fashion, at the father's death the children are forbidden entry into his village. That is, as soon as the exigencies of the marital alliance no longer have to be considered, the mother's village claims them to the exclusion of any contact with the outlawed line. When as adults or old people they must carry food to the village of their father in a ritual exchange, on the outskirts they stand motionless with bowed head while others take their burdens into the village The village of one's father is called ' the place of bowing one's head ' . . . "

Matrilocal custom deprives the man of all rights of ownership which are the wife's sole prerogatives. It is her lot, as holder of the purse-strings, to supervise all work connected with the household and family property. She often actively participates in the daily toil, while the husband tends the herd or goes hunting or warring. He even assumes her name just as in patriarchal society the woman takes on her husband's name. Such matriarchal supremacy exists amongst the Hemitic tribes of North Africa. It is the woman who, among them, selects her spouse and conducts the courtship. Should she, after marriage, be drawn to a more attractive male, she can divorce her spouse, but should he be reluctant to be thus treated, he is cavalierly dismissed. The husband, on the other hand, cannot divorce his wife. As the matriarch's eldest brother is her chief adviser, often he is better treated than the husband.

We shall later deal with marriage by capture in patriarchal society. But this custom also exists, in reverse, among the Khassi tribe of

Assam. The woman often has the man on whom she has set her cap
abducted, and he has to put up a show of resistance before he is
eventually captured, in the same way as a captive bride has to defend
herself against her abductors.

The inferior position of the husband in a matriarchate becomes
evident in David Livingstone's description of the Banyai in the region
of the Zambesi. We are told that the husband is bound to his mother-
in-law to carry out certain tasks, one of which is to provide her with
firewood. The most humiliating rule is that he must approach her
on his knees so as not to affront her dignity by pointing his feet at
her ! In the event of his wishing to forego such abject behaviour,
he is free to return to his family but cannot take his children with him
as they are the property of his wife.

A strange kind of matriarchate exists among the Kasa and Osage
tribes. In his informative work, **Strange Customs of Courtship and
Marriage,** William J. Fielding describes it thus: " Upon the marriage
of the eldest daughter . . . she became the mistress of the maternal
home and her parents were subordinate to her. Her sisters as they
grew up, became the wives of the same husband. A great chief was
usually attended by one or two wives who looked after his establishment, but the majority of his spouses remained with their own
relatives, and the husband visited them as he pleased."

Similarly, we are told that among the Caribbean tribes the women
continued to be members of the parental home even after marriage,
and the polygynous husband would visit, in turn, each of his several
wives and cohabit with her in her mother's home. Again, among
certain Malayans, neither partner in marriage leaves his or her matriarchal home. Unlike the custom of the matriarchates previously
described, this one does not even hold the husband responsible for the
maintenance of his wife and the children of his loins. His attachment
is more to to his mother's or his sister's home in which he acts as
administrator of the family estate. However, the family wealth
remains in the hands of his sister. On his death, anything owned by
him passes on to his sisters and brothers, and after them, to the
children of the former. His wife and the children of his blood would
have no claims on his worldly goods.

Fielding is indeed a mine of information on matrilocal customs.
From him one learns that in some matrist societies even the men have
something to gain out of marriage. Thus, among the aborigines of
Vancouver, " . . . the new husband acquired hunting and fishing
rights over his wife's property . . . " If the couple separated, the
ownership reverted to the wife and became, one presumes, an induce-
ment to marriage for another prospective partner. We are told that
in British Columbia, the Kwakiutl tribes permitted the husband the
luxury of owning his own wife and removing her from the matriarchal
roof provided that, after three months of dwelling under it himself, he

paid the family for her.   A bride-price such as this exists even in patriarchal societies.

Unbelievable though it may sound, the Khasi tribe of Assam appoint a woman as a pontiff (pope), and when she dies, the office passes on to one of her female relatives. The maternal line inherits the family possession from mother to daughter. It is understandable that among all matrist societies the birth of a girl is a joyful event, whereas a boy causes the same disappointment as the female child often does in patrist communities. Similarly, infanticide would claim more male than female children.

Having dealt with the matriarchate as it exists today among some primitive tribes, it is interesting to glance back to ancient civilisations which gave woman an honourable if not always domineering position. About half a century before Christ, daughters played an important role in Egyptian family life.   In their old age, the parents turned to the daughter for support. The bridegroom had even to promise to obey his wife !   This is not as surprising as it at first sounds, considering that women did the wooing.   Similarly, women took the initiative in love and romance among the Lydians, as reported by Herodotus.   Even Manu, the Indian law-giver, bequeathed on the female the right to select her partner—a right hardly ever exercised, one would imagine, in the predominantly patriarchal society that India became.

In most matriarchies, the woman's legal position is sounder than that of the man.   A veritable form of slavery awaits the husband among the Balonda tribe of Africa. He is not merely at his wife's beck and call, but also has to render service to her mother. The poor man cannot move a step without first obtaining his wife's sanction to do this or that. In return, of course, she must help him to keep body and soul together.

From the anthropologist Bronislaw Malinowski's work, **Sex and Repression in Savage Society,** we learn that in North Eastern New Guinea the Trobriand Islanders are matrilineal and monogamous, except for the chiefs who are polygynous. " To begin with," says the author, " the husband is not regarded as the father of the children in the sense in which we use this word; physiologically he has nothing to do with their birth, according to the ideas of the natives, who are ignorant of physical fatherhood. Children, in native belief, are inserted into the mother's womb as tiny spirits, generally by the agency of the spirit of a deceased kinswoman of the mother. Her husband has then to protect and cherish the children, to ' receive them in his arms ' when they are born, but they are not ' his ' in the sense that he has had a share in their procreation.

" The father is thus a beloved, benevolent friend, but not a recognised kinsman of the children.   He is a stranger, having authority through his personal relations to the child, but not through his sociological position in the lineage. Real kinship, that is identity of substance, ' same body ', exists only through the mother. The authority over the children is vested in the mother's brother . . . Her children are . . . his only heirs and successors . . . At his death his worldly goods pass into their keeping, and during his lifetime he has to hand over to them any special accomplishment he may possess—dances, song myths, magic, and crafts. He also it is who supplies his sister and her household with food, the greater part of his garden produce going to them. To the father, therefore, the children look for loving care and tender companionship. Their mother's brother represents the principle of discipline, authority, and executive power within the family.

"The bearing of the wife towards her husband is not at all servile. She has her own possessions and her own sphere of influence, private and public. It never happens that the children see their mother bullied by the father. On the other hand, the father is only partially the bread-winner, and has to work mainly for his own sisters, while the boys know that when they grow up they in turn will have to work for their sisters' households."

We have quoted Malinowski at length because his is surely the most graphic picture of a matriarchal household. But among the Trobrianders, whose case he cites, marriage is not matrilocal as in most matrist societies, but rather patrilocal, *i.e.*, the wife forsakes her home and goes with her husband to his. Hence their children grow up as aliens with no property rights in the community in which they are brought up, their own rights and fealty being vested in their mother's home.

It will be readily understood that just as in a patrist society the men attempt to concentrate in their own hands the monopoly of power by legal sanction, so in matrist communties the women do likewise. Women among the Iroquois Indians enjoy equal suffrage with men on the village council; they can make and unmake chiefs; divorce their husbands as they wish, and be the sole arbiters of disposal of family property.

While women suffer limitations of sexual freedom in a patriarchal society, in a matriarchate they enjoy complete sexual independence. They can indulge in promiscuous love affairs to their hearts' content, but should their husbands stray, they are severely punished for their adulterous conduct by the women of the tribe. The man himself cannot raise a murmur against his wife's wanton behaviour with other men.

Incest Taboo
and Exogamy

Matrilineal society has a horror of incest, *i.e.*, sexual relations between near kin or even between members of the same clan. Hence endogamy or marriage outside the clan is insisted upon. Almost from childhood brothers and sisters are kept apart. The taboo operates right into adulthood, and though the brother is really the head of his sister's house and responsible for the welfare of her family, yet between him and her there can be no sentimental attachment of even a fraternal kind. He serves merely as a counsellor and guide and provider of her household. She respects him and even bows before him as before a chief. He exercises authority over her children who will, one day, be his successors. In the Melanesian matriarchate he is called *kada*.

Owing to the existing brother and sister taboo, no allusion to sex in connection with either is ever made. Between them a veil is drawn so far as each other's love affairs are concerned. Even the grown-up brother who plays so important a role in his sister's family life has no part in the selection of her husband. This is one responsibility which matrilinear society places on the shoulder of the father who is bound to assist his wife in finding a suitor for their daughter. The incest prohibition spreads over most female relatives from the mother's side, but it is directed with marked emphasis against the sister. It is very likely that, as Malinowski observes, "This taboo also, since it makes even an accidental contact in sexual matters a crime, causes the thought of the sister to be always present, as well as consistently repressed." This must result in the matrilinear counterpart of the Œdipus Complex in patriarchal society, as will be presently explained.

In matrilineal society, the father-son relationship is amicable, and there is no rivalry, as no economic influence or paternal authority is vested in the father, nor does the boy ever see the latter treat his mother with brutality or arrogance as so often happens in a patriarchate. But the maternal uncle's position in the matriarchate is analagous to the father's in patriarchal society, as it is the mother's brother who exercises economic control and parental authority over the matriarchal household, so that resentment of his economic power becomes crystallised in the boy against the uncle. However, the boy's ambivalent sexual envy is not over the mother as the maternal uncle's relationship with his own sister is distantly benevolent rather than affectionate owing to the brother-sister taboo, but rather over the boy's own sister, for the maternal uncle wields parental authority, bound up with an element of emotional ambivalence, over his niece. It can now be understood how the Œdipus Complex of the patriarchate, with its envy of the father and the repressed wish to kill him and marry the mother, is replaced, in the matriarchate, with jealousy of the maternal uncle and the desire to kill him and marry the sister.

The taboo against any incipient emotion for the sister undoubtedly accounts for the Matrilineal Complex if we may thus call it. Extreme measures are taken to enforce the taboo. We learn from Sigmund Freud's classic, **Totem and Taboo,** that in New Mecklenburg the restriction is extended to cover cousins as well, who may address each other only from a distance, and never exchange gifts or shake hands. If incest is committed with a sister, it is punished with death by hanging. It is not surprising to learn that such extreme measures serve to bring about deliberate defiance of the taboo. Thus we learn that in Fiji, where such rules are particularly stringent, orgies occur in which coitus or sexual intercourse takes place precisely among kindred falling into the forbidden degrees of blood-relationship.

Sexual Freedom and Sexual Taboos

Mostly in the interests of keeping incest from their doors, matriarchal communities are very liberal in allowing the growing children easy sexual outlet. The danger of concupiscence between brothers and sisters, or cousins, is overcome by an institution known as the *bukumatula* among the Trobriand Islanders. There are quite a few of these ' club-houses ' to which repair unmarried male adolescents with their sweethearts. Each *bukumatula* houses up to four couples or so, and is run by a male adult, either a bachelor or a widower, who is the nominal owner of the house which is, in actuality, owned by all the youths who share it. This, of course, leads to the family breaking up early, but the boys and girls do go to their homes for food, and often labour for their parents.

In a Trobriand village, the *bukumatula* are found in the inner ring in the midst of huts belonging to the chieftan and his kinsfolk, and yam houses which have a sacred character. The *bukumatula* may be called a house of love. No compulsion binds a pair. The only code is nature's law of sexual attraction. Licence has no place here; mating is carried out in the dormitory without any attempt at either exhibitionism or lascivious scoptophilia by watching one another in the sexual act—degeneracies that ' civilisation ' tends to breed. No obligations and duties are involved except for temporary or permanent fidelity acording to the lovers' inclinations. A couple may extend their relationship into marriage or they may not as they wish.

This pre-nuptial cohabitation rules out propinquity as a brother and a sister would, naturally, not frequent the same *bukumatula* even with their respective partners. The dread of incest takes absurd forms. Thus when a boy in one of the islands of the New Hebrides goes home from his 'club-house' for food, should his sister be in, he must leave immediately. Should either of them detect each other's footprints, each must go another way to avoid the other. From puberty onwards, brother and sister do not even utter each other's names. As the boy grows up, the incest taboo makes his relationship with the sister a distant one indeed. Among the Battas of Sumatra, a son is not allowed to be in the same room as his mother, nor a daughter with her father.

Freud gives us many instances of the dread of propinquity among primitive tribes though not all are confined to matrilineal societies

However, while on the subject of incest, we may as well examine some of the other taboos:

" By far the most widespread and strictest avoidance (and the most interesting from the point of view of civilised races) is that which restricts a man's intercourse with his mother-in-law ", maintains Freud. Thus, we are told, among the Melanesians of the Banks' Islands, and in the Solomans, a man may not come near or speak to his wife's mother. If they meet by chance, he must disappear and must certainly give no sign of recognition. Among Eastern Bantus, a man must take precautions to avoid his mother-in-law. They must both shun each other during a chance encounter, " . . . she perhaps hiding behind a bush, while he screens his face with a shield. If they cannot avoid each other, and the mother-in-law has nothing else to cover herself with, she will tie a wisp of grass round her head as a token of cere-monial avoidance . . . " Certainly a very charming even if tedious custom.

All communication between the two is via an intermediary, but should such a one not be present, the two in-laws must shout at each other with, perforce, a barrier of some sort, such as a fence, dividing them. Freud tells us that among the Basoga tribe of the Bantus the son-in-law may speak to his wife's mother only when the older woman is not in the same room and therefore not within his view.

To us in civilised society, these taboos seem fantastic. Yet when one examines them carefully, they seem to contain a great deal of understanding of the complexities of the human mind and nature. Why is the mother-in-law such a figure of fun in advanced societies, and why do sons-in-law and daughters-in-law seldom hit it off with her ?

One is aware of the Narcissus Complex that causes parents to identify themselves with their children in whom they see a reflection of themselves, and through whose youth they often strive to relive their own. The mother in particular is known to do her best to make her daughter achieve an ambition she herself failed to realise, such as becoming an actress or marrying a title. It is not difficult to visu-alise such a mother identifying herself with her daughter, particularly if she is emotionally frustrated, and thus finding herself attracted to her son-in-law. He, in turn, may see in her many facets that attract him in his own wife, and perhaps even some pleasanter ones which may be missing in her daughter. This attraction becomes even stronger if the man in early adolescence has suffered, even slightly, from the Œdipus Complex drawing him to his mother. He now substitutes his wife's mother for his own, and the old complex rears its head in new guise, with the incest taboo not quite apparent as the mother-in-law is not related to him by blood but only through marriage.

It is the struggle in both son-in-law and mother-in-law to fight the attraction which society makes them consider ' unholy ', that results in the conflict between the two. Of course the same process may be

reversed in the case of a woman and her father-in-law, substituting for
the Œdipus Complex the Electra Complex which, during pubescence
or adolescence, may have caused her to be attracted to her own father
for whom the father-in-law may now serve as a substitute. Such cases
are, of course, not very common in civilised societies, but in rare cases
they do exist and create quite a few complications. Much commoner
is the case of the daughter-in-law not being able to pull on with her
husband's mother, and here it is easy enough to pin-point the causes:
the mother's extreme possessiveness and the son's mother-fixation
which may be a sublimation of the Œdipus Complex.

Totemism and Exogamy

What is a *totem*? Freud's entire work, **Totem and Taboo,** is
devoted to explaining totemism and the taboos that arise from it, as
well as the complexes resulting from them, with particular emphasis
on the fear of incest that seems to haunt primitive tribes. He takes
for his example the totemic aborigines of Australia, who, he claims,
are the most backward primitives still extant. We shall endeavour
to compress, in a very limited space, some of the theories Freud
propounds.

First of all, the totem is an animal, be it mild or aggressive,
edible or inspiring fear. It can also, but rarely, be a plant or a natural
element such as water. The important thing to note is that *the totem
is looked upon and revered as the clan's common ancestor.* It protects
its family like a guardian angel. It is strictly enjoined that *the totem
must never be killed or done away with,* and when, as usually, it is
a plant or animal, it must never be eaten. Every single member of the
clan is said to inherit the totemic character, and, at festivals, the clansmen often imitate the movements or the characteristics of their
particular totem.

When the tribal society is patriarchal, the totem is inherited
through the father; if matriarchal, then through the mother. It need
not be confined to one spot, that is to say the clansmen may live away
from their own clan in close proximity to other clans which have
other totems. However, far or near, *those who claim descent from
the same totem are considered to be blood-relations,* and the entire
clan is looked upon as a single family.

Just as in civilised society incest between near kin is looked upon
with horror and legally forbidden, so also in totemism is it marked
by a taboo or ban, but with this difference, that while in our society
the family is a comparatively small unit, and the incest taboo covers
only very near blood-relatives, often excluding first cousins though
not always, under totemism it spreadeagles the entire clan who are
all considered to be blood-relations. Hence sexual intercourse, and,
of course, marriage, within the clan, in other words, endogamy, is
forbidden, and exogamy or marriage outside the clan is made
compulsory.

Totemic blood-relationship poses a question: Is incest among these tribes merely totemic, *i.e.*, is it restricted to sexual relations only between persons of one clan so that the father or mother, whichever happens to belong to another clan as one of them must—which one depends on whether it is a matrilineal or patrilineal community—is free to commit natural incest with his or her children who belong to the opposite partner's clan? Freud would, at least at first, lead us to believe that such consanguineous, as opposed to clan, incest of a son or a daughter with the parent of another totem or clan is permissible, for he says: " Since totems are hereditary and not changed by marriage, it is easy to follow the consequence of the prohibition. Where, for instance, descent is though the female line, if a man of the Kangaroo totem marries a woman of the Emu totem, all the children, both boys and girls, belong to the Emu clan. The totem regulation will therefore make it impossible for a son of this marriage to have incestuous intercourse with his mother or sisters, who are Emus like himself." He then adds in a footnote: " On the other hand, at all events so far as this prohibition is concerned, the father who is a Kangaroo, is free to commit incest with his daughters who are Emus. If the totem descended through the male line, however, the Kangaroo father would be prohibited from incest with his daughters (since all his children would be Kangaroos), whereas the son would be free to commit incest with his mother. These implications of totem prohibitions suggest that descent through the female line is older than through the male, since there are grounds for thinking that totem prohibitions were principally directed against the incestuous desires of the son."

After, however, leading us to believe that such consanguineous, as opposed to totemic, incest with the parent of a different clan is permissible, Freud declares only two paragraphs later: " We see, then, that these savages have an unusually great horror of incest, or are sensitive on the subject to an unusual degree, and that they combine this with a peculiarity which remains obscure to us—of replacing real blood-relationship by totem kinship. This latter contrast must not, however, be too much exaggerated, and we must remember that *the totem prohibitions include that against real incest as a special case."* (Italics ours.) We can but assume that by 'real incest', Freud meant consanguineous and not clan incest, so that then, sexual intercourse between father and daughter, or mother and son, even when belonging to different clans, *would still constitute punishable incest.*

Why is a clansman taught to regard every other woman, apart from his consanguineous sister, as a blood sister, and, therefore, not a prospective wife? The origin of this taboo goes back to the days of group marriage, and it was obviously introduced to prevent group incest. Among the Trobriand Islanders, sexual relation between a clansman and a clanswoman of the same totem though not consanguineous, is termed *suvasova, i.e.,* a breach of the rule of exogamy or compulsory marriage outside the clan, and such a breach carries with it a penalty, amongst most savage tribes, most often death for both the

man and the woman, or in some cases the female is spared for fear
of her having been coerced; she is, nevertheless, brutally chastised
when not put to death. This taboo accounts for the speech of tribal
people in which every man or woman, of the same clan, is addressed
as ' brother ' or ' sister ', irrespective of consanguineity.

Horror of Incest analysed

From the foregoing it would appear that totemism and exogamy,
i.e., marriage outside the clan, are interlocked. However, there are
two schools of thought on this—one that claims that totemism and
exogamy are " . . . fundamentally distinct in origin and nature,
though they have accidentally crossed and blended in many tribes,"
as J. G. Frazer, author of **Totemism and Exogamy,** maintains, and
another that exogamy is the direct outcome of the basic principles of
totemism.   With the arguments of the two schools we are not concerned.   But before we end this chapter, Freud's ingenious explanation
of the reason for exogamy is worth examining.

The two main taboos of totemism, declares Freud, are avoidance
of incest and the need to refrain from destroying the totem—usually
an animal—which constitutes the father-figure revered as ancestor of
the clan.   The two totemic ordinances—*no incest and no killing of the
father*—are but counterparts of the two crimes of Œdipus: incest with
his mother Jocasta, and the killing of his father Laïus.

Freud quotes William Robertson Smith, physicist, philologist,
Bible critic, and archæologist, as declaring that an integral part of the
totemic system is the ' totem meal '.   There is no gathering of a clan
without an animal sacrifice.   The sacrificial animal of ancient religious
ritual is identified with the totem-animal.   Now, in the Pastoral Period,
the priest who made the sacrifice had often to flee as if to escape retri-
bution for the killing.   In classical Greece, when oxen were slaughtered
at the Athenian festival of Buphonia there was held a trial after the
sacrifice, and all those who had participated gave witness, in the end
all deciding that the blood-stained knife should bear the guilt and be
cast into the sea.

Robertson Smith came to the conclusion that a feature of the
totemic religion was the periodic *killing and eating* of the totem-animal
whose consumption, however, was forbidden at all other times.   Since
the individual could never kill the totem-animal, but only the entire
clan, the members shared collective responsibility which they exhibited,
after the totem meal, with moans and groans of regret at their guilt.

The totem-animal, we know, is a substitute for the father, being
looked upon as an ancestor.   Therefore by *collectively* killing and
consuming the beast, the clansmen sought to escape guilt yet to imbibe
some of the father-substitute's strength.   Thus restrengthened, and
having no longer to fear the dead father-substitute, they bewailed the
killing, and forbade the *individual* destruction of the totem-animal

as a kind of 'deferred' obedience to the dead father's wishes. The death of the father, as in the case of Œdipus's killing of Laïus, set the clansmen free to claim their clanswomen who were daughters of the totem-animal or clan-ancestor. But to escape the consequences of their murderous guilt, they voluntarily forfeited the prize—the daughters of their clan-ancestor, just as Œdipus remorsefully gave up the mother he had won after killing his father, and gouged out his own eyes by way of reparation. Thus exogamy or marriage outside of the clan crystallises the sacrifice of the clansmen of their right to possess the daughters of their clan, as a measure of atonement for killing and eating the totem-animal collectively.

Freud very aptly says: " They thus created out of their filial sense of guilt the two fundamental taboos of totemism, which for that very reason inevitably corresponded to the two repressed wishes of the Œdipus Complex. Whoever contravened these taboos became guilty of the only two crimes with which primitive society concerned itself."

The horror of incest, particularly between mother and son, is explained very well by Simone de Beauvoir: " . . . through menstrual blood is expressed the horror inspired in man by woman's fecundity . . . More vaguely, man finds it repugnant to come upon the dreadful essence of the mother in the woman he possesses; he is determined to dissociate these two aspects of femininity. Hence the universal law prohibiting incest expressed in the rule of exogamy or in more modern forms; this is why man tends to keep away from woman at the times when she is especially taken up with her reproductive role: during her menses, when she is pregnant, in lactation. The Œdipus Complex . . . does not deny this attitute, but on the contrary implies it. Man is on the defensive against woman in sofar as she represents the vague source of the world and obscure organic development."

And again: " But more often man is in revolt against his carnal state; he sees himself as a fallen god: his curse is to be fallen from a bright and ordered heaven into the chaotic shadows of his mother's womb. This fire, this pure and active exhalation in which he likes to recognise himself, is imprisoned by a woman in the mud of the earth. He would be inevitable, like a pure Idea, like the One, the All, the absolute Spirit; and he finds himself shut up in a body of limited powers, in a place and time he never chose, where he was not called for, useless, cumbersome, absurd . . . She also dooms him to death. This quivering jelly which is elaborated in the womb (the womb, secret and sealed like the tomb) evokes too clearly the soft viscosity of carrion for him not to turn shuddering away. Wherever life is in the making —germination, fermentation—it arouses disgust because it is made only in being destroyed; the slimy embryo begins the cycle that is completed in the putrefaction of death. Because he is horrified by needlessness and death, man feels horror at having been engendered; he would fain deny his animal ties; through the fact of his birth murderous Nature has a hold upon him."

CHAPTER 2

RIGOURS AND HUNGER OF THE FLESH

Primitive Man's Sexuality—Male Puberty Rites—Clitoridectomy— Female Puberty Rites and Menstrual Taboos—Akambas encourage Coitus during Menstruation—Chastity and Sexual Modesty—Nudity and Unashamedness—Nudity and Prudery—Nude Customs— Virginity: A Cult—Peruvian Virgin Sun-Brides—Vestal Virgins— Chastity Girdles symbolise Man's Possessiveness—Infibulation and Defibulation—Infibulation: Infallible Method of preserving Virginity —Defloration Customs: ' Jus Primæ Noctis' (Right of the First Night)—Public Defloration—Digital Defloration—Roman Method of Defloration on Ithyphallic Image of Tutunus or Priapus—Proof of Bride's Virginity on Bridal Night—Public Exhibition of Blood-stained Proofs—Woman: ' the Kernel, the Marrow '.

C IVILISED man—that strange admixture of sophistication and naïvety, prudery and debauchery, repression and excess, religiousness and agnosticism—is apt to despise the down-to-earth, closer-to-nature composition of primitive society and to deplore what he regards as the sexual gluttony of ' savages '. This ' holier than thou ' attitude, may, of course, be a defence mechanism to cover up his own inhibitions while subconsciously envying primitive man his spontaneous abandon. He also takes an exaggerated view of the virility and libido of the primitive, not pausing to think that, in actuality, the latter's sexuality is not stronger, but far more natural in the outlet it is allowed, than his.

A complex system of codes governs the social structure of aboriginal society. Civilisation's view of it is often one-sided. We are too apt to look upon primitive sexuality as being rooted in the distant past, and, therefore, as having become arrested at a certain stage in its development. For instance, we are inclined to think that the modesty and chastity we ostensibly prize are conspicuously missing from the sexual lives of backward peoples. But are the orgiastic rituals that admittedly occur among them any more shameful than the manner in which we titillate ourselves with strip-tease, nude shows, and the

20

Bacchanalian cavortings and perversions that are widely practised in sections of our own society?

Primitive man's sexuality is based on traditions which take cognizance of the fundamental needs of the sex urge, and rather than pretend as we do, out of notions of false prudery, that they do not exist and thereby create fresh inhibitions, they encourage and tend a healthy growth of the libido. With so much talk of sex education in the air, the present writer has come across numerous parents, many among his own friends, who ignore the factor of sexual curiosity among pubescents and adolescents, and discourage the reading of works that would enlighten the young, thus often laying in store for them an unhappy, and perhaps inhibited, sex-life. One does not, of course, wish to promote unrestricted licence, but a careful examination of the sexual customs of aborigines is very likely to open our eyes as to the defects inherent in our own priggish and puritanical approach to matters sexual.

Fernando Henriques makes some sage observations in his excellent sociological study of sex called **Love in Action** : " All individuals pass through phases of development from birth to death. These phases, depending upon the society, are either marked by elaborate rites and ceremonies, or emphasised in a moderate way, or partially ignored. For example, no people allows death to pass unnoticed—it is a time of crisis for those related to the dead person . . . Again marriage in a majority of societies is regarded as an event of major importance. It creates new social bonds and is the precursor of a new family . . . Of these phases of development adolescence is as much a time of crisis as death or marriage . . . "

Yet what do advanced societies do to guide and harness the energies of the young at the critical period of their youth ? The elders of society stand bewildered and disgruntled as they watch each decade produce its crop of irrepressible, and seemingly unfathomable, youngsters, be they Oxford hedonists of the 'nineties led by Walter Pater, the gay young things of the 'twenties, the Teds of the early 'fifties, or the beatniks of the late 'fifties and the 'sixties. The sap of the young coursing merrily through their veins impels them to exhibit their mounting energy which, undirected, finds an outlet in attitudinising.

Male Puberty Rites

In so-called savage society, puberty and adolescence are doorways through which the young pass to become respected—rather than despised as amongst us—members of their community. This is the time when their mettle is tested and a sense of their duty and responsibility to their tribe is inculcated in them before the mantle of manhood or womanhood is, so to say, wrapped around them. Initiation ceremonies and puberty rites mark the transition from childhood to adulthood. Such rites differ from tribe to tribe. Henriques gives us a fascinating account of the customs of circumcision for boys, and clitoridectomy for girls, among the Kipsigi tribe of Kenya.

A group of boys is placed under the care of an elderly man called the *pamango*, or father, who instructs them in preparation for their forthcoming initiation. In a hut, called the *menjit*, which the boys are made to build, the ceremony begins in the midst of revelry. Warriors sing and dance round a fire and even married women exult in sexual abandon. As dawn breaks, the boys are stripped to the buff inside the *menjit*. Two sponsors, called *motiryots*, now lead them to a corridor of sticks—a pathway of stinging nettles which they must traverse four times without a murmur. Each youngster is then taken to a dark corner and questioned as to whether he has had carnal knowledge of the opposite sex. There follows a little game with an *Arap Mogoss*, a man covered with monkey skins, who, the youth is told, will perform sodomy on him if he does not reveal the truth.

Before the actual ceremony, the boys are led to a fire which is supposed to contain the knife with which the circumcision is to be carried out, the young men being told that if they brave the fire they will emerge circumcised; however, they are not allowed to enter the flames. Each boy is then made to sit four times on a stool plastered with nettles, while his head is covered. Having passed the preliminary ordeals, the boys are lined up before the 'Elder of the Ceremony' on whom devolves the task of marking the spot where incision will be made on the foreskin. The boy is then made to look at a stick planted in the ground before him by a man of about his father's age standing behind him. Then either the Elder, or should he be feeble a man skilful in handling the circumcision-knife, lops off part of the marked foreskin, while the remaining portion is pulled over the *glans penis*, and secured with thorns on either side.

The initiate is not supposed to display any signs of pain. When undergoing this test, he wears an amulet given him by his chosen girl. If he passes the test with flying colours, she treasures it; if not, he must throw it away. However, this is the least humiliation for him who fails the test, for failure is followed by ostracism for his lack of courage and perhaps even banishment from the village.

Following the circumcision ceremony, the boy's hands are not to be used for eating as he is considered unclean; he must, therefore, use leaves to convey his food to his mouth, or pick up the food straight into his mouth. Other rites ensue and half a year goes by before his full initiation, after which he can indulge in sexual intimacy with maidens who are not taboo to him.

Girls have to submit themselves to the ceremony of clitoridectomy in which the clitoris is removed. The procedure leading up to the final cutting off of the clitoris is somewhat similar to that employed for the boys who take almost six months to recover from the effects of the severe tortures they have endured, often losing the power of sensible speech. Female circumcision probably has behind it the object of artificial defloration. Among the Aruntas of Australia the hymen is pierced and often the clitoris is cut away. On the other hand, in parts of Africa, the *labia minora* or inner lips of the vagina, are partly excised, as well as the clitoris, but the hymen is left intact. The most surprising custom is that of the Amazonian and North Peruvian tribes. Clitoridectomy is performed after a state of intoxication has been artificially induced in the girl. Then, for the purpose of defloration, a clay model, supposedly of the penis of her prospective spouse, is inserted into the vagina. She is now ready to be a bride.

Among the Züni tribe of New Mexico, the initiatory rites for young men seem to consist mostly of whipping. When a child enters a *kiva, i.e.,* the ceremonial chamber of one of six groups into which male tribal society is divided, masked 'gods' wield yucca whips on him in order to exorcise the forces of evil. If the child cries, the amiable Zuni do not take it amiss; rather do they look on it as an auspicious sign. When the boy is older, he receives a far severer whipping from the masked 'gods'.

After the 'scare *kachinas*' as the masked men are called, have administered the last whipping, four of them face four of the tallest boys who have been initiated. The *kachinas* now remove their masks, the boys signify horror at the revelation, and, in their turn, are made to whip their former tormentors as a reminder that they will have to initiate, likewise, the younger generation. While free to mimic the gods, the newly initiated boys can have masks made only when they marry. When a man does acquire such a mask, there is yet another whipping ceremony followed by a feast. In life, the mask is supposed to protect the man's home; in death, it is buried with him. The *kachina* priests have special masks to which many cult ceremonies are attached, and these masks are passed down the family line.

In South Africa, long sticks are used on the boys instead of whips. The novices are submitted to heavy blows from the sticks. In her **Patterns of Culture,** Ruth Benedict tells us that for the entire period of three months of initiation, not a drop of water must pass their lips, while the food given them is revolting. No matter how cold it may be, they must yet sleep naked, and not even attempt to squash the worms that sting them. On waking at dawn, they must plunge into a pool of cold water and remain submerged till sun-rise.

Endurance tests of fasting or lying sleepless, feats such as scalping an enemy, or the capture of big game and various other exploits are the striking rods of a youth's manhood. In the Cameroons, the initiation course for boys takes almost six months during which they live in the forest with the priests. At the end of the novitiate, a spear is thrust out of their hut to symbolise the death of their boyhood, and they are reckoned to have been swallowed by monsters. They are now resurrected in their newly-found manhood as indicated by their tattooed faces. Wearing banana girdles, they face their female counterparts who are similarly attired. The banana girdles are torn away and the couples mate, the boys no longer recognising their parents from then on.

The generally painful induction of the growing boy into savage society is, of course, a purely practical measure and the first major crisis in his life. On his powers of endurance and courage may rest the safety of his family, for at this level of society where man is exposed to threats from man and beast alike, he must be able to defend himself and put up with pain and hardship.

Female Puberty Rites and Menstrual Taboos

Female puberty rites often revolve round menstruation. There is either reverence for the menstruating woman or fear of her. Among Apache tribes it would seem that even the priests seek the blessing of the touch of girls who are just beginning their menstrual life. Illness, too, is considered to respond favourably to their magic touch. On the other hand, among Carrier Indians of British Columbia, menstruation is looked upon as a form of defilement. Accordingly, the first period is followed by a 'living burial', in other words, the girl is banished for some years to exist in a remote hut in the fields, being considered not merely dangerous to herself, but also to all and sundry. An animal skin is made to cover her face and breasts. Similarly, among the Tlingit Indians of the same region, the girl is isolated in a hut. The sun's light is not to shine on her face which is rubbed over with charcoal. Female relatives alone can visit her and supply her with previously masticated food. She must not even lie down but rest against logs.

These menstrual taboos are not confined to savage tribes. Even the civilised Zoroastrians of ancient Persia, the Hindus of Arya-varta, and the Greeks, considered a menstruating woman to be unclean. Henriques, on the authority of Verrier Elwin, mentions that the Laws of Manu of the Hindus laid down that a man becomes impure through touching "' . . . a menstruating woman, an outcast, a woman in childbed or a corpse . . . '"; also that "' . . . The wisdom, the energy, the strength, the sight, and the vitality of a man who approaches a woman covered with menstrual excretions utterly perish . . . '" Euripides, too, we are told, likened the uncleanness of a woman during her period as being akin to the impurity of a corpse. The sacred books of Zoroaster, prophet of ancient Persia, specifically pronounce menstruation as a fiend that "smites with a look . . . " During menstruation, the Zoroastrian woman dwelt in a special chamber, and at the end of her period, her clothes were done away with. If a man infringed the taboo, he received a flogging in public. This custom of segregation of a menstruating woman was still partially observed among the Zoroastrian Parsis of India till about a generation and a half ago.

In Central India, the Gonds isolated their menstruating women in huts far from view of the village. Food would be placed outside the huts. The post-menstrual period was entered into with rites of purification. Among the Kikuyus, a similar custom prevails, but should there be a violation of the taboo, the hut is destroyed. Some of the more drastic measures provide an interesting study.

The Guarani Indians of South America would fumigate the girl after her menstrual period by suspending her in a hammock over an open fire. Some tribes of Australian aborigines in Queensland adopt the cruel practice of sand burial with the sand reaching the poor menstruating woman's waist. Surrounded by a thorny bush fence, she would be fed by her mother, and she could scratch herself only with a stick but not with her hands. Among the Tahitians, the woman is not isolated but must keep herself apart from the family group. Among the Kikuyus, a breach of the menstruation taboo leads to destruction of the hut polluted by the woman's presence. Even the free and easy Hawaiians, and the rest of the Polynesians, dread the menstruating woman. She is sent to the *hale pea* or places of segregation, and even her own husband must come nowhere near her, nor any other man, as infringement of this taboo means death for him.

As a startling contrast, the Akambas of East Africa, instead of tabooing coitus during menstruation, as is generally the rule among savages as well as most civilised people, actually insist on the husband having sexual intercourse with his wife on the first night of her menstruation as the period is considered favourable to fecundity.

Matriarchal societies adopted an ambivalent attitude to menstruation, granting it both favourable and destructive powers. The use of the menstrual fluid in love potions was meant to increase the potency of its effect, yet menstruation was blamed for the failure or ruin of crops, or for lack of rain. Patriarchal society, naturally enough, attributed only evil powers to the menstrual period. Strange as it may seem, we learn from Simone de Beauvoir's **A History of Sex,** that the British Medical Journal declared in 1878 that " ' it is an undoubted fact that meat spoils when touched by menstruating women ' "; and in Northern France, at the turn of the century, women having ' the curse ' were kept away from the sugar refineries lest their touch should blacken the sugar. The authoress maintains that in France such ideas " . . . still persist in rural districts, where every cook knows that a mayonnaise will not be successful if a menstruating woman is about; some rustics believe cider will not ferment, others that bacon cannot be salted and will spoil under these circumstances. A few vaguely factual reports may offer some slight support for such beliefs; but it is obvious from their importance and universality that they must have had a superstitious or mystical origin."

Chastity and Sexual Modesty

Womanly chastity is a virtue that is greatly prized in civilised society in which it is a moral abstraction. Codes of morality, as we well know, differ from society to society; nor do they remain static in one particular society. Hence morality must be judged strictly in its own special environment rather than by standards alien, and perhaps repugnant, to it. The morality that attaches itself to chastity amongst civilised man is somewhat dubious. Is he really so interested in a woman's purity for its own sake, or is it more likely the desire for exclusive possession of a woman that leads to his exaggerated passion for chastity and virginity ?

For primitive man, chastity, where it exists and is not despised, is not an abstruse morality but a substantial factor contributing to the welfare of his tribe, whether in the matter of combatting the ills of nature such as famine and drought, or overcoming an enemy. Superstition involving belief in magic and its manifestations, good or evil, through human agencies, makes him esteem chastity as a placatory factor in interceding for the help of the world of spirits. This apart, there is, of course, the more practical value of chastity today, which, in more ancient times when marriage by capture was the normal mode of winning a bride, did not exist. Only when society had evolved and marriage by purchase reared its head, did pre-nuptial chastity assume the guise of a virtue, for it now carried with it a price.

Modesty, which is chastity's handmaiden, is the blush of the body, its expression of shyness and coyness. It is not an innate instinct, for were it so, children would be ashamed of their nakedness and attempt to conceal, rather than revel in it as they are known to do. It undoubtedly springs from social conditioning, and in earlier times, especially in the case of women, had its roots in fear. Prehistoric man, as we saw in the previous chapter, held the woman in awe, carried away as he was by the magic of her fecundity. However, woman, being weaker than the man, had and still has perforce to protect herself from his amorous advances when she does not crave them or considers them out of keeping with the social mores of the time.

It was precisely this dread of the aggressive male that led the woman to conceal the parts of her body that would serve as temptation to his libido, and expose her to his lust. If this feminine fear persists today, either in the conscious or the subconscious of the woman, it is because so-called civilised man often gives vent to his atavistic urges in the commission of rape and other sexual crimes.

" Modesty ", avers William J. Fielding in his **Strange Customs of Courtship and Marriage,** " is largely contingent upon the sense of vision. For this reason darkness greatly facilitates sexual indiscretion, often without a full realisation of any change in attitude, or without causing offence to the sense of modesty. In the dark, nakedness seems less naked, because the condition is no longer apparent to sight, but only to touch . . . shame becomes less intense when the observer is unable to see one's face and eyes and cheeks. The defensive mechanism of modesty tends to lose its effectiveness under the spell of darkness."

Thus in Shakespeare's tragedy, **Romeo and Juliet,** we have the ill-fated heroine expressing her modesty in Act II, Scene II:

" Thou knowst the mask of night is on my face,
Else would a maiden blush bepaint my cheek
For that which thou hast heard me speak tonight.
Fain would I dwell on form, fain, fain deny
What I have spoke; but farewell compliment ! . . . "

Various social cultures differ on their ideas of modesty, so that it becomes a mere convention. Women in many primitive societies think nothing of exposing their bare breasts to public view, whereas in civilised communities it is done only in sophisticated places of entertainment by nude show girls and strip-tease cabaret artistes. According to Lombroso, the Dinka tribe of Africa have developed modesty to so high and absurd a pitch that both the sexes have been known to refuse medical examination of their genitals, and the women even of their breasts.

Among some people, there exists an indifference to nudity. G. Rattray Taylor, in his stimulating work, **Sex in History,** tells us that in pre-Christian Ireland, " Nudity was no cause for shame: not only were warriors normally naked, except for their accoutrements, but women also undressed freely: thus the Queen of Ulster and all the ladies of the Court, to the number of 610, came to meet Cuchulainn, naked above the waist, and raising their skirts ' so as to expose their private parts ', by which they showed how greatly they honoured him."

Till the last century, mixed bathing in Japan produced but little licentiousness and even children joined the men and women in the communal bathroom. This practice still prevails but in a modified form. Similarly families in Finland collectively take the Sauna or steam bath in which water is poured on hot stone while they beat one another with birches, no doubt to stimulate circulation, and not, except perhaps in very isolated cases, for reasons of sado-masochistic gratification. Mixed bathing was not uncommon in mediæval times either.

In Polynesia, the male can expose his genitals so long as the fore-skin is kept concealed with a string ! The women have no shame in exposing their bare breasts, but they keep their genitals well covered. Those who admire Gaugin's nudes may find this surprising, but Bengt Danielsson, in his diverting account of the Polynesians, titled **Love in the South Seas,** tells us that the artist " often complained of the difficulty of finding models." We learn, further, that except in Tahiti, which is probably commercialised due to tourist traffic, it is a problem to find nude models in any of the other South Sea Islands. Further testimony is quoted by Danielsson from the diary of Morrison, one of the boatswains among the men who mutinied on the ship Bounty: " ' It being deemed shameful for either Sex to expose themselves Naked even to each other and they are more remarkable for hiding their Nakedness in Bathing than many Europeans, always supplying the place of Cloaths *(sic)* with leaves going in and coming out of the water.' "

While the Japanese do not fight shy of mixed bathing, the women's national costumes conceal their contours and the *obi* or girdle serves to cover the posterior more or less as did the bustle of Victorian women's dresses. In modern Western society, the shoulders are often exposed, and so also the entire back sometimes, and much more often the cleavage of the bosom in evening dress. Every device is adopted to outline the female contours, thus making clothing more salacious than nudity. Men's attire, from the Victorian era, became drab and concealing, but with the present outburst of jeans, drain-pipe trousers, and short Italian jackets, the young men at least look as if their masculinity is coming in for its fair share of display. Perhaps the bathing beach, with its bikinis and men with only trunks and bare chests, are the places that provide the least salacious atmosphere in Western society.

The most startling case of semi-nudity is to be found among South American aborigines. The women of the far south go around as nature made them except for an animal skin thrown over their shoulders. However, they sit with decorum, concealing their genitals artfully. In the Sudan, according to Henriques, the men of the Suk and Nandi tribes wear elaborate clothing, yet leave their sexual organs exposed ! However, he adds : " But such disregard of the genitals is somewhat rare : for what is of great importance to the savage is the possibility of magic being directed against the most vital part of the anatomy." Again : " All the openings of the body are regarded as being particularly defenceless against magic . . . Thus it is fairly common practice amongst a great number of peoples for the ears, mouth, nose, anus, vagina, and penis to be guarded by some object, design, or material having the power to ward off evil . . . In many instances tattooing serves the purpose of providing a symbolic covering. Examples can be drawn from peoples of the Congo, such as the Mangbettu and the Basonge : the Tupi Indians of Brazil, and Polynesian tribes. In all these cases women are either tattooed or painted in the pubic region . . . A striking instance of this type of protection comes from Ponape in the Caroline Islands in the Pacific where the most intricate and elaborate designs were woven round the vulva. In most Polynesian societies a prospective bridegroom had the right to demand a view of the tattooing before marriage, to see whether his wife-to-be was adequately defended."

The ancient Adamites who imitated Adam in his state of unclothedness before the Fall, even went naked to receive or administer communion. Similarly the Quakers created a stir in England by exposing their nudity to the elements and, no doubt, the horrified gaze of the onlookers, particularly in Yorkshire.

Virginity—a Cult

It was belief in the magical charms of womanly chastity in particular, more even than the custom of marriage by purchase, that originally led to the Cult of Virginity which, in our time, seems to have become over-emphasised. It is a virgin who in the Congo is made the custodian of a Chief's fighting paraphernalia such as his bows and arrows, shields and spears. She keeps them in her chamber or they are hung on a tree guarded by her. Her solicitude is supposed to endow the articles with powers that the Chief is considered to absorb automatically. Should she lose her virginity, the taint is said to enter the weapons which are forthwith destroyed.

In Tonga and Samoa, where young men and women have pre-marital sexual freedom, the daughters of the Chiefs are compelled to remain virgins till their marriage. To this end, they are watched over perpetually by attendants, at least in Tonga. The virgin daughters of Samoa, known as *taupos,* are well fed and cared for and not sub-mitted to work more difficult than weaving, but they are members of the Chiefs' Council. Similar rules prevail among the high-born maidens of other South Sea Islands, including Tahiti where sexual freedom attains its zenith.

The insistence on the Chiefs' daughters retaining their virginity is apparently not due to sexual prudery, but rather to acute class-consciousness, for the daughters of chiefs must marry only men of their own social status. These same societies, being patriarchal, do not taboo the sexual intercourse of the sons of Chiefs with lower class women, as, by such liaisons, men cannot adulterate the blood of their noble families, whereas females exercising similar licence would through conception. The men, on the contrary, are looked upon as conferring a favour on the women with whom they fornicate by contributing their noble blood to women of lesser rank.

Early Christianity exhorted maidens to remain virgins. St. Augustine went so far as to say that the virginal state was superior to the marital, and Jovinian was excommunicated for his denial of this doctrine. Nuns are, to this day, referred to as ' the brides of Christ ', But in earlier Christian times, the designation was applied to lay virgins as well, so that if a man seduced a virgin, it was not merely fornication, but adultery, for he was stealing Christ's bride from Him, and she, on her part, was being unfaithful to her divine Spouse. How-ever, we are not told that on marrying, she, being united to Christ, committed bigamy. The cult over-reached itself and the virgin Gorgonia preferred suffering bodily injury and pain to exposing her precious virginity to the gaze of a physician—just like the savage Dinka tribes of Africa we encountered, only a few pages ago, who for precisely the same reasons refused medical inspection.

So obsessed is the European mind with virginity that in **Romeo and Juliet** Shakespeare makes Juliet's old nurse swear by it in Act I, Scene III :

> " *Now, by my maidenhead, at twelve year old,*
> *I bade her come . . .* "

In war-like societies, the virgin is highly revered. Hence when a famous prince of Peru won a victory over a tribe known as the

Chancas, he expressed his gratitude to the Peruvian Virgin Sun-Brides
for their prayers and their chaste lives. An echo of this custom rings
through the corridors of time to the Rome of the Vestal Virgins who
were also credited with magical powers. From Fielding we learn that
their prayers could "rivet runaway slaves where they stood, if they
were still within the city." He narrates a story told by Ovid of the
Vestal Claudia who was suspected of having broken her vow of
chastity. To prove her innocence, she stepped forth from the group
of Vestal Virgins who had gone to Ostia to welcome with a chaste
hand a statue of the goddess Cybele that was being borne to Rome
in a vessel which got stuck at the Tiber's mouth. Claudia placed her
hand before the vessel and called upon Cybele to help prove her innocence. Lo and behold the vessel started moving and Claudia won
back her honour.

The Vestal Virgin had to remain chaste for almost three decades
during which she carried on with her task of attending to temple sacri-
fices and other ritual. If, during that period, she broke her vow of
chastity, a hideous death awaited her. There was also a superstition
that marrying after their full term of temple service, as they were
permitted to do, brought calamities in its wake. Hence many of them
stayed on in the service of the temples. It is, however, quite easy
to see that their prospects of marriage at such a late age for those
days, must have been few and far between; it was probably this factor,
rather than the hoary superstition, that influenced their decision. These
Vestals apart, in ancient Rome, there were also the *Occlos*, women of
royal blood who, while not deserting the world, yet remained virgins.
Breaking such a vow meant a cruel death, either a 'living burial' or
immolation by fire.

In mediæval times, novel devices came to the help of the men who
sought jealous and exclusive possession of their women folk, *viz.*
chastity girdles and padlocks. They were widely used in England and
France, as well as in Italy, judging by the still existing relics to be
found in the museums of these countries. Fielding tells us of one such
relic to be found in the Farnham Museum in Blandford, Dorset,
England. The belt is made of steel with designs at front and back,
and open-work ornamentation cut out of the metal; " . . . the hip-
band is equipped with two alternative clasps for securing it around
the body. There are small holes around the edges of the plates for
the purpose of sewing on a lining of velvet or other soft material."
Of course such belts had locking devices, and, presumably, the husband
or lover kept the key. Such belts are reminiscent of classical Hellenic
times when a girl, on attaining puberty, had the Herculean knot tied
on to her woollen maiden's sash, the knot being removed when she
married. This custom was obviously to protect her virginity, whereas
the chastity girdles of mediæval times were forced on married or
wanton women by jealous husbands and lovers whose desire for their
women's purity was governed by their male property-consciousness.

American folk-lore reveals that the New World, too, had its

chastity belts of leather. The main strap that passed between the legs, was held in place by back-straps suspended around the shoulders, and a padlock to ensure security. From Fielding we learn that such devices, known as *eiholders* or *futsashduppers*, were used among the mountain folk of Pennsylvania till quite recent times when sending their daughters to picnics or similar jaunts. However, whether in old times or today, it is certain that man's concern for woman's chastity is due to his power complex which motivates the yearning to plough a virgin field and make it yield its wealth for his pleasure and his alone.

Infibulation and Defibulation

We are inclined to think that savage tribes do not prize virginity; this is only partly true. Some of those which do, resort to the practice of *infibulation*, the only infallible method of ensuring virginity. This necessitates the cutting of both the *labia minora* or inner lips, and the *labia majora* or the outer lips. A congealed scar results from the raw tissue which blocks the *vulva* or entrance to the vagina, or the flesh is sewn together with a minute orifice left for the purposes of menstruation and urination. The extreme painfulness and cruelty of this procedure becomes obvious from Henriques's quotation of F. Peney describing an infibulation accompanied by female circumcision, *i.e.*, clitoridectomy:

" ' . . . When the hour comes, the child is laid on a bed and held down and in position by the assembled women, while the matron . . . begins by slicing off the top of the clitoris and the edges of the inner lips, then the razor shears along the rims of the outer lips, removing a ribbon of flesh about two inches wide. It lasts between four and five minutes. In order to drown the shrieks of the girl, the assembled guests and kin raise the loudest and shrillest din conceivable until the process is over. Then, when the flowing blood has been staunched, the girl is laid flat on her back, her legs extended and tied firmly together so that she cannot walk . . . Before leaving the girl to the healing process of nature, the matron introduces a hollow cylinder of wood . . . into the lower portion of the vagina, between the bleeding edges of the wound, and this is kept in place until the scar is completely formed, for purposes of menstruation and micturition . . . ' "

On marriage, natural defloration of an infibulated vagina is out of the question as even the best equipped husband is unable to penetrate the inelastic orifice. Hence the services of the matron are called in again for the purpose of defibulation. A fresh cylinder of wood or tube, even larger than the one used for infibulation, has to be inserted into the vagina where it is made to remain for about a fortnight till the wound heals up. Should the woman become pregnant, the knife has again to come into play, as the scars that made coitus impractic-

able now block the outward passing of the child. This time the knife
has to slash wider and deeper, and often the emerging babe receives
injuries. To our horror, we are told that after childbirth the husband
may insist on partial infibulation, and the knife again has to do its
cruel work.

Henriques quotes M. Helber's statement in an article entitled
Female Circumcision published in the Journal of the Medical
Women's Federation (April 1951, pp. 24-27), to the effect that
" 'Pharaonic circumcision or infibulation was prohibited by a law of
the Sudan Government in 1947. Sunna circumcision or clitoridectomy
was the only type to be permitted henceforth. Unfortunately this has
not proved successful as only the pharaonic type is acceptable to the
majority of the Sudanese . . . ' "

Defloration Customs :

Jus Primæ Noctis

Since the beginning of mankind's existence on this globe, the
attitude of man towards woman has been ambivalent. Accordingly,
while the desire to marry a virgin seems to remain constant, whether
the obsession is due to property-consciounsness or fear of the feminine
mystery, the wish to take a *virgo intacta* to the nuptial bed for the
purpose of natural defloration is confined to the former and not the
latter. Generally, in savage society wherein dread of woman's mystery
remains, the bride must be deprived of her virginity before the first
intercourse. As to who is to undertake this office, is decided by every
society's particular sexual code.

Tracing the history of defloration, one learns, from a mediæval
source, of the royal prerogative of the kings of Ireland to deflower the
brides in their realm. Rattray Taylor tells us of the feudal lord's right
to take the bride's maidenhead: " In early feudal times, the marriage
day might have ended differently, with the feudal lord deflowering
the new bride, before releasing her to her husband. The existence
of this *jus primæ noctis** also known in France as *jus cunni,* in England
as *marchette,* in Piedmont as *cazzagio,* has been much disputed, but
Ducange has provided detailed evidence and the best authorities now
accept that it existed; cases are even known where monks, being at
the same time feudal lords, held this right—for instance the monks of
St. Thiodard enjoyed the right over the inhabitants of Mount Auriol
. . . The psychological purpose of the custom, derived from fertility-
religion, is said to be the diversion from the husband of the resentment
which a woman generally feels for the man who deprives her of her
virginity. Whether or not this is an adequate explanation, it would
certainly be misleading to regard the *jus cunni* simply as the cruel and
wilful exercise of a feudal power, even if that is what it finally became.

* *Right of the first night.*

It is chiefly of interest as evidence of the survival of magical beliefs."

While the foregoing explanation for the feudal lord's right seems feasible enough, others have their own arguments. Henriques maintains that no such right prevailed, but rather the payment of a fine to the Lord of the Manor by his vassal, the bride's father, which came to be regarded as a payment made in place of the Lord's right to sleep with the bride. " A more sensible explanation is that the lord was entitled to service from the girl ", explains Henriques. " On marriage, she might, following her husband, leave the estate. Thus the fine was recompense for loss of services . . . "

A modern counterpart of the feudal lord's *droit de seigneur* or the lord's right, is said to have been exercised, not so long ago, by the local chieftain among the Bhutanese and Hunza tribes of the North-West Frontier, as well as by a Nigerian tribe.

Herodotus's ' **Historiæ** ' reveals a similar custom among the Nasamonians of Cyrenaica who indulged in public defloration. Every guest at the wedding feast would lie with the bride and give her a gift on the first night. Hence the custom is often referred to as the Nasamonian rite. The bridegroom was the last to partake of the shared sexual bliss. This custom, however, was definitely a transference from the bridegroom to a group, of the danger said to be attendant on the virgin's first participation in coitus. In a few isolated communities, this group responsibility still prevails, and the Nasamonian rite is re-enacted in New Guinea and parts of South America.

Public digital defloration existed in ancient Peru. The mother would take her daughter to a public place and would deflower her by inserting her finger into the girl's vagina, so that prospective suitors might be convinced of her viriginty. Digital defloration is, of course, sometimes resorted to by a bridegroom when he is averse to breaking the maidenhead in the normal way with thrusts of the phallus, or when he has to contend with an inelastic hymen.

At one time, in the South Seas island of Samoa, a ritualitic public defloration of the bride by the tribal chief was the custom. The bride was led to the *malae* or scene of the wedding feast, and older women removed her garments. She was now paraded in the nude before the assembled guests, then made to sit with her legs crossed in the midst of the gathering. The Chief then advanced to her and seated himself opposite her in a similar attitude. He would then proceed to grip her right shoulder with his left hand so as to steady her, while two women would stand behind her holding her firmly at the waist. The Chief now inserted two fingers of his right hand deep into her vulvar entrance, and having broken the hymen, would hold up his right hand with the two fingers extended and the others folded. At the sight of drops of blood trickling down the fingers, the assembly would give out cries of joy. The two women who had held her at the waist would then again parade her among the guests so that they could feast their eyes on the blood pouring down her thighs. This ritual, be it understood, was only carried out in the case of a daughter of a chieftain who alone, of all women, had to remain a virgin till marriage, as observed earlier. Should the ceremony, however, have proved that she had not been chaste, either the disgraced father, or his son, would rush on the poor girl and club her to death for having dishonoured the tribe.

The shifting of group to individual responsibility is, of course, much more common today. Amongst the Todas of India, just before puberty, a ritual is performed, after which a stranger arrives from any clan except the girl's own, and spends a night with her. According to W. H. R. Rivers' **The Todas,** the ceremony could on no account be put off till after puberty which would constitute a matter of disgrace and even result in no man being willing to marry the poor girl. In the Phillipine Islands, as well as among some tribes of Central Africa, defloration by a stranger is the favoured method.

Defloration by a stranger attains an element of sacredness or pride when he who performs the deed is a tribal chieftain, a priest, a king, or a medicine man. In the palm-fringed land of Malabar in South-West India, up to the last century, the chief priest, a Nabudri Brahmin, deflowered the bride on the wedding night, and could, if he desired, extend his pleasure for the next two nights. However, the priestly function was exercised only with the high-class bride, and the girls of lower castes had to be satisfied with humbler strangers.

The ' **Rig Veda** ' or Book of Hymns of the ancient Aryan Hindus does not confer on the priest the right to takes the bride's virginity; but it does give gods of the Hindu Pantheon the divine right of defloration. Similarly, in yet another country that attained almost as high a civilisation as ancient India, the gods had the prerogative to break the bride's maidenhead: none other than ancient Rome. The Romans used the stone image of the god Tutunus or Priapus, with an enormous phallus, on which the bride was made to sit before the bridegroom had his initial coitus with her. That the shifting of responsibility from the husband to a priest or a god was akin to a sacrament to these ancients, is not hard to fathom. Childless women of Rome would often bestride the ithyphallic god who was credited with the power of imbuing her with fecundity.

Virginity is despised on Easter Island which belongs to the South Seas group. Older women instruct the growing girl and she is broken in usually by an older male relative. Similarly, the Slavs were reported, by an Arab, to despise a woman who had had no carnal experience prior to marriage, their reasoning being that if a woman were worthy of sexual seduction no young man would leave her hymen intact. The Tibetans, according to Marco Polo, also despised virginity and would not marry a girl who had never had children. Bertrand Russell, the great contemporary sage who is in favour of companionate marriage, has suggested that until the birth of a child a couple should not bind themselves to each other permanently.

Proof of Virginity
of the Bride

Amongst those who value virginity, there is the old custom of furnishing proof of it on, or soon after, the bridal night. Simone de Beauvoir declares: "Through a transvaluation that is classical in the realm of the sacred, virginal blood becomes in less primitive societies a propitious symbol. There are villages in France where, on the morning after the wedding, the bloodstained sheets are displayed before relatives and friends. What happened is that in the patriarchal regime man became master of woman; and the very powers that are frightening in wild beasts or in unconquered elements became qualities valuable to the owner able to domesticate them.

"A virgin body has the freshness of secret springs, the morning sheen of an unopened flower, the orient lustre of a pearl on which the sun has never shone. Grotto, temple, sanctuary, secret garden—man, like the child, is fascinated by enclosed and shadowy places not yet animated by any consciousness, which wait to be given a soul: what he alone is to take and to penetrate seems to be in truth created by him. And more, one of the ends sought by all desire is the using up of the desired object, which implies its destruction. In breaking the hymen man takes possession of the feminine body more intimately than by a penetration that leaves it intact; in the irreversible act of defloration he makes of that body unequivocally a passive object, he affirms his capture of it . . . "

France apart, in eastern and southern Europe evidence of virginity had to be publicly exhibited. In Sicily and Greece, the bride had to hang her nightdress on the window. In Spain, at royal weddings, proofs had to be provided before the assembled court. In Bedawi camps or villages, the garment of proof flutters from a lance in the centre of the camp.

All the obsessions with virginity and its mystical powers are nowhere better crystallised than in the Virgin Mary of Christianity. Simone de Beauvoir, for ever poetic, describes this concept with beautiful imagery: " . . . The Virgin is fecundity, dew, wellspring of life; many statuettes show her at the well, the spring, the fountain . . . she is not creative but she fructifies, she makes what was hidden in the earth spring forth into the light of day. She is the deep reality hidden under the appearance of things: the Kernel, the Marrow. Through her is desire appeased: she is what is given to man for his satisfaction . . She heals and strengthens; she is intermediary between man and life . . . Tertullian called her ' the devil's doorway '; but, transfigured, she is the doorway to heaven . . . She is shown more directly as advocate pleading for man before her Son, and on the Day of Judgment, her bosom bared, making supplication to Christ in the name of her glorious maternity . . .

"The Christian God is full of the rigours of Justice, the Virgin is full of the gentleness of charity . . . She heals the wounds of males, she nurses the newborn, and she lays out the dead; she knows everything about man that attacks his pride and humiliates his self-will. While she inclines before him and humbles the flesh to the spirit, she stays on the fleshly frontiers of the spirit . . . Woman's power over men comes from the fact that she gently recalls them to a modest realisation of their true condition; it is the secret of her disillusioned, sorrowful, ironical, and loving wisdom . . . she wafts the breath of poetry through city streets, over cultivated fields . . . She incarnates the Dream, which is for man most intimate and most strange: what he does not wish and does not do, towards which he aspires and which cannot be obtained . . . "

One may be inclined to feel that Simone de Beauvoir places her sex on too lofty a pedestal; yet have not men also sung woman's praise ?   It is fitting to end this chapter with Sir Walter Scott's famous lines, which we quote from memory:

> " *O Woman, in our hours of ease,*
> *Uncertain, coy, and hard to please,*
> *And variable as the shade*
> *By the light quivering aspen made;*
> *When pain and anguish wring the brow,*
> *A minist'ring angel thou!* "

CHAPTER 3

CELIBACY AND PRE-MARITAL EROTISM

Celibacy and Magic—Celibacy and Spiritual Power—Buddha renounces the Flesh—Christianity and Celibacy—Catholic Priests permitted to marry till Fourth Century A.D.—Priestly Revolt against Celibacy—Pope Gregory VII condemns Priestly ' Whoredom '—Priestly Sexual Capers—Mediæval Priests use Confessional Box to seduce Women—Nuns and Sexual Hallucinations—Licentious Popes : John XII, Leo VIII, Benedict IX, Alexander VI—Tragic Romance of Abelard and Héloïse—Abelard forcibly castrated—Pre-marital Erotic Customs—Captain Cook reports on Sexual Demonstration—Free Love among Adolescents in Indian ' Ghotul '—Free Love among Polynesians—Strange Courtship Customs—Women woo Men in Some Tribal Societies—Bride-Winning Feats—Quaint Courtship in W e s t e r n Communities—' Queesten ', ' Probenàchte ', ' Night-Running ', ' Frieri ', ' Bundling ', ' Tarrying '—Agapemonites and ' Agapæ ' : Fleshly or Spiritual Love ?—Self-Castration among Valesians.

MAN'S sexual abstinence does not, in modern society, carry with it the same respect or awe that woman's virginity and purity arouse, except that it is enjoined on the priesthood of many world faiths. Yet, among primitives, male continence is looked up to, probably from reasons of superstition, and also for practical purposes such as conservation of energy. Thus hunting expeditions and war-like pursuits are often preceded among them by abstention from sexual intercourse.

Even in civilised communities it is believed that too frequent coitus can result in a certain depletion of energy and muscular strength, a dulling of the senses owing to expenditure of phosphorus. There is also the factor that in male-female sexual relationships there is always a current of natural antagonism, so that, subconsciously, the man may feel that while outwardly he possesses and conquers the woman, in actuality she overcomes him and possesses him, for with every orgasm in which coitus ends, he, in a sense, renounces his own life for the life of the species, and each ejaculation is, therefore, akin to death.

Man glories in his phallus when he looks upon it as a symbol of transcendence, of power, but he shrinks from it when, following orgasm, he realises that it is flesh that enmeshes him, making him nature's plaything.   In the arms of woman, man finds momentary contentment; but he also discovers satiety and the certainty that he is but a finite being doomed to an inevitable end.   Hence he recoils from woman, from the mother; hence the fear of incest; hence exogamy.

With conservation of the semen, man feels intact, master of his fate, removed, however temporarily, from nothingness.   The Tahitians believe that continence before death can gain a man a better lot in the next life.   For this reason, many tribes refrain from sexual inter-course after the death of a Chieftain or relative or fellow-tribesman, for a certain period, so as to help the departed man to win for himself a good place in the hereafter.

Male chastity is esteemed among more advanced savages for its inherent value of self-control leading to a desired goal.   The endurance tests and the uncrying patience they instil in him before he can partake of the joys and responsibilities of life, engender in him the idea that self-control does lead to attainment of the object for which he aspires.

Fertility rites among savages often involve continence.   The Karamundi tribes of South-West Australia do not touch their wives during the rain-making rites till the rains have come, partly they imagine, due to their self-control.   Similarly, the Nicaraguans observe conjugal abstinence when they sow crops, and the Panaians taboo sexual intercourse from the community while the ceremony for en-suring a rich harvest is in progress.   When the ancient Mexicans held the feasts of their gods, Tlaloc the god of rain, and Mixcoatl the god of the tornado, they remained continent.   Hunters such as the Eskimaux segregate themselves from their women folk before starting out on an expedition.

Contemplatives and the religious have always related spiritual power to celibacy.   Perhaps the earliest instances history provides are the Hindu *sadhoos* or holy men who, from time immemorial, have gone to forests and mountain tops to meditate in solitude after re-nouncing the flesh.   Buddha, who lived in about 500 B.C., born Prince Siddârtha, forsook his kingdom, wife, and child, and the world, to seek the mystery of old age, illness, and death, in the forest, as Sir Edwin Arnold describes so lyrically in his poem, **The Light of Asia :**

> "*I will depart . . . the hour is come !*
> *. . . . . .Unto this*
> *Came I, and unto this all nights and days*
> *Have led me; for I will not have that crown*
> *Which may be mine : I lay aside those realms*
> *Which await the gleaming of my naked sword :*
> *My chariot shall not roll with bloody wheels*

From victory to victory, till earth
Wears the red record of my name. I choose
To tread its paths with patient, stainless feet,
Making its dust my bed, its loneliest wastes
My dwelling, and its meanest things my mates;
Clad in no prouder garb than outcasts wear,
Fed with no meats save what the charitable
Give of their will, sheltered by no more pomp
Than the dim cave lends or the jungle-bush.
This will I do because the woeful cry
Of life and all flesh living cometh up
Into my ears, and all my soul is full
Of pity for the sickness of this world;
Which I will heal, if healing may be found
By uttermost renouncing and strong strife . . .
Oh, summoning stars! I come! Oh, mournful earth,
For thee and thine I lay aside my youth,
My throne, my joys, my golden days, my nights
My happy palace—and thine arms, sweet Queen!
Harder to put aside than all the rest!

It is not difficult to imagine that when Prince Siddârtha returned to the world as the Buddha, the Wise or Enlightened One, in saffron robes of humility and poverty, the order of Buddhist priests which he founded, known as *bhikkus*, took celibacy as the fifth of their five major vows.

Christianity and Celibacy

Jesus Christ, too, remained celibate, but he for the whole of his life, not just a part of it as in the case of the Buddha. Yet for the first three hundred years after the death of Christ, celibacy was not demanded of the lower ranks of the clergy, though it was considered unbecoming if a young man already ordained while a bachelor, chose to marry subsequently. St. Paul himself, though enamoured of celibacy, yet appointed married men to be bishops.

In the fourth century A.D., a movement started in favour of celibacy and some of its advocates wished even the married clergy to give up their wives, or at least forfeit sexual indulgence with them. Ironically enough it was Bishop Paphnutius, himself a celibate, who saved the day for the married priests. But, in course of time, the demand for celibacy became more vociferous, starting in Spain and spreading over the south of France and Italy. The papacy bowed before the storm. It was decreed that consecrated priests must be celibate, though there was nothing against a married man entering the priesthood so long as, after he had been ordained, he became a confirmed celibate. Pope Innocent I introduced a penalty for those who scorned the order.

Surprising though it sounds, for another three hundred years after this, almost till the end of the seventh century, vows of chastity had not become compulsory. The Council of Trullo even permitted priests to continue living with their wives till they came to be consecrated bishops, in which case their spouses had to take the veil. Complete celibacy became obligatory only in the course of the next few centuries. It was over this question of permitting the marriage of priests that the Orthodox Church, which approved of the practice, broke away from the Roman Church.

However, even in the West, priests and concubines did not part easily. In England, the Archbishop of Canterbury's order that married clergy should cease conjugal relations with their wives, fell on deaf ears. The Milanese priests, most of whom were married, cited St. Ambrose as their shining example. For Rome, so near to Milan, this was the thin edge of the wedge. The priestly resistance in Lombardy ushered in the final struggle with the recalcitrant married and fornicating clergy. It was the monks, as opposed to the secular priests, who gave the movement for celibacy its staunchest support, for the monastic orders inspired respect among the populace. Richard Lewinsohn, in his work titled **A History of Sexual Customs,** gives a graphic picture of the times: " . . . Married priests were pilloried as lustful voluptuaries, men who had succumbed to the woman-demon. No mercy for them ! Rome still hoped, however, to bring the priests to see reason without expelling them from the Church. In 1018, Pope Benedict VII enacted that the children of clergy should be perpetual serfs of the Church. After the children, it was the women's turn to be blacklisted; wives of priests were placed on an equal footing with concubines."

The battle continued till the advent of Pope Leo IX who succeeded to the papacy in 1048 and consolidated the Church till his death in 1054. He boldly enjoined chastity on priests and decreed disobedience of the command would constitute heresy. Priests who refused to separate from their wives were pounced upon by the populace led by monks. What is more, about four years after Leo IX's death, a Council in Rome prohibited the lay congregation from hearing Mass said by a priest with a woman in his house.

Two years before the start of the last quarter of the eleventh century, the Tuscan monk, Hildebrand, became Pope Gregory VII. He labelled all priestly sexual contacts with women with the odious term 'Whoredom'. As the Church would not permit divorce, he compelled priests to leave their wives. At the Councils of Mainz, Erfurt, and Paris, there were stormy debates on the question and even high dignitaries of the Church still spoke in favour of priestly marriages. Once again the monks rallied to the help of the Church.

"Nevertheless," declares Lewinsohn, "decades more passed before celibacy was generally practised—at least nominally—in the West. No more priestly marriages were concluded, except in the

Eastern Churches in union with Rome, where they are still allowed today. Concubinage went on, however, almost openly." As if this were not enough, the erstwhile props of the Church, the monks, also seemed to fall by the wayside, for Lewinsohn tells us, " Monastic morality, too, became laxer; there were innumerable scandals in the monasteries and convents. The question of celibacy continued to smoulder throughout the Middle Ages, like fire under ashes, till Martin Luther blew it into a leaping flame which split the Church for the second time."

Priestly Sexual Capers

It is interesting to survey some of the cases of wayward clergy in the Church's hierarchy, both before and after Pope Gregory VII's accession to the papal throne.

One Archembald, Bishop of Sens, evicted the monks from the Abbey of St. Peter and established a veritable harem in the refectory. When the Council of Spalato forbade priests to contract a second marriage (apparently being resigned to their taking one wife each) in 925 A.D., there was a hue and cry. About a century later, Roman nobility and bishops of Lombardy set up an Antipope in the person of Cadalus, Bishop of Parma, who, under the nomenclature, Honorius II, marched on and captured Rome, till, two years later, he and his recalcitrant followers were defeated.

From H. C. Lea's **History of Sacerdotal Celibacy,** we learn that when Rome made marriage difficult for her clergy, the latter resorted to fornication. What's more, so common did this practice become that in Germany a bastard was jokingly referred to as a *pfaffenkind* or parson's child ! No less than sixty-five bastards were said to have been fathered by the Bishop of Liége. " So serious did the situation become", we are informed by G. Rattray Taylor in **Sex in History,** " that in many parishes—at least in Spain and Switzerland—the parishioners insisted that the priest *must* have a concubine as a measure of protection for their wives."

What is most revolting is that mediæval priests are reported as having used the confessional to compel a woman confessor to submit to their lecherous advances on pain of being refused absolution for their sins. The ecclesiastical courts were, unfortunately, much too lenient with these culprits. Lea cites the case of a priest, one Valdelamar, who as late as the second quarter of the sixteenth century, was brought to trial at Toledo for the seduction of two women and the additional attempt to seduce another by a threat of withholding absolution. The penalty of the court was as little as two ducats, and one month's confinement to church !

As a counter-measure to the immorality of the priests, the confessional box was evolved by the Council of Valencia in 1565, and its general adoption, decreed in the early part of the seventeeth century, was flouted right up to the middle of the eighteenth century. However, the confessional box brought other evils in its train. For instance, if a man confessed to having fornicated, the priest insisted on the name and whereabouts of the woman so as to further his own lecherous pursuit. Even laymen would take advantage of the semi-secrecy of the confessional box to enter it and regale their ears with confessions of fornication and lechery. If they dared to give abso-lution at the end of the confession, the Church took a more than dim view of it since they were poaching on the clergy's preserves. Such masqueraders were burnt alive when found guilty. Drastic diseases may require drastic remedies, but when the Church thus punished a man, was she not usurping to herself the Divine Prerogative that vengeance is the Lord's and he alone must repay ?

To cover up or punish with leniency the sacerdotal offences of the priests, theology and its endless quibbles intervened in the trials of priestly offenders. The poor woman who had fallen a prey to the lust of the priest did not seem to count with the judges as much as whether the improper advances had been made prior to, or following, the giving of absolution. " Thus ", says Rattray Taylor, " it was argued that to give a woman a love-letter in the confessional was only ' solicitation ' (as the offence came to be called) if it was intended that she should read it on the spot, before being absolved. Once the question of intention had been introduced the casuists were able to confuse the issue still further: it became possible to argue that a conditional statement, such as ' If I were not a priest, I should like to seduce you ', was innocuous."

From Coryat's Crudities, we also learn of pregnancies among nuns and manifestations of hysteria, the latter due most probably to sexual repression. We get a clue to these self-induced states from the explanation of a German doctor who investigated several cases of nuns becoming ' possessed' in the Convent of Nazareth at Cologne. Their bodies generally contorted themselves in the coital position described as *arc-en-cercle*, with the entire body arched and the genital region thrust upward as if engaged in coitus. When they opened their eyes, there was guilt and shame in them. This mass outburst of hallu-cinations was diagnosed as being imitative of a girl in their care who had been a victim of such a condition, imagining that a lover was paying her nightly visits during which he raped her against her wishes. Her condition seemed to infect the nuns. Later it was discovered that more than just hallucinations haunted the nuns, for it was found on inquiry that many of them had been indulging in sexual relations with the young men of the neighbourhood, and their convulsions had developed due to their liaisons having been discovered and stopped.

To get back to the male clergy, their sexual exploits were far more realistic, particularly in the hierarchy of the Church. The basilica of St. John Lateran was once converted into a brothel and by none other than Pope John XII who was, subsequently, tried on manifold charges including incest, perjury, adultery, sacrilege, and even murder ! His successor, Leo VIII, ended up by getting a paralytic stroke while engaged in adultery. Lea comments thus on the licence of many of the Popes: " . . . the vilest issues were the pastime of pontifical ease. Chastity was a reproach and licentiousness a vice."

A typical example of that unbridled age, was Benedict IX who succeeded to the papacy while yet a child and led a thoroughly profligate existence. The Council of Constance heard from the lips of Balthasar Crossa a lurid confession of crimes of the flesh embracing murder, adultery, incest, and even lack of belief in God ! As a punishment, he was packed off to Bologna where he seduced numberless women. Yet this was the man who was created Pope to put an end to the Great Schism.

Perhaps the most debauched Pope of all was Alexander VI, father of the notorious poisoners, Cesare and Lucrezia Borgia. Havelock Ellis, in his **Sex in Relation to Society,** gives us a nauseating picture of Alexander's papal court: In the first year of the sixteenth century, Alexander VI gave a banquet at which his son and daughter were both present. Among the guests were prostitutes who danced with the Pope's henchmen as well as with Cesare and Lucrezia. Clothes were gradually cast off and the women were goaded on to crawl and pick up chestnuts thrown at them between rows of lighted candles placed on the marble floor. Prizes were offered to such men as could seduce the maximum number of women. And these were the Vicars of the Church of Christ !

What were the might-be Vicars like—the men who in solemn conclave would elect, usually from among themselves, the next Pope ? Rattray Taylor declares : " The same was true of the Cardinalate, from whom the popes were normally selected, and the whole Curia. Here, too, the trend is found at least as early as the eleventh century, when Cardinal Pierleone had children by his sister, and regularly took with him a concubine on his journeys—*actions which did not debar him from being considered for the Papal throne.* (Italics ours.) By the sixteenth century, the higher echelons of the church display all the signs of moral anarchy, epitomised in the rape of the Bishop of Fano by Pierluigi Farnese, son of Paul III . . . "

When Pope Gregory VII (the former Tuscan monk Hildebrand) sat on the papal throne, a boy was born, in 1079, who was to win both fame and notoriety about forty years from then, for this child was Pierre Abelard who grew up to be a great scholar, and a student of theology, though he did not take Orders, preferring the worldly life. Where the Sorbonne stands today in the *quartier latin* of Paris, Abelard ran a school of philosophy and theology, to which came a vast throng of pupils.

Abelard lived in the home of one Canon Fulbert who had with him a young niece called Héloïse. Here, in this house on the Mont

Sainte Genevieve, a ghastly and tragic drama was enacted in 1119. Héloïse was a pupil of Abelard and admiration of him soon changed to love. She bore him a son in Brittainy where he sent her to the house of his sister in order to conceal their secret from the Canon The latter, however, discovered the truth and took a bitter revenge: entering Abelard's room forcibly with fellow plotters, he had the latter overpower Abelard and castrate him. The unfortunate man retired to a monastery, while Héloïse became a nun. Earlier, she had refused to marry him believing that such a brilliant scholar, a genius in fact, should be free of a family to pursue his career.

The love of Héloïse for Abelard remained an unceasing yearning even in the convent. Lewinsohn provides several extracts from her passionate letters to Abelard. In one of them she declares: " . . . The name 'wife' might sound to thee nobler and more honourable, but to me it was ever more delightful to be thy 'beloved' or even—take it not amiss of me—thy 'mistress', thy 'strumpet'." In another, she vowed: "'Tis thou whom I would please, not God. 'Twas thy word, not the love of God, made me into a nun . . . "

Years later, in Champagne, Abelard was again allowed to found a school where thousands came to learn under him. It was here he taught " the *Universalia,* the relationship between ideas and things." Héloïse came to stay in a nunnery which he also opened. But they were a pair of ill-starred lovers both in flesh and spirit, for the monks opposed him and aroused his ire, which led to his giving battle to the Church. This man of genius ended his days as a simple monk in a monastery to enter which the Pope had to give him a special dispensation. Two decades after his death, Héloïse breathed her last, highly revered.

Thus it will be seen that while savage, and civilised Eastern races find in fleshly and worldly renunciation a challenge they readily accept, the basically pagan European—from whom the creed of the mid-Eastern, Jesus Christ, was very remote, and still remains so in the present writer's opinion—took centuries to adapt himself to the principle of renunciation of the flesh; and, then too, but a tiny section adhered to it when Luther appeared on the scene and restored to them the right to appease the hungry flesh, himself, as an excommuni- cated monk, setting an example by marrying a nun, one Katherine von Bora, who had run away from a convent.

Pre-Marital Erotic Customs

The sexual mores of the civilised world, particularly in some countries of the Orient, and in Europe, are based mostly on prudery and hypocrisy. Hence the sexual customs of backward and so-called savage people are apt to outrage our sense of modesty as we view them disdainfully with the beam of puritanism lurking in our critical eyes. What is more, we generally, and with great impertinence, apply the yardstick of our own cramped, repressed, and complex standards of morality to measure their infinitely freer, more natural, and more robust sexuality. Perhaps our judgment is tinged with envy of the uncomplicated pattern of their sex-lives and with subconscious resentment of the anti-sexual code of our society which presents the ludicrous spectacle of sexual restraint and prohibitions in the midst of synthetically manufactured temptations dangled perpetually before us to titillate our senses and tantalise them with denial of the very allurements we are artificially induced to crave.

Bengt Danielsson gives an entrancing and almost idyllic picture of free love among the Polynesians on the island of Tahiti, in **Love in the South Seas.** The *arioi* society was first mentioned in Captain Cook's official reports on his voyage in the last quarter of the eighteenth century. Cook is quoted by Danielsson as declaring: " ' A very considerable number of the principal people of Otaheiti, of both sexes, have formed themselves into a society in which every woman is common to every man, thus securing a perpetual variety as often as their inclination prompts them to seek it, which is so frequent that the same man and woman seldom cohabit together more than two or three days '."

The Christian missionaries who visited the island in the wake of Captain Cook, stigmatised the *arioi* as 'privileged libertines' and strolling players who spread 'moral contagion' throughout the island. However, it would appear that the missionaries were jealous of the popularity of the *arioi* among the people which served to establish a rivalry in which these self-appointed 'do-gooders' had to play second fiddle, for even their head, Ellis, admitted that the native islanders considered the players to be superior beings related to the gods. Apart from being entertainers, they were also missionaries and apostles of these same gods, and all their large festivals started with a kind of religious sermon describing the two principles of life, the god Taaroa, and his cosmic creation. Hymns, dancing, and wrestling, as well as pantomime, formed part of their shows.

Needless to say that what went most against the puritanical grain of the bible-thumping missionaries were the dances in the nude, and the public exhibitions of sexual intimacy. Yet " even these bore the marks rather of natural innocence than of conscious immorality." We have Captain Cook's own account of one such procedure which seems to have been penned with hardly any trace of hypocrisy or disapproval :

" A young man, nearly six foot high, performed the rites of Venus with a little girl about eleven or twelve years of age, before several of our people, and a great number of natives, without the least sense of its being indecent or improper, but, as appeared, in perfect conformity to the custom of the place. Among the spectators were several women of superior rank, who may properly be said to have assisted at the ceremony; for they gave instructions to the girl how to perform her part, which, young as she was, she did not seem much to stand in need of."

Danielsson tells us that when the famous Voltaire read **Voyage Round the World,** such a description made him comment: ". . . I see with edification the queen of the country taking part in the communion of the Anglican Church and inviting the English to divine service as conducted in her Kingdom. This divine service consists in making a young man and a girl, quite naked, have intercourse in the presence of Her Majesty and 500 ladies and gentlemen of the Court. It can be affirmed that the inhabitants of Tahiti have preserved the oldest religion on earth in all its purity."

The *arioi* who were confined to the Society Islands, are supposed to have originiated from a similar group called the *karioi* or *kaioi* in the Marquesas, Cook, and other islands. This group consisted of young unmarried members of both sexes who were also troupers and generally ended their shows with demonstrations of coitus. They were very promiscuous and the girls gave freely of themselves to men visiting their islands. Marriage ended membership of the group which could not be obtained till a boy or a girl had attained puberty. The narrow-minded Christian missionaries were instrumental in abolishing these societies over a century ago on the excuse that its members were apt to be anarchic. What they actually did was to rid themselves of formidable rivals.

In Chapter I, was narrated the custom of the Trobrianders of sending growing children to the *bukumatula* where sexual indulgence between the couples was the rule so long as they stuck to each other for reasonable periods and were not too promiscuous amongst themselves. Similar institutions exist in other societies, notably among the Muria aborigines of the Central Provinces of India.

The Muria *ghotul* is a communal dormitory, as well as a guesthouse mostly for officials, the advantage of this being that there are plenty of young people available to provide service for the guests. These *ghotuls* are large and well ventilated, usually standing in the midst of the village and surrounded by a wooden fence. A central hall, wooden huts, and sheds, provide ample accommodation. The dormitories are of two kinds: One, called the *jodidar* (literally, ' pair ') accommodates couples who are considered partners almost as in a marriage, and strict fidelity is binding on them, though 'divorce' is permitted. Infidelity is not countenanced, and when it occurs, is punished. When mature, the partners may marry each other, a ceremony taking place in the institution itself to mark the event. On the other hand, they may part on leaving the *jodidar ghotul*, and select mates in the world outside. This is preferred as it prevents clan incest and also because many of these young people may have been betrothed in childhood to members of other tribes.

The second type of dormitory *ghotul* is the *mundi-badalna*, being a reverse of the first type. In this one, no boy or girl may mate with the same partner for more than three nights, infringement of the rule of permissive cohabitation carrying with it a penalty. This arrangement is by no means devoid of a practical purpose. It takes into account the psychology of lovers, seeking to eliminate the strong attachments that cohabitation may breed, and rendering it easier for partners to marry in the outside world in their maturity, particularly as marriages within the same clan are tabooed. By the quick change of partners, the Murias also imagine that they are nipping fecundity in the bud. There are about a score of sleeping mates to choose from, and one presumes that though no more than three nights may be spent by the same couple together, their turn to pair off does recur. The partners are allocated by the senior boy or girl who acts as a ' prefect ', and is known as a *diwan* in the case of a male, and a *belosa* in the case of the female, so that another practical measure of the *mundi-badalna* is that even the plain ones do not find themselves neglected.

Yet another variety of *ghotul* exists to which girls come only of a rare evening, many not staying overnight. The inmates come with their mats in the evenings and these *ghotuls* serve also as clubs where the young, who generally begin attending from the age of eight or so, can enjoy recreation by way of dancing, games, music, or discussions about picnics and excursions of a like nature. A firm and healthy discipline prevails. As the evening lengthens, the junior boys offer salutation to their seniors, and one of the girls distributes tobacco, after which there follows a period of hair-combing and massaging of the boys by the girls. They then retire with their respective partners, those desiring privacy for their sexual acts going to the huts and sheds. The younger ones sleep in the dormitory, boys and girls together, but in such an order that sex-play is not possible.

Aborigines, all over the world, do not believe in individuality, but rather the stability of the group. Hence a sense of responsibility and loyalty to the group is inculcated in the young. Gossip is, therefore, forbidden and the internal affairs of the *ghotul* are not to be discussed outside. Jealousy, unresponsiveness, lack of co-operation, are all severely dealt with. But punishment is not of the corporal variety; rather does it take what one may call a ' homeopathic ' form. Thus punishment for breach of the rule of cleanliness may be meted out to, say, a boy who does not keep his face clean by smearing it with dirt.

Marriage terminates a girl's membership of the *ghotul*, but not the boy's till he has earned enough to throw a feast for his companions, after which he must bid adieu to the *ghotul* and never return to it. These institutions to a great extent free the parents of the responsibility of looking after their children constantly, besides ensuring their own privacy; as a matter of fact it is the desire to conduct their own sex-lives without the anxiety of being watched in the act of coitus by their children, and the fear of incest in cramped quarters that are the prime reasons for the existence of the club-houses, and their wisdom is obvious when one reads of the cases of incest in the slums of industrial civilisations.   Indeed the *ghotuls* are training grounds not merely of sexuality, but also for life in general.

Peculiarly, clan incest, as distinct from family incest, is not frowned upon at the *ghotul* stage of life.   But pregnancy must be avoided.   When it does occur, the boy has to pay a fine, and in extreme cases, he may be banished from the tribe.   The girl, if as a child she has already been betrothed to a boy of another clan, is made to marry the latter, and he normally accepts legal paternity of the child.

Free Love

The pleasure-houses of Polynesia, called *whare tapere* by New Zealanders, and *hare nui* on Easter Island, have often been likened to our brothels.   Yet they are vastly different, and if promiscuity be accepted as a natural adherence to man's polyerotism, far more moral. For one thing, in the old days, money never changed hands in the pleasure-houses.   Love in Polynesia, before the advent of corrupt foreigners, was a pleasure shared with neither partner owing the other anything more than making the intimacy of their moments together supremely satisfying.   The girls would not sleep with any and every man, but would select their own partners, whereas common prostitutes in the civilised world cannot afford to be selective nor to dispense of their charms without monetary considerations.   What is striking among the Polynesians is that only unmarried people visited the pleasure-houses, unlike our own brothels which give free rein to both pre-marital and post-nuptial sexuality in a purely physical sense.

On one of the islands, called Pukapuka, a son or daughter invited friends to live in the parental home on the understanding that the outsiders provided extra food.   If the parents did not like the ways of their children's companions, he or she would be asked to build a special hut for himself or herself and his or her friends.   This house would be used by the young for general merriment and sex-play, whereas the parental home would still be frequented for meals and the youngsters would continue to help out with the food.   Eminently sensible arrangements, we think, as, in our own society, the petting and other pre-marital affairs take on a hypocritical note with youngsters inventing lies to cover up their underground escapades.

Astonishing as is may seem, in view of the open promiscuity of Polynesians, we are assured by Danielsson that venereal diseases " . . . were quite unknown in Polynesia before the arrival of the first Europeans."   Contraceptives, too, one presumes, were unknown to these apostles of free love· but no doubt in the pre-marital stage they resorted to sexual techniques such as *coitus interruptus, i.e.,* interruption of sexual intercourse so that the man achieves orgasm without the semen entering the woman's vagina.

It is a fact that adolescent Polynesian girls are not prone to pregnancy, and this the native islanders attribute to frequent change of partners. In any case, illegitimacy carries no stigma among these sensible children of nature, and a girl, if reasonably attractive, does not lose her marriage prospects by being an unmarried mother, even if she keeps the child herself, though, frequently, a relative might gladly adopt it.

In keeping with their broad-minded outlook on sex, the Polynesians imparted practical sex knowledge to their children, leaving the initiation usually to an older and experienced man or woman. Even an uncle or aunt would perform the task. Often the *karios*, already referred to, instructed the boys, while the girls were taught by priestesses. On Tongareva Island, the ceremony of initiation was entrusted to an older woman. The boy and the woman would retire to the privacy of a hut, and she would pull his foreskin over the *glans*, after which coitus generally took place between them. With the official dawning of sexual knowledge, his penis had, in future, to be covered.

A similar custom prevails in the New Hebrides. The initiatory rite is carried out by a woman called the *Iowhanan* who is painted, and adorned with turtle-shell ear-rings as marks of her profession. Till this woman has laid hands on a young man, he cannot even become betrothed. She visits the *imeium* or young men's hostel where circumcised bachelors live, and dwells in their midst, during which time she is apparently shared by them. When she departs, they are supposed to remain continent. There is no bar to her marrying subsequently, as she is not looked down upon. She receives no payment for her services to the *imeium*, but her tribe is compensated for loaning her.

Social approval of pre-marital sexual intercourse is to be found among the Masais, an East African tribe. The boys, according to their age groups, live in villages called *manyatta*. Their sisters and mothers are also entitled to live in the *manyatta*, but the sons do not sleep in the huts of their mothers, though their sisters do. The older woman and her young children sleep in one corner of the hut, while in the other corner, the daughters may sleep with warriors. It is incumbent on the girls to be in the nude while sleeping in their lovers' arms. A girl may have a favourite among these casual amorists, and she is permitted to choose him for a husband provided she has not already been betrothed as a child. If a girl in such a predicament conceives a child by her favoured lover, she is allowed to renounce the betrothed of her childhood and marry the father of her child.

Strange Courtship
Customs

In animal, bird, and insect life, we find that nature is partial to one or other of the sexes inasmuch as it endows it, on maturity, with physical attributes that by virtue of their beauty, colourfulness, and formation, dazzle the opposite sex. Amongst animals, the male is generally the superior in strength and appearance. The lordly lion overshadows, with his bushy mane and majesty, his less prepossessing mate. Among birds, too, the male is the more splendiferous, and, in the mating season, his colours seem to become even more vivid. The peacock, with his gorgeous tail, struts and preens himself before the peahen who cannot but respond to such magnificence, and so inviting a courtship. Only in insect life does the female often dominate the male, with her larger size and greater hideousness, as in the case of the Queen Bee in comparison to the drones.

Among humans, it is a moot point as to which of the two sexes is the more attractive. It is generally recognised that, from at least an æsthetic point of view, the male, with his harmonious proportions and greater muscularity, is woman's superior. On the other hand, man's normal sex instinct colours his vision and to him the woman, being sexually desirable, is the more attractive.

From the point of view of courtship, the initiative seems to rest with the man, at least in most patriarchal societies; but we shall find that in a number of matriarchal orders, it is the woman who makes the preliminary advances. As in a matriarchate, marriage is most often, though not always, matrilocal, and the husband leaves his maternal home to go to the bride's, it does not seem so very surprising that the woman should take the lead. In his work, **Becoming a Kwoma**, J. A. Whiting points out that amongst the Kwoma tribe of New Guinea a male will not pursue a female, lest by calling out for help and accusing him of intended rape, she draws the attention of her menfolk who would seek to protect her by killing him. Hence it is left to the woman to initiate the courtship.   ,

Margaret Mead, in **Sex and Temperament**, reveals a similar practice among the Tchambulis of New Guinea. The men of this community are lackadaisical and epicene, while their women are industrious and energetic. Hence they play the domineering role in courtship, despite the fact that their tribe is polygynous. Among the Pueblo Indians of South America, though the woman selects her partner, the procedure is carried out with more delicacy amounting to a sort of match-making. According to H. H. Bancroft's **Native Races of the Pacific States,** the female confides in her father who forthwith visits the home of the desired male to obtain the permission of his parents to the match. This is the reverse of the normal custom of the boy, or his parents, asking for the girl's hand in a patriarchal society.

In some savage societies, the method of approach employed by the female is somewhat lewd. In **Love in Action,** Fernando Henriques quotes from B. Blackwood's " Both Sides of Buka Passage ", the author's description of such an invitation on the part of a woman of the Kurtatchi tribe of the Solomons. Should a woman find that the man she desires does not court her, she will seek an opportunity to lie before him with her legs wide apart, a posture normally considered taboo, as the women of the tribe are taught to stretch their legs out decorously and keep them close together while lying down or when standing, so as not to arouse a man's libido. Among the Melanesians, this custom also prevails in the Lesu tribe.

Coming to Europe, Rattray Taylor gives us an insight into the role played by women. in courtship in pre-Christian Ireland: " . . . In this pre-Christian era, even more notably than in the Middle Ages, the running was made by the woman. Their method of wooing was often most determined: Deidre seizes Naoise by the ears, tells him that she is a young cow and wants him as her bull, and refuses to release him until he promises to elope with her."

Bride-Winning Feats

Custom apart, as far as one can judge nature's plan, it is the male who is meant to initiate the courtship and to impress the female with his strength and prowess. The woman's role is that of the pursued and sought after, turning coyly away and offering modest resistance, but eventually capitulating to the masculine charms of her pursuer, the conquering male. In accordance with this concept, in ancient and modern times, custom has decreed in certain societies that the man win the woman by entering a contest in which he proves his skill superior to that of several rivals. Thus among the ancient Persians there was the practice of single combat. In mediæval times in Europe knights entered tournaments in which they vied gallantly for a woman's favour, the contest not necessarily resulting in death but merely in the rival's defeat such as his being unseated from his horse or suffering an injury.

In the Epic period (1200-1000 B.C.) of Arya-varta, the modern India, royal brides were often won in a *swayamvara*, a contest in which the prospective husbands had to try their mettle against one another by attempting a tremendous feat. He who succeeded, won the bride The Hindu epic, **The ' Ramayana ',** begins with the hero, Rama, prince of Ayodhya, entering the lists of suitors for the fair hand of Sita, daughter of Janak, king of the Videhas. The task set before the suitors is the bending of the mighty bow of Rudra which feat even the mythological gods and demons have failed to accomplish. Then comes Rama's turn:

" *Wond'ring gazed the kings assembled as*
                              the son of Raghu's race
Proudly raised the bow of Rudra with
                              a warrior's stately grace,
Proudly strung the bow of Rudra
                              which the kings had tried in vain,
Drew the cord wth force resistless till
                              the weapon snapped in twain! "*

Rama's feat is acclaimed by the assembly, and King Janak awards him the victor's prize: his daughter, the princess Sita's hand in marriage :

" ' *Now my ancient eyes have witnessed*
                              wond'rous deed by Rama done,
Deed surpassing thought or fancy
                              wrought by Dasaratha's son,
And the proud and peerless princess,
                              Sita, glory of my house,
Sheds on me an added lustre as she
                              weds a god-like spouse;
True shall be my plighted promise,
                              Sita, dearer than my life,
Won by worth and wond'rous valour
                              shall be Rama's faithful wife! ' " *

This is the same Sita who in Hindu mythology, as explained in Chapter 1, is a daughter of the field-furrow.   In India's other great epic, **The ' Mahabharata ',** there is a similar *swayamvara* in which the princess Draupadi is won as a bride by the warrior Arjuna's skill in piercing with his arrow the eye of a golden fish fixed high aloft on a tall pole.

Yet another kind of contest, but perhaps a more thrilling one, is the love-chase of the Kirghiz of Turkey. The prospective suitors of a girl gave her chase as she gallops off on horseback wielding a whip in her fair hands. The speed with which she makes her horse run away is a little less dangerous than the stinging cuts she inflicts on her pursuers to prevent them from catching up with her.

Horseplay of another kind entered the competition among poor young men of ancient Ireland who ' horsed ' a particular woman by carrying her on their backs in turn. As the prospective bride of one of them, who was generally selected before the contest, she had to entertain them at her expense with cider and whisky. She was then ' horsed ' and the Irish game of ' hurling ' would begin. If the chosen suitor did not come off best, whichever of the lads did, won the girl as his bride.

---

* *These couplets are reproduced from a translation of the ' Ramayana '*
by Romesh C. Dutt.

In the Egyptian Sudan, suitors are submitted to an endurance feat: The rivals sit on logs on either side of the bride-to-be who has sharp knives fastened to both her arms, the points of the blades sticking out from under her elbows. The men's legs touch hers. She raises her arms and then plunges the blades into the thighs of her suitors. To the man whose endurance of the sharp pain is greater goes the fair prize.

Tests of courage, skill, intelligence, and endurance, gradually gave way to the commercial test in later times. Men were valued by the heads of cattle they had or the number of sheep and goats they owned. Eventually, on the same commercial plane, came the means test whereby the financial worth of a man became a matter of the utmost importance. Money and not the man often does the talking in our modern age, and in the land of the Almighty Dollar it talks the most.

Quaint Courtship in Western Communities

In civilised countries, particularly in Europe and among the people of the United States of America, there is generally an attitude of revulsion at the ' savage ' customs of primitive tribes. But in the matter of courtship, there will have to be a revision of this basically hollow evaluation. Apart from the fact that pre-marital sexuality is very common, but surreptitious, in both Europe and the States, both worlds have passed through phases of a quaint custom of courtship, with its own peculiar variations in different countries and regions, in all of which it is called by different names, and in a few of which it is still said to exist on a limited scale. In general, however, it may be referred to as ' night-courtship '. In origin it seems to have been a peasant custom and probably sprang from the mediæval practice of hospitality in which the host offered his wife or daughters to his honoured guests as the Eskimo is still reputed to do. Climate and limitations of house space had probably a great deal to do with it. The courting male would call on the female and spend the night with her in her parents' home, making love to her generally fully clothed, and in bed.

Queesten was the name the Dutch gave the custom which, in the seventeenth century, was very popular amongst them, being considered the proper and formal mode of courtship. They even built houses with an easily accessible entrance to the girl's bedroom so that the lover could slip in. However, sexual intercourse between the couple was strictly forbidden and if ever a girl got into trouble, the villagers would deal severely with him, sometimes even wounding or killing him. A girl without a *queester* was despised as being a wall-flower. This manner of courting prevailed in Holland till the end of the eighteenth century.

Night-running was how the custom was dubbed in Norway. The girl would don not one, but a number of skirts, presumably hoping for safety in numbers. She would then wait for her lover to enter her bedroom through the window. As distances between homesteads in the rural areas were considerable, the name they gave this form of wooing seems to have been very apt.

In the British Isles, the custom seemed to prevail in one form or another for hundreds of years. Every county had its own variation, and the most popular name for it was *sitting-up*, a misnomer, one would imagine. Among the primitive Celtic races of Scotland, Wales, and Ireland, the custom seems to have flourished even more than amongst the comparatively more civilised English. It also appears to have evolved or degenerated, whichever you wish, into a kind of 'trial marriage' similar to the hand-fasting of the Scots, as in the case of the 'island custom' in Portland which will be dealt with later.

Probenächte was the German name for night-courting. The boy would visit the girl by night. Fully clothed, they would converse with each other in the first stages of the courtship, though, having young blood and its impetuous ways, it is more than likely that they beguiled the hours in amorous dalliance. As soon as the girl fell asleep—but how did she with her gallant in the room?—the boy had to leave. Only with time was he permitted to make far more intimate advances. One imagines that the girl did a very slow strip-tease, over a long period, letting the wooer at first see her in fewer and fewer clothes. Eventually, she would surrender to his manly charms provided he proved his atavistic virility by taking her by force. After that, the visiting nights probably became 'trial nights' as a preliminary to marriage. In Germany's Black Forest, it appears, this custom has not quite died out, though, no doubt, today's parents are probably not party to the liaison as in the old days.

Frieri was the term for the Swedish version of night-courting. The wooing was hardly ever carried out in the home; at least in the summer, the barns of the homesteads or pastures some way from home, were the places of assignation. To begin with, the boy could never visit the girl alone, but had to be accompanied by a group of his friends. There then ensued a party and only when this had broken up would all except the suitor leave. The girl could remove her clothes but not her undergarments. The boy was not permitted to get in between the sheets but had to lie on top of them. In course of time, gifts were exchanged and this was considered as a token of their 'going steady' to use the modern phrase.

It was the Dutch settlers who took their practice of *queesten* to rural New England where it gained firm footing under the name of *hundling* or *tarrying*. But no less a person than Washington Irving, letting his sense of humour run away with him, jocularly fostered the idea that the custom originated with the Janokie tribe of Connecticut—from whom is derived the term 'Yankee'—affirming what advocates of free love have always expounded: " This ceremony was likewise . . . considered as an indispensable preliminary to matrimony; their courtships commencing where ours usually finish, by which means they acquired that intimate acquaintance with each other before marriage, which has been pronounced by philosophers the sure basis of a happy union . . . "

Bundling was undoubtedly a practical arrangement in pioneering times in New England. The young man would probably walk miles from the farm where he worked, to his sweetheart's home where, as was usual in those days, the family probably slept in one long room. The suitor would have to bestir himself early in the morning to return to his farm for work. Rather than let him court the girl in a cold room, it was more hospitable to let them carry on their love-making under a cosy eiderdown. Very often a thin wooden board divided the two lovers in bed, and it is most probable that this kind of courtship was encouraged mostly when the couple was engaged.

Clergymen berated the practice all over the country and its death-knell was rung in the late eighteenth century. From Rattray Taylor we learn that both in New England and New York state there was, in 1832, " a religious revival . . . based on a doctrine commonly called Perfectionism, the main tenets of which were the leadership of women, chastity and spiritual wifehood . . . " This apparently involved the habit of bundling which the Rev. Simon Lovett, who had led the revival, is said to have practised with two women. The Lovett sect soon acquired the name of ' the Pauline Church ' as a reminder of St. Paul's sojourns in the company of a " wife who was sister to him ".

One Father Noyes is reported to have founded a sect called the Oneida Community, and other such communities sprang up with names like ' Shakers ' and ' Angel Dancers ', the latter a charitable group, which was accused of practising free love. In Pennsylvania, bundling is said to have been definitely continued in isolated cases, well into the nineteenth century. No doubt improvements in housing, and changing moral values which sometimes, alas, meant growing ideas of prudery, helped to bury the custom in the end.

Tarrying was strictly not synonymous with bundling, being allowed for but one solitary night which really seems to have been a ' trial night '. If, in the morning, the couple still wished to be united, their marriage was forthwith planned; if not, they went their own separate ways.

Akin to the free love sects of America were the Agapemonites of Somerset, England, their founder being a parson, one H. J. Prince, who started the sect in 1850. As the name—derived from the Greek *Agape* or chaste love, as opposed to the sensual love of Eros—suggests, the members wished to establish a form of Platonic relationship between the sexes, but amongst several men and women, not just a couple.

The forerunners of the Agapemonites of England had been the *Agapetæ* of early Christianity, one of whom, the deacon Nicolas, had been willing to share the love of his wife with the other Christian members of the coterie to which he belonged. Though later writers have accused him of immorality, it would seem to us that it was of spiritual and not carnal love he was speaking when he made his offer, as many sects of this nature then existed, one such, the Valesians, even going so far as to castrate themselves to be the better able to practise their doctrines with no fleshly temptation to deflect them.

Prince's sect of Agapemonites fell into disrepute because, though he observed for long the chastity which he preached, he finally seems to have fallen and seduced the daughter of one of the members, which led to many resigning from the sect, and, of course, added grist to the mills of those who accused the sect of carrying on free love under false pretences.

With these instances in mind, it will be seen that the Companionate Marriage advocated by Judge Ben B. Lindsey who belonged to the Juvenile and Family Court of Denver, in the state of Colorado, was by no means a charter for free love, though in the late 'twenties it created a great stir not only in the United States of America but all over the civilised world, and was *misinterpreted* as being synonymous with ' trial marriage ' as will be proved in the next chapter.

CHAPTER 4

PIQUANT MARRIAGE CUSTOMS

Human Sexuality : Biological and Metaphysical Elements—Varying Sexual Mores—Trial and Companionate Marriages—Judge Ben Lindsey vis-à-vis Bertrand Russell—The 'Isle Custom' of Portland —Scottish Handfasting—Gretna Green : Runaway Marriages—Marriage by Capture, Rape, and Abduction—Rape of the Sabines and of Lucretia—The 'Rakshasa' Capture Marriage of Arya-varta— Mock Marriage Customs—Group or Multiple Marriages—Marriage by Elopement—Marriage by Purchase—Bidding for the Bride—Brides on Hire Purchase—Marriage by Service—Survivals of the Bride-Price—The 'Bewuddung' of the Anglo-Saxons—The Dowry System —Wives for Sale in Merrie England—Smithfield : Market of Human Flesh—Mock or 'Tree' Marriages—Symbolic Transvestitism— Morganatic and Quaker Marriages—Marriage by Exchange—Marriage : a Universal Institution.

MARRIAGE is an institution which has existed from very early stages in mankind's evolution. Analogous mating is to be found amongst some animals and birds. Amongst the latter, especially, it has been observed that a pair will keep together long past the breeding season. The sexual urge is, of course, the mainspring of these selective matings to be found in nature.

Human sexual codes are a mosaic of fragments of customs and taboos pieced together to make a somewhat complex pattern over a few thousand years and varying periods of history. Anthropologists and sexologists admit that the human sex instinct is not monoerotic but rather polyerotic, *i.e.*, directed not towards one but several objects of attraction. Hence polygamy—whereby, as explained earlier, we mean in general both polygyny or a man's marriage to several wives at the same time, and polyandry or a woman's marital alliance with a number of simultaneous husbands—was, in early times, an accepted form of marriage. Polygyny still persists in many communities such as the Arabs and Muslims in general, and, till not not long ago, among Hindus and the Mormons; polyandry has not died out either, and is to be found among primitive tribes, and also on the Malabar coast of South India. In these societies, polygamy is sanctioned by custom, law, and religion.

Monogamy evolved out of primitive group and polygamous marriages, and no doubt was buttressed with the growth of private property and ownership, though many ethnologists and writers are inclined to refute such an evolution. As proof that man's sexual urge is by no means monoerotic, *i.e.*, attraction confined to but one person, we have the recorded history of man's extra-marital escapades outside his monogamous relationship with his wife, and we know such a state of affairs to prevail today as well even in civilised societies .

Though human sexuality is fundamentally biological, it certainly has a metaphysical element—that which often leads to its being canalised into creative work, or to its degenerating into destructive ends. As G. Rattray Taylor puts it so succinctly in his **Sex in History,** " There is Eros, which is love and creativity, but also lust; and there is Thanatos, which is hate and destruction, but may also become the power to control and manipulate for useful purposes . . . "

It is the metaphysical element in the human sex urge that helps to promote family welfare, and monogamy seems best suited to maintain a community of interests, ownership, and responsibility and care of the children. As to the antiquity of marriage itself, whatever form it took when time began for the human creature, bird and lower animal life, in which one finds various monogamous species, seems to indicate that the pairing, or limited group, instinct most probably existed in our prehistoric ancestors, and, before them, amongst our sub-human ancestors. Yet though Edward Westermarck, author of **The History of Human Marriage,** points out that marriage has its roots in family life, other authorities, such as Iwan Bloch, maintain that promiscuity prevailed amongst the earliest human beings.

Sexual *mores* differ with the races and the times. This Latin term which has come to be accepted, and somewhat overworked, in modern parlance, originates from *mos* meaning ' custom ', the plural being *mores* which we interpret as ' morals '. What is customary today may be out of fashion tomorrow. Hence human morality is far from constant, particularly in the matter of sexual codes. Among the Hindus of old, as we shall see, marriage was a sacrament over which a priest had to preside. But in the pre-Christian era, and in the early days of Christianity, it was a simple private ceremony between the bridal pair itself. Occasionally the couple did ask a priest's blessing after the clandestine ceremony, but irrespective of whether they did this or not, their marriage remained valid in the eyes of both State and Church.

Only after the first millennium, and half of the next, from the death of Christ, did the Council of Trent, in 1563, take the step that St. Augustine had advocated long before, and make sacerdotal marriage mandatory. A non-sacerdotal marriage performed in the absence of a priest, and without witnesses, remained legal, but not valid in the eyes of the Church. This dogma of the Catholic Church pertaining to marriage had better be further elucidated: the Church maintains so far that although the priest administers the sacrament, it is, actually, the couple who do the marrying. Should they, therefore, be so circumstanced that a Catholic priest is not available to minister to them, they could yet cohabit, provided they genuinely desire a permanent union and seek a priest's blessing immediately they are in a position to do so.

Even the Reformation, and Luther's refutation of marriage as a sacerdotal, rather than a purely civic, affair, as he wished it once again to become, did not change matters in many Protestant countries where the practice of a sacerdotal ceremony continued. It was the French Revolution that altered the process and made civil marriage obligatory. A priest's blessing could be sought if desired, but by itself, and without a civil marriage, it did not constitute a valid marriage. Government and state control over marriage seems a happy arrangement, as it enables records to be maintained and prevents malpractices.

Having traced, in a nutshell, the evolution of marriage as an institution, let us now examine many of the quaint forms it has taken among various races, primitive and civilised, in different periods of mankind's history.

Trial Marriage

This section can well begin by explaining the *Companionate Marriage* recommended by Judge Ben B. Lindsey. It created quite a furore, and was and even still is, looked upon as a form of trial marriage, most erroneously in our opinion. It was, actually, a legal marriage with all the approved trappings of the usual marriage. At best, one may call it—and then not very justifiably—a temporary marriage, as it was dissoluble by mutual consent in case it turned out to be barren. The marriage advocated by the philosopher, Earl Russell, seems the true form of trial marriage, for Bertrand Russell, unlike Judge Lindsey, is in favour of a couple not marrying officially till such time as pregnancy occurs. In this kind of alliance, should the couple wish to part in the absence of conception, there would be no need for dissolution as no official marriage exists but only cohabitation as a kind of trial run.

The measures advocated by the sagacious Judge Lindsey were profoundly sensible ones and worth examining: In the case of dissolution, since it would be with the mutual consent of both parties, there was to be no arbitrary right to alimony, though it could be arranged on a friendly basis. Another measure was that birth control was obligatory for a certain undefined period, and such couples were to be given legal assistance in obtaining knowledge of prevention of birth. The idea behind this, of course, was that if, after a certain time, the couple decided that they were unable to hit it off together, there would be no children to suffer through their parting. On the other hand, if they discovered that they got on together, they could continue to share their lives together and begin to have children. However, if there were an accidental conception despite birth control measures, the marriage would automatically take on the guise of a normal family marriage and the husband would be responsible for his wife and child.

The most important factor in companionate marriage was that till such time as the couple definitely decided to share the rest of their existence together, and altered their companionate marriage to a family union, neither was to be financially responsible for the other's welfare. They need never convert their companionate association into a family one should no children arrive and should both wish to be economically independent of each other. Could there be a freer, happier, and yet perfectly legal, type of association between two people in love with each other yet wishing to remain untrammelled by family cares and responsibilities ?   This was no licentious cohabitation passing off under the guise of a trial marriage, nor even yet entirely a temporary marriage limited to a definite period. Its essence was freedom from the twin responsibilities of economic and child ties.

Trial marriage occurs only when there is cohabitation or regular sexual association even without the pair necessarily living together, with the express purpose of discovering whether a man and a woman are sexually well suited to each other or can adapt themselves in this, as well as other, respects. Legal, *i.e.*, normal family marriage follows if they consider themselves suitable partners; if not, they part. Hence such a marriage is an experiment pure and simple.

When trial marriages were instituted in the old societies, it was not so much a question of the partners' suitability as the desire to discover whether their union could be fruitful. Thus in Yorkshire, in the last century, when a couple embarked on a trial marriage, the man solemnly swore to marry the woman legally if she proved fertile. Similarly, the wish for proof of pregnancy seems to have motivated the trial marriages of the Dalmatians, also in the last century.

The trial marriage custom on the Dorsetshire Island of Portland was also for the purpose of discovering the prospective mate's fertility or barrenness. Behind this desire for children was property-conscious-ness and the need for heirs to inherit the name and estates of the father. However, a love of family life may also have come to play in many cases, as it would seem that the custom was resorted to by high and low, the latter, in those times, having no worldly goods of any con-sequence to pass on. Why was the Portland practice called 'the isle custom ' ? Because, in those days, Portland became, in bad weather, virtually an island, as the primitive shingle track that connected it to the mainland was practically uncrossable. Unfortunately, Londoners who went to work there, took advantage of the trial marriage practice for mere gratification of their lusts, shirking the responsibility of marriage and fatherhood when it did occur. Hence, somewhere in the middle of the nineteeth century, the custom died a natural death.

In Germany, as pointed out, night-courtship or *probenächte* often merged into trial nights. But there, as in Portland, a promiscuous young man was likely to break off his affair and seek fresh pastures. Perhaps a friend of his, or some other young man, took his place and carried on with the girl where he had left off. So long as the succession of beaux did not degenerate into a procession, the switchovers were tolerated, but an unending stream of fresh lovers would be decried on the grounds that the girl was probably lacking in some essential, and, therefore, unable to rivet a man's permanent attention.

Scotland seems to have had very broad-minded marriage arrangements. The clasping of hands and the exchange of vows, presumably of fidelity, constituted legal marriage for just one day over a year, after which the couple could part or live together as they wished. Even the birth of a child was not a binding ground for marriage, and should one partner alone dissent at the union being made permanent, the partner who objected to the breakup would have to support the child. The phrase " to be left holding the baby " probably dates back to this singular Scottish practice. Fortunately, in those days, bastardy was not stigmatised among Highlanders, and many a bastard was supported by his clansmen in the matter of inheriting property that rightly belonged to the feudal or legitimate heir. For a long time, laws of heredity prevailed over feudal laws. Apparently, *handfasting,* as the custom was called, between the children of chiefs necessitated the marriage of the pair should there be a pregnancy during the year and a day's cohabitation.

Though there are many church weddings in Scotland, the people do not seem to place great store by marriage as a sacrament. Hence the old tradition of non-sacramental marriage, in which the couple can declare, before two witnesses, that they wish to be man and wife, constituted a marriage. It is still symbolised in Gretna Green, the famous Mecca of eloping lovers wishing to contract runaway marriages in the face of the disapproval of the parents or guardians of one or both of them. The brief ceremony, if such it can be called, takes place in the blacksmith's shop. Here, a myth must be exploded : The first ' blacksmith ' of mythical fame, was, alas, a tobacconist; being a Justice of the Peace, he could join a couple in wedlock. Subsequent ' blacksmiths ' came from divergent walks of life, some being fishermen, others craftsmen. The advantage of marriage at Gretna Green is that Scottish magistrates have the right to make out marriage certificates which are recognised by English law. As a result of a law passed in the middle of the last century, one of the candidates for marriage must have resided in Scotland for twenty-one days prior to the ' ceremony ' taking place.

In the pre-Christian era, promiscuity is said to have run rampant among the passionate, romantic Irish. Virginity had little or no value, and polygamy flourished. Temporary marriages were often contracted, some for merely a year. Marital partners, too, were changed quite rapidly. The Irish believed in spicing their sexual activities with variety. What a far cry from the Church-dominated parish-pump prudery of the modern Irish, which, of course, does not include many of the young, a study of whose romantic adventures reveals that Celtic blood still courses merrily through their veins and even Roman Catholicism cannot dilute its wild richness.

Though, in the mid-sixteenth century, the Council of Trent made sacerdotal marriage compulsory, the masses seemed to be completely unaffected and did not hesitate to contract private marriages. However, the Church differentiated between invalid and illegal marriages. One that took place without the presence of a priest was considered illegal but valid. The illegality would affect rights of inheritance, but the poor of the time could hardly have bothered about that. Penalties could also be imposed for contracting non-sacerdotal marriages.

In France, in the reign of Louis XV, Maurice of Saxony, the illegitimate son of the Elector, Augustus, and the Countess Aurora of Königsmark, boldly recommended temporary marriages in a book, advocating that they should be confined to a set number of years. Though a famous general and in the service of the king, the author's views, daring for the times, were not taken seriously but used as joking points, in much the same way as, one supposes, Lawrence's **Lady Chatterley's Lover** is used today by the hoi-polloi who, for the most part, did not know of its existence till the trial case.

After the foregoing lightning survey of pre-marital customs in the West, one could hardly be justified in sniggering at the customs of either older but industrially backward civilisations, or more primitive tribes.

Equivalent to the New England custom of ' tarrying ', the Lolos of Tonkin uphold a practice of one night's experiment between a young couple; they, however, reverse the procedure, and instead of the boy visiting the girl, it is the latter who goes to the boy's house and spends the night with him. Should she return to him pregnant at a later date, he accepts her as his wife even though, meanwhile, she may have conceived a child by another experimental lover. The Munshis of Northern Nigeria permit a young man to cohabit with a girl provided the girl's mother is given so many pigs and so much cloth. Any children of the union belong to the matriarchate.

The South American Indians and Mexicans have a custom akin to Scottish handfasting. With the consent of the girl's father, a youth would live with her for a fixed period. If the union turned out to be fruitful, he was yet not compelled to marry her, unless he did so of his own free will. If the girl remained barren, the young man would seek another mate. Among the Peruvians of old, no regular marriage took place as it was not considered respectable to marry until a year of cohabitation had taken place between the intended husband and wife. The trial marriage could terminate at the end of the year unless the partners wished to perpetuate it. A West African tribe had a custom permitting a boy and a girl to live together for a short period of about a fortnight. They would then part. If she bore him a son subsequently, she would send for him, but he was not bound to respond to her message unless he felt inclined to do so.

We shall wind up this whirlwind account of trial and temporary marriage—binding, with their similarity, the different races and nationalities, the civilised and the primitive, into one erotic family—with an instance of a temporary form of marriage among Mohammedans. It is called the *mut'a* and is a contract. A woman may sign it without her family's approval. During the period of cohabitation, the man is bound to look after the woman as in a normal marriage; he may even have to confer a settlement on her. But when the limited period expires, he owes her no further sum of money. For a woman who does not desire the stability of family life, the *mut'a* is a convenient practice, as, if she exercises her business acumen, she can by such recurring marriages, fill her coffers through demanding handsome settlements. Should offspring result from such casual unions, the Mohammedans very sensibly consider them legitimate and with rights of inheritance. In North Africa, a woman who continually contracts such marriages is looked upon as no more than a glorified courtesan, envy probably having a great deal to do with such a sentiment.

Trial marriages have apparently woven an erratic but continuous pattern in the human fabric. If one is to judge married happiness in terms of sexual compatibility and fulfilment, the custom seems a very logical one. All the modern horrors of adjustment, immediately following marriage, are obliviated and the way paved for a smoother path than at present obtains. Judge Lindsey's companionate marriage seems the highest evolved form of temporary union laying the basis for a more enduring arrangement should it be desired, and granting both partners full equality of status, with no family or economic dependence, and freedom to opt out of any emotional attachment, or to stabilise it into an everlasting accord of body and mind.

Marriage by Capture, Rape, and Abduction

In every tribe, country, and race, marriage by capture has been known to exist in some epoch or other. Hostility among primitive tribes sometimes arose over such cases of abduction. Mock capture of the bride still remains a part of marriage rites among certain tribes and races. Many Christian marriage practices derive from those early days of bride capture and symbolise the winning of the bride by force in opposition to the wish of her parents and kin.

The best known case was the mass rape of the Sabines, immortalised by Rubens in his famous painting hanging in the National Gallery, London. This, perhaps, is the earliest romantic exploit of the early Romans whose descendants were to win renown and notoriety in this field. Romulus, co-founder, with his brother, of the city of Rome, let his men invite the Sabine men and women to the feast of the god Consus. At a signal given by their leader, the Romans fell on the male guests and drove them away keeping their wives as captive brides for themselves. The Sabine men waged war against Rome, and defeat seemed evident for the villainous Romans who had shamelessly infringed the rules of hospitality. But peace was brought about by the captive women who rushed between the opponents and bade them live in amity as one community. This legend symbolises woman's part in life as the mediator, the forgiving one, who is the healing balm, the link in the human chain. Racial animosity and class barriers evaporate when the potent power of sex works through her as a cohesive force.

The rape of Lucretia is another instance of sexual ravishment which, with its tragic end, goes to prove the horrors of violation, though once again the victim emerged triumphant in a manner of speaking, for Lucretia, who preferred honour to life, remains the Western model of Chastity to this day. Rome, defending her daughter's honour even against a royal seducer, fared no better over the affair than the brave but treacherous Tarquinians. Lucretia has her parallel in Sita, the Indian symbol of wifely chastity. Abducted by Ravana, the lecherous king of Lanka, the modern Ceylon, while in exile with her husband in the forest, it took a war between Arya-varta and Lanka before she was rescued and proved her chastity by surviving ordeal by fire.

In the Old Testament, the tribe of Benjamin slew the men of Jabesh-gilead and such women as the men had lain with. "And they found among the inhabitants of Jabesh-gilead four hundred young virgins that had known no men by lying with any male: and they brought them unto the camp to Shiloh, which is in the land of Canaan" (Judges, 21: 12). However, as this number was not sufficient, the order was given to the men: "And see, and behold, if the daughters of Shiloh come out to dance in dances, then come ye out of the vineyards, and catch you every man his wife of the daughters of Shiloh, and go to the land of Benjamin" (Judges, 21: 21). Accordingly, this was done, till every man had found himself a wife among the daughters of Shiloh.

Among certain Australian aborigines, abduction still occurs. A young man may lurk around another tribe's camp and club any women whom he finds alone and to whom he takes a fancy. He would then drag her to his own camp and establish his right over her by raping her in full view of his tribesmen. Sometimes, tribesmen would awaken sleeping women of a neighbouring village and abduct them at spear-point. Such a fate could, of course, befall their own wives or sisters. The women of these Australian aborigines are used to such modes of capture and of passing from one pair of hands to another pair, time and time again. The kinsmen would often wage war against the adductors, but as the custom of bride-capture was commonly prac-tised, the two parties would settle matters by the captor of the bride submitting himself to a symbolic punishment. Thus he might face a number of the woman's kinsmen and dodge their spears or arrows, thus atoning for his misdeeds.

The South American tribes and the Papuans of New Guinea followed similar customs. The bride would be abducted in reality, or the ravishment was purely symbolic. The crime was expunged by offering compensation to the aggrieved tribe. The North American tribes, being matriarchal, were gallant to their female captives. The latter were looked after by their own women folk and were adopted into the conquering tribe, after which they were married in keeping with tribal rites, and enjoyed the same rights as if they had from first belonged to their husbands' clan.

The *Rakshasa* form of marriage was looked upon as one of the eight legal types of marriage in Aryan Hindustan's Code of Manu the law-giver. The *kshatriya* or warrior, had the right to capture a woman in battle and to carry her off after having slain her relatives. Among the aborigines of ancient India, the Dravidians, the Gond tribe still permits bride-capture. In the face of opposition from the girl herself and her kin, the seducer can, with the aid of a friend or friends, abduct the unwilling bride and make her his own—a state of affairs to which she will resign herself in due course.

Among the Tibetans of Purang, a similar practice prevails with friends assisting the bride's capture. However, the suitor, rather than ravish her, would treat her kindly and court her to win her love. If she remains adamant, and he is unable to influence her parents to consent to her being married to him, his case is put before the elders of the village, or the local chief, whose verdict, favourable or other-wise, has to be abided by.

Simulation of Capture

Where the customs of capture and forcible marriage have died out, there still persists among some people, the custom of simulating capture. Thus a certain sect among the Bantus has the quaint pro-cedure of the bridegroom leading the bride from her family home to the throng of wedding guests. His relatives then tie a rope round one of her legs, and his family and hers vie with each other in a mock game of tug-o'-war. The game is won not by the physically superior

party but by the bridegroom's family, as the bride's people must relin-
quish her after a show of force and resistance.

A most fervent mock battle occurs among New Guinea's Roro
tribe. The bridegroom's friends attack the girl's family residence in
a sham invasion of the household, during which the bride has to run
away and offer strong resistance to her pursuers, employing all her
feminine tactics in the process, not excluding biting. Meanwhile, the
mother of the bride bewails the loss of her daughter's virginity and
eventually feigns a complete collapse which has to be simulated for
three whole days ! During this time, the bride is lodged in her new
home.

Marriage by capture is the only way of procuring a bride among
certain Eskimo tribes. The young man must take his bride away from
her parental home by force, and she, on her part, must defend her
honour by fighting him tooth and nail in the most literal sense. Once
he has got her to his home, the pretence is done away with and she
offers no more sham resistance. He may, however, have to curb his
sexual ardour and not consummate the marriage till he has proved his
manhood by bagging his first seal. The friendly Greenlanders have
a similar custom of abduction and resistance with the bride's final
capitulation.

A rather more elaborate form of capture exists among the
Koryaks according to William J. Fielding's **Strange Customs of
Courtship and Marriage :** " When the bride's father decides it is time
to get the marriage under way, he tells the bridegroom he may seize
the girl. *i.e.,* marry her. The mother warns the bride that the groom
has obtained the right to take her." The bride's duty is to make herself as hard to ravish as possible, so as to prove that she is chaste.
Accordingly, she " . . . ties up with thongs the sleeves and trousers
of her combination suit, so that it cannot be taken off without cutting
or untying the thongs. . . . " The bridegroom has to take hold of
her and cut open the knots. He must then touch her with an intimate
gesture indicating bodily possession, after which she ceases to resist
him and leads him to her bridal tent.

Roman brides of the plebeian class were also ceremoniously abducted in a mock capture. Though this sham pursuit-and-flight
mimicry was less extreme among those higher up the social scale, it
had none the less to be observed, and custom decreed that the bride's
hair be parted by a javelin, preferably one that had slain a gladiator.
The bride could not step over her husband's threshold as if a willing
party to the marriage, but had to be carried over to complete the
symbolic capture—a custom retained in Western marriages to this
day, though perhaps not all but the very romantic practise it.

Violence, again simulated, was also resorted to in classical Greece,
the Spartans being particularly addicted to it. The bride was left in
a dark room in men's clothes. The bridegroom would enter and take
her captive and have coitus with her in a bed other than the one he

had found her in. He would then join his companions. The bride and groom had to meet in a clandestine manner lest her family should discover the 'liaison' and her ravisher !

These piquant mock customs were, one presumes, merely to accentuate the bride's modesty and her pride in her chastity as is becoming in a virgin. 'Playing hard to get' is quite a popular phrase in the language of modern young lovers when referring to girls who do just that because they feel it makes them more desirable, and sometimes, no doubt, it does. The bridegroom's aggressiveness was meant to be a sign of his manhood and the domineering role he would play thenceforth as her lord and master. One can clearly see here th concessions the ancients made to woman's natural masochistic instincts which make her exult in domination by the male, and man's symbolic sadism making him the pursuer and conqueror, the two instincts being complementary to each other.

Group or Multiple Marriages

Marriage by capture was evolved as man's revolt against group marriages which are said to have prevailed as the earliest forms of sexual union among humans. Fielding explains it lucidly: "Group marriage is the marriage of one totem with another—that is, the men of one totem group marry the women of another, and *vice versa*. No individual man, however, has any particular wife. To illustrate, if twelve men of the first totem married twelve women of the second totem, then each one of the dozen men has an equal share of each of the women, and *vice versa*."

This kind of marriage was evidently a slight advance on total promiscuity. Such marriages have been known to occur among a few tribes till very recently. What emerges as most interesting is the fact that a little over two thousand years ago, group marriages existed in Britain. Fielding quotes none other than Julius Cæsar on this point: "'The husbands possess their wives to the number of ten or twelve in common, and more especially brothers with brothers, or parents with children.'"

As women in primitive societies did not leave their homes under the matriarchate, their husbands, who often had to visit their own sisters' homes where they enjoyed more prestige and played the important role of advisers, probably brought back with them their brothers who would thus, in a group, meet the sisters in the home of their brother's wife, and thus the group marriages would be formed. To judge by Cæsar's description of the early Britons, they were most probably matrilineal.

With the gradual evolution of primitive societies, taboos came into being, and, as was explained in Chapter 1, the strictest of them all was the incest or clan taboo whereby there could be no endogamy within the clan as all the men were brothers and all the women were sisters.   Hence arose marriage by capture which made women the property of the captor.   This spelt the beginning of the end of the matrilineal system, and the commencement of the patriarchate with men beginning to assert themselves.   The patriarchy, then, was clearly a revolt against matriarchy which tore a man away from his own children and in which his own possessions could not pass on to his own flesh and blood, but went rather to his sister's children, his nieces and nephews.

Marriage by Elopement

Whereas in marriage by capture, the bride is a helpless victim and the bridegroom an aggressor, marriage by elopement is by mutual agreement between two lovers in opposition to dissenting parents or guardians.   The classic case of elopement was of Helen, the wife of Menelaus, King of Sparta, with Paris of Troy, which precipitated the Trojan wars and ended in the death of Paris and the return of Helen to her royal spouse.

Elopement has a romantic element about it which appeals to lovers and to the world at large, unless it is your own daughter or son, sister or brother, indulging in such madness.   One has only to observe the reaction to the Gretna Green marriages of today to realise how such a runaway match can arouse either the tenderest feelings and fervent championship of " the poor young things ", or the most violent opposition and criticism.

Among primitive tribes such as the Kurnai of Australia, since clan-incest is very strict and every woman of the clan is a young man's ' sister ', exogamy or marriage outside the clan is compulsory and infringement of the taboo can bring death upon the lovers should their liaison be discovered.   If they manage to disappear till the birth of a child, they may be accepted back after they " have run the gauntlet and been given their drubbing ", as Ruth Benedict puts it in her work, **Patterns of Culture.**

If the eloping couple does not belong to the category of clan-incest taboo, then the medicine-men of these aboriginal tribes would help the elopers.   Should the girl, however, have been betrothed in her childhood, the lover has to engage in combat with her fiancé.   Sometimes the respective families are drawn into the battle.   Among the Wallari, should a man escape with another's wife, he has to face the woman's tribesmen, and she is his if he can evade their spears.

Runaway matches among aborigines in India, such as those in the Chittagong Hills, do not arouse fervent hatreds.   The young man has to perform several abductions as after the first three he is bound to restore the girl to her kith and kin when they ask for her return. If he succeeds in conjuring her away for the fourth time, he can keep her as his wife.   This seems to be a test of any young man's sincerity and perseverance, and is, perhaps, a good thing for the future happiness of the pair as his mettle is thus properly sounded.

Many modern marriage customs are symbolic echoes of the rituals of marriage by capture and mock capture. Thus the best man is a reminder of the captor's friend who assisted him to carry away his bride and to hold at bay her pursuing relatives and friends; hence also the origin of the phrase many a man uses when questioning his prospective best man: " Will you stand up for me ? " As already pointed out, when the bridegroom carries his bride over the threshold, he is doing precisely what the old Roman bridegroom did in his mock symbolism of the bride's captivity. The honeymoon is a relic of the time an eloping couple had to remain hidden to evade their pursuers, or an abductor to conceal himself and his fair booty.

Marriage by Purchase

Ruth Benedict tells us of the custom of paying a price for the bride which prevailed among the Kwakiutl tribe of the North-West coast of America: " . . . a bride was obtained exactly after the manner of a copper. Just as in any economic exchange, there was a down payment which validated the transaction. The greater the amount of the bride-price at marriage, the more glory the clan of the groom could claim, and this payment had to be returned with great interest at a return potlatch usually held at the birth of the first child . . . "

This return was the conferment by the bride's father of privileges on the son-in-law; however, privileges were not acquired by the son-in-law in the sense of their becoming his private possessions, but were rather " held in trust for his relatives, and especially for the donor's daughter's children. In this way matrilineal inheritance was secured, though there were no matrilineal groups."

The conferment of privileges was regarded as a repayment of the bride-price wherewith the bride's people ' won ' her back, so that the son-in-law had to pay yet another bride-price to his in-laws in return for which the bride's father transferred fresh wealth to him. This kind of exchange apparently took place at the birth or maturity of every child, but the accumulated wealth stayed in the daughter's family for the use of her children.

The actual bidding for the bride was a fascinating ritual when the bridegroom was somebody of importance. It had the semblance of a war between the tribes of the groom and the bride, but the weapons were, of course, blankets and coppers. Ruth Benedict provides an amusing description of the goings on: " . . . The bride-price the bridegroom paid for the bride was bid up and up as in the case of the purchase of a copper. The bridegroom and his retainers went in a party to the house of the father of the bride. Each of the nobles brought forward a part of his property 'to lift the bride from the floor' and 'to make a seat for the bride'. More and more blankets were counted out, to overpower the family of the father-in-law, and to show the greatness of the bridegroom."

We are told, however, that sometimes the transactions went awry and fights ensued between the two groups even resulting in fisticuffs and slayings. "Other families owned as their prerogative the right of building a tremendous fire in the feasting home beside which the groom's party must sit without flinching till they were burned. Meanwhile, out of the mouth of the carved sea monster which might be another heraldic prerogative of the bride's family were vomitted seven skulls, while the father of the bride mocked the groom's party: 'Beware . . . These are the bones of the suitors who came to marry my daughters and who ran away from my fire.'"

In other parts of the world, such as the Philippines, Malaya, and in Ceylon among the Vedda tribe, the bride-price is merely a token, either a weapon, some sort of gift, or food. In Africa, in districts where livestock abounds, the payments naturally take the form of cattle, goats, and sheep. Here, too, weapons and tobacco, and comparatively small sums of money, may be added on. Among the Melenesians and Polynesians, shell money is used, while the Siberians favour reindeer and furs. The Mekeo tribes of British Guinea raise the bride-price from both the maternal and the paternal branch members of the two families.

The tribes of West Africa, and the Yakuts, despise a bride if no purchase price has been paid for her, as she is then considered to be of little worth. The bride in civilised society would be to them a contemptible woman fetching no price. Pride and prestige are involved in the price given and received. An African chief has, on occasion, to pay as much as a hundred head of cattle for his bride. In Uganda, men of standing pay with as many goats and about a score of cows, while men of lesser degree would pay with perhaps half a dozen, or less, bullocks. Fielding tells us that in the Bangala tribe, " . . . a free man marrying a free woman was formerly required to give her parents four slaves, two male and two female, and no money or goods would be taken in lieu of them."

Brides on Hire-Purchase

Among the Yakut, the Tungo, and the Ostyak tribes of Siberia, a bride may be hire-purchased. The marriage takes place before the instalments are paid up, but should the bridegroom default, he very often forfeits full rights to his wife and to his children by her. If the marriage takes place when the bride and groom are yet children, as among the Kirgiz, a Turkish Muslim tribe of South-West Siberia, the instalments start from then and continue till the parties reach maturity. When the girl's family has received a considerable portion ɔf the bride-price, the boy may visit his betrothed but not marry her till the entire sum of the bride-price has been handed over.

Sometimes a bride is sold on hire-purchase even before her birth, as in the Ho tribe of West Africa. If a girl is indeed born, the future bridegroom may make payments in various ways, one of them being by his service to the household. When the girl is grown, if the parents feel they can get a bigger price for her elsewhere, they can withdraw from their pledge and buy off the fiancé with some cowrie shell coins. However, as mentioned before, other Siberians permit marriage while the instalments are still under way. Sometimes, as among West Africans, a time limit is specified, such as one or two years.

These hire-purchase bride contracts present some of the same features as similar commercial transactions amongst us, if one substitutes human flesh for inanimate objects. Thus among the Banyoro of Central Africa, the groom pays for his bride by instalments with cattle, and each of his children becomes for the father-in-law a collateral security that may be redeemed with one cow per child. Similarly, wife and children in Tenimber, we are told, serve as hostages in the maternal home where the husband and father also lives till such time as he has paid the full bride-price.

A more civilised and practical measure than the father of the bride claiming a price, is the handing over of it to his daughter for her use in case of her future widowhood or divorce. Such a gift is very often made by the in-laws direct to the bride, particularly among Semites such as Jews and Muslims. Under Judaic law, the bridegroom had to sign a written statement, called the *kethubhah* or marriage deed, promising that, in the event of his death, his widow would receive a set sum from his estate, or the same sum if he chose to divorce her. The minimum sum was two hundred silver denarii in the case of a virgin, and half that amount if the bride were a widow marrying for the second time. The husband's property was mortgaged to provide security for the wife's claim, and Fielding tells us that this custom, still prevalent, " is atributed to Simon ben Shatach, about 100 B.C."

Equivalent to the *kethubhah* of the Jews, is the *sadaq* of the Mohammedan which the Koranic law lays down as the bride's share of the husband's property. No Muslim marriage is valid til the *sadaq* is given. However, even if a legal marriage takes place without the *sadaq*, the Koranic law would presume that the wife was given such a promise, and would decide in her favour in case of divorce or her widowhood. In India also, the bride-price was converted, with time, into a gift for the bride for her future security. It would be given to her either direct by the groom, or paid to her parents and then passed on to her. It is pertinent to point out that though women in Jewish, Mohammedan, and Hindu society, occupy a somewhat inferior status, the communities yet look well after their security.

One could go on endlessly citing cases of the bride-purchase custom among ancient races and primitive tribes. We must now pass on to civilised societies in classical times, and to modern society. In classical Greece, where the wife was looked upon as the husband's property, he had to pay a price for her to her family, after which she became wholly his, in token of which the carriage that brought her to the bridegroom's home was burnt. In China, right up to 1949, the bride-price was a prerequisite of marriage. The same rule exists among Mohammedans, though in their case the father-in-law often turns over the funds to his daughter so that they may be of assistance to her.

Gold, silver, clothing, land, cattle, and other such commodities, were the purchase price paid for the bride by the Celts of olden times. The Irish called the bride-price *coibche*. Prior to the Russian Revolution, haggling over the price of the bride was common in that country too, where the custom was very popular among the peasantry. In England, King Alfred permitted the payment of cattle for the *weotuma* or bride-price. Just as among the Jews, a virgin fetched a higher price than a widow remarrying. An interesting law of King Alfred was that a freeman who had committed adultery had to compensate the husband he had cuckolded by buying him a fresh bride in more senses than one.

Marriage by Service

Amongst poorer people who could not afford the bride-price in terms of cattle, precious articles, or gold and silver, human ingenuity discovered a way out: the suitor had to 'pay' his bride-price with the sweat of his brow, *i.e.*, in service to the girl's family. A period was often specified as the young man's term of service. In the matrilineal society, the husband remained in the service of his wife's family for the whole of his married life. In Africa, South America, China, Indo-China, among the Anu of Japan, and the aborigines of India, this system still prevails. The minimum period of service seems about a year, but the maximum is an indefinite number of years, sometimes as much as, or more than, a year. Marital relations may, or may not, be allowed during the period. Of course in newer guise we have a similar arrangement in modern times when a wealthy father-in-law allows his daughter to marry an impecunious young man of her fancy and then ropes in the son-in-law to serve on his firm's staff.

The Kenai Eskimo of Alaska does domestic chores for his prospective father-in-law for a year in order to 'earn' his bride. The Yucatan Indians contribute five years, while the Ainu bridegroom of Japan must serve for a year during which he is allowed intimacy with the chosen daughter. His term may continue even after marriage or till the birth of a child.

The classical case of marriage by service is to be found in the Old Testament which tells of Jacob falling in love with his uncle Laban's daughter: "And Jacob loved Rachel; and said, I will serve thee seven years for Rachel thy younger daughter " (**Genesis,** 29: 18). But Laban substituted his older daughter, Leah, for Rachel, on the wedding night. When Jacob complained about this, his uncle gave him Rachel as his second wife: " And he went in also unto Rachel . . . and served with him yet another seven years " (**Genesis,** 29: 30).

The advantage of marriage by service, from the point of view of the girl's family, was that the potential son-in-law's worth and utility were well tested, and if he were found wanting, he could always be dispensed with so long as he had not been permitted sexual indulgence.

Survivals of the
Bride-Price

Marriage among the Anglo-Saxons, even after the advent of Christianity, but before sacerdotal marriage became compulsory in the mid-sixteenth century, was a simple affair. The self-administered ceremony consisted of the bride and groom plighting their troth while the latter would fit the ring, in turn, round every finger of the bride's left hand, in the name of the Father, the Son, and the Holy Ghost, with an ' Amen ', as he slipped the ring on to the last finger. The pledge had the same words that are incorporated in modern church ceremonies, having come to us through the long ages: " . . . for better or worse, for richer or poorer . . . " A simple wedding, yet not without solemnity.

The Anglo-Saxons of early times had the custom of child marriage, and, of course, as we have seen, the *weotuma* or bride-price. When the bride was a child, her father gave her future bridegroom's family a *wed* or pledge, which took concrete form by way of security. From this arose the word ' wedding ' which we apply to the marriage ceremonial. The old English word *wed* has its equivalent in the *wedden* of the Dutch, and the *wetten* of the Germans.

Fielding tells us: " Among the early Teutonic and English peoples marriage took the form of a sale of the bride by the father, or other legal guardian, to the bridegroom. The *beweddung* was a genuine contract of sale. Sale-marriage was the common form of nuptials. The marriage ring at this period was evidence that the bride-price had been paid." Prior to the French Revolution, thirteen deniers had to be laid down when the marriage contract had been made, a symbolic link with the bride-price of old.

The marriage contract of today is, of course, a throw-back to the *beweddung* of the Anglo-Saxons. So is the custom of the father or near-relative giving the bride away, the only difference being that in olden times he ' sold ' her away. Perhaps the most interesting of all the survivals is that of the bridal veil. Brides in many countries were, in ancient days, covered from head to foot, and their faces veiled as they were, so to say, ceremonially ' sold ' in the marriage mart. From these survivals of hoary customs, one can sense that the woman was valued, as a piece of property or goods, for the price she would fetch in terms of cattle, gifts, and, later, money.

Having served her father's interests by bringing him substantial return for her upbringing, she then became her husband's property, promising not merely to love and honour, but also to obey him. It was, in actuality, a glorified form of slavery. This degradation was symbolised in many ancient rites which have culminated in the placing of the wedding ring round her finger. In England of old, the ring merely symbolised the fulfilment of the *beweddung* or marriage contract, but in token of her newly begun servitude, the bride had to kiss her husband's right foot, whereas in Russia, both his feet had to be so touched with her lips. The French, with some subtlety, converted the degrading custom into an ' accident ', the bride merely dropping the ring, as if by chance, at the altar, and then herself stooping at her bridegroom's feet to retrieve it, thereby symbolising her servility.

The Dowry

Just as the bride-price was converted, in course of time, to a gift for the bride among Jews, Mohammedans, and Hindus, so also did the same change take place among the Teutons at a much later date, some time in the sixth century A.D. The Teutonic races were patriarchal so that even the wife's possessions were controlled by her husband, but in case she became widowed, the same price was rightly hers from her husband's estate.

It has been observed that even among primitive tribes the bride-price was returned by the bride's father in excess of the amount paid to him. This apparently was the commencement of the well-known *dowry* system. But wife-purchase, and the bride-price, existed side by side to begin with. Classical Greece, India, and Rome, show evidence of this. Greek families of standing would not permit a daughter to leave their home without giving her at least one-tenth of their wealth. In Sparta, more than half of the land had thus been doled out to the women by way of their dowries.

The *dos* or dower of the Roman bride was the property of the bride herself. During the marriage, the husband could use it, but he could not, under Roman law, squander it away or mortgage it. Even in ancient Babylonia, almost two thousand years before Christ, the famous Laws of Hammurabi decreed that should a wife leave her husband on good grounds, and should he divorce her, she had the right to take back her dowry, provided her father returned the bride-price. If the dowry exceeded the latter, which it mostly did, the husband could deduct the bride-price and give the parting wife the balance.

It must be made clear that while, amongst almost all people, the husband could use the interest from the dowry, he could not touch the capital as it was meant for the wife's future security if she became widowed, or if the husband divorced her. After the advent of Christianity, the dowry system continued as the Catholic church saw in it the protection of the widow and the woman separated from her husband. Today, in most Catholic countries, as in Asian lands, the dowry is still bestowed on a daughter at marriage, if her parents can afford it. However, even in Protestant lands, among families of great wealth, while the custom may not be carried on under the old name of 'dowry' which suggests, and in a sense *is* a 'husband-price', a daughter may often receive a settlement, or a fixed weekly, monthly, or annual income.

Wives for Sale in
Merrie England

A most intriguing custom, which is recorded as having existed in England right up to the last century, was that of bride-sale. Fernando Henriques in his **Love in Action** quotes from two sources. The first is 'The Times' of July 22, 1797, from which he reproduces the following extract: "'By an oversight in the report on Smithfield Market we are not in a position to quote this week the price of women. The increasing value of the fairer sex is considered by various celebrated writers to be a sure sign of increasing civilisation. On these grounds Smithfield may raise a claim to rank as a place of special advance in refinement, for at its Market the price of women has lately risen from half a guinea to three guineas and a half . . . '"

The other source, a magazine called 'All the Year Round', is cited by Henriques as reporting on December 20, 1884, " twenty cases in which the price given for women varied from twenty-five guineas to a penny."

Apparently the traditional system of paying a man the price for his daughter's hand in marriage degenerated into husbands selling their wives. English law, it would appear, insisted that such sales should be carried out in the presence of witnesses in the manner of auction sales. Smithfield Market, even in Victorian times, must have resembled the slave markets of Rome where human flesh was sold openly for servitude. The wives who were led before the gaze of prospective buyers. and, no doubt, mere spectators who found the proceedings a sport, were sold into a different kind of servitude none the less degrading, with, as we are told, a halter or rope round their necks. Describing such a scene, Henriques says: " . . . bids were taken, and she was knocked down to the highest bidder. The attitude of the mass of the people towards such sales was curiously ambivalent. On the one hand magistrates who attempted to frustrate such auctions were sent about their business. On the other husband-vendors were frequently assaulted by the market crowds." What, one wonders, was the treatment accorded the buyers ?

Mock or Tree
Marriages

The object of mock marriages is to thwart ' the evil eye ' and to deflect the harm that evil spirits may do to the actual bride or bridegroom. It is a custom which occurs among the Tamilian Brahmans of South India, and its origin is probably rooted in the old superstitition that initial sexual intercourse can be harmful. Hence a girl who is not the bride will dress as one and avert the evil eye from the real bride, while the latter will dress as a boy and masquerade as the bridegroom in a procession through the streets with the false bride. Later, the sham bridegroom will insult the real one by calling him humiliating names. This is symbolic transvestitism, the identification of the bride with the opposite sex destroying antagonism.

In the Punjab, once a province of Northern India, now a part of Pakistan, if an old widower married for the third time, the young bride's place was taken either by a tree, or a sheep, the idea being to protect the man from the evil fate that had resulted in death taking from him his two former wives, and to avert from the new bride the malicious hatred of the first wife whose jealousy is held responsible for the death of the second ! However, such a bride-substitute is not necessary for a fourth marriage, for by then, the first wife's wrath is supposed to have exhausted itself.

Again, among the Tamil tribes of South India, a younger brother's marriage is not supposed to take precedence over an elder brother's. If the latter, for some reason, cannot find himself a suitable bride, the tree is substituted for her, its spirit being his bride according to the theory of animism which accords spirits to every living thing. This tree marriage, then, clears the younger brother's path to matrimony.

Among the Somali tribe, the mock marriage impersonation is adopted by neither of the bridal pair, but by several completely bogus couples who resort to transvestitism, the boys dressed as girls with padding to imitate feminine curves, and the girls masquerading in bridegrooms' costumes. These latter horsewhip the former, and the horseplay continues for a whole week in return for payment from the actual bridegroom.

This custom of tree and mock marriages is not confined to Asia or Africa. Europe, too, has her versions. In Greek mythology is an episode in which Zeus was married to an oak. This is the origin of the custom, during the Dædala festival, of felling an oak and dressing it as a bride used as a substitute in the procession. In Teutonic and Slav countries a false bride in the person of an old woman, a young girl, or even an old man in disguise, is handed over to the bridegroom and his party when they call at the bride's house for her.

Tree marriages among Hindus are best explained by the belief which some of them have in animism, the transmigration of souls according to which doctrine spirits dwell in trees, in animals, in everything that lives, and even a human being's spirit can enter an animal or a plant after death. The mock marriages are obviously designed to avert the evil eye from the chief actors in the actual drama of marriage.

Morganatic and Quaker Marriages

A union between a man of exalted rank and a woman of lower social status is referred to as a *morganatic* marriage, which derives from the Latin term, *morganatica,* meaning ' morning gift '. There is also an old German term, *morganeba,* which was the husband's morning gift to his bride after consummation of their marriage. Though regarded by some as the ' price of virginity ', as if the husband were compensating his bride for having deflowered her, the fact that even a widow who had remarried a man of high rank received such a gift, indicates that the theory is not soundly based.

Since a woman who married far above her could not herself acquire either the husband's title or inherit his property, and since no children of hers by him could do so either, the marriage was referred to as morganatic, implying that the morning gift was all she was entitled to. This of course, was merely a symbolism, for actually such a wife was given a handsome settlement for her own and her children's maintenance.

In a socialist state, one presumes, such a term would not exist as the society would be a classless one. But in a class-conscious democracy, such a marriage can wreak havoc with the lives of the lovers unless they are ready to resort to a clandestine affair. The most conspicuous instance of such a marriage is, of course, that of the popular but ill-fated Edward VIII, who was faced with the choice of forfeiting the love of the woman he adored, or renouncing his throne. He chose the latter course as everyone knows.

One of the simplest forms of marriage is that of the Quakers who are noted for their simplicity and sobriety. To this day, they dispense with the existence of a clergy and require a couple to appear amidst a congregation and declare themselves man and wife, in keeping with George Fox's words: " We marry none, but are witness to it."

Marriage by Exchange

The winning of a wife by exchange is not to be interpreted as an exchange of wives. Rather is it the exchange of daughters, by their respective parents, as wives for their respective sons. Where there are no daughters, female relatives or sisters may be exchanged. The permutations can be of an infinite variety.

In Sumatra, the bridal price is sometimes foregone provided each side furnishes a wife for the other side. On the other hand, a father, in return for a wife for his son, may exchange for her his own daughter wnom the son's father-in-law may himself marry or whom he may treat as his own daughter. Should the old man marry his son-in-law's sister, she, in turn, becomes the step-mother of her blood brother. Some tribes expect a bridegroom to contribute a bride-price along with the consanguineous or clan sister he may provide in exchange.

If a prospective groom has no sister of his own, he can purchase from his closest relative a sister of the latter and hand her over in exchange for a bride for himself. This is because the relative's sister is still the bridegroom's clan sister. This kind of exchange, with a few local variations, prevails among the tribes of South Australia, New Guinea, and the New Hebrides.

Ruth Benedict tells us that the exchange of wives among the Kurnai of Australia is restricted to groups: " Sometimes two localities, out of the fifteen or sixteen of which the tribe is composed, must exchange women, and can have no mates in any other group. Sometimes there is a group of two or three localities that may exchange with two or three others."

It will be seen from this merry-go-round of bewildering marital customs that marriage, whatever form it takes, is a universally common institution treated with respect in every society, primitive or civilised. It is the basis of family life, and being tied up with rights of inheritance and man's need for transcendence, is an incentive to perpetuation of the human species.

CHAPTER 5

POLYGAMOUS AND INCESTUOUS LOVE

*Polygamy : Generalisation—Polyandry : Fraternal and Non-Fraternal
—Blood Brothers with Common Wife—Polyandry in Classical India
—Polygamy among Ancient and Modern Races—Substitute Husbands among Spartans—Jewish ' Levirate' : Polygynous Custom in
a Sense—Wife-lending—The ' Sororate' : Man married to Several
Sisters—Polygamy ropes in More Hands for Labour—Mohammedan
Tetragamy : Marriage limited to Four Wives at a Time—Polynesian
' Punalua' Marriage—Why Mormon Polygamy failed—Incestuous
Love and Marriage—Incest in Egyptian Ruling Dynasties—Rameses
II and Nefretiri, Cleopatra and Ptolemy : Brother-Sister Marriages
—Incest in the Old Testament—Polygamy in Europe—The Incestuous Pope Alexander VI—Child Marriage—Early Christian and
Hindu Child Marriages—Ghost Marriage and ' Shamanism'—
Ghandi Condemned Child Marriages—Endogamy among Modern
Zoroastrians.*

THE term *polygamy*, as previously explained, applies to the
practice of a man or a woman having more than one spouse.
Hence it covers both *polygyny* or the right of a man to have
several wives simultaneously, and *polyandry* or the right of a woman
to have more than one husband at the same time.

Polyandry is, obviously, a hangover from the matriarchal period.
It may have been due to an insufficiency of women in a totem. That
polyandry existed in classical India is evidenced by the Hindu epic,
The ' Mahabharata ', whose heroine, Draupadi, is married in fraternal
polyandry to the five Pandava brothers who lose her in a game of dice
to their hundred Kaurava cousins. As in the case of Helen and the
Trojan wars, the Pandavas and the Kauravas go to war on the battlefield to which the warrior Arjuna, one of the five Pandavas, is driven
by Lord Krishna himself in the guise of a charioteer. When Arjuna
hesitates to pull the bow against his cousins arrayed on the opposite
side, it is here on Kurukshetra (symbolic of the battlefield of Life),
that there ensues the famous discourse, embodied in the Song Celestial
or the *Bhagavat Gita,* between the hesitant warrior and the disguised
divinity who spurs him on to place duty higher even than love. The

polyandrous Draupadi is won back in the end, with her chastity untouched, for, when the Kauravas attempt to humiliate her in their father's royal court, by undraping her, she prays to the Lord Krishna for help and he causes her *sari* to be of unending length so that she remains undisrobed.

Among the Nairs or Nayars of South India, the Sakai of Tibet, and certain matrilineal tribes of Burma, polyandry of the non-fraternal variety, flourishes. Among the Polynesians, it holds sway only in the Marquesas. The argument that this custom of plurality of husbands may be due to scarcity of women, certainly does not apply in the case of Tibet which is one of the leading polyandrous countries and yet has an almost equal proportion of men and women. Tradition alone must here account for the prevalence of the custom.

The Todas practise not merely fraternal polyandry, in which a girl's marriage to a man automatically makes her the wife of his brothers, but also a similar polygyny whereby the husband of a woman becomes her sisters' husband as well. A quaint custom of the polyandrous Nairs of South India is worth describing: In Travancore, Cochin, and Malabar, where the Nairs live, a girl is married before puberty to a ' nominal ' husband. The latter places a collar round her neck, consummates the marriage, and disappears from the girl's life for ever. This may originally have been a method of averting the evil eye from the man who will, one day, be the first of her several real husbands and will not have to deflorate her. When the girl is old enough to select her spouses, she can go to a maximum of twelve. The selection of these husbands takes place with the help of her mother.

Maintenance of the common wife is the responsibility of her several husbands who generally divide among themselves the several tasks of providing food, shelter, clothes, and other necessities. As to sexual union, each takes his own turn, and whenever so inclined, he hangs on the door of the house a personal possession such as a knife, so that the other spouses may not intrude. This is matriarchal polyandry, but there is the patriarchal variety too. Here, however, the wife does not exercise the same dominance as under the matriarchate. She becomes rather the plaything of her husbands who are always greatly concerned with her fidelity to them.

Among the Todas, polyandry is strictly fraternal, the brothers of the suitor becoming his wife's husbands jointly. These are generally blood brothers, but, occasionally, they may be clan brothers of a like generation. When a child is born, paternity, or to be more precise, legal fatherhood, is shared by all the husbands. If the husbands do not all live in the same place, then it is the wife's duty to visit each one in turn. Among the Lepchas, in the North-East of India, polygyny, polyandry, and monogamy, all exist side by side.

Polyandry was also a custom with the ancient Spartans. It was motivated by economic reasons. Despite the richness of the soil of Sparta, the majority of its people were poor. Hence it was cheaper for several brothers to marry and jointly support one wife and their offspring by her than to marry separately and each support his own family. The Spartans also allowed a substitute husband. This was sanctioned by law in Sparta when the husband happened to be impotent, or if a man did not wish to marry yet desired a child of his own. According to Fernando Henriques's **Love in Action,** the Hindu Laws of Manu also gave permission for a substitute to be employed in the same circumstances.

One would imagine that while an impotent husband would, perhaps, find it not so difficult to sanction the use of a substitute husband, particularly to satisfy the wife's desire for maternity, it seems odd that a husband, even if impotent, and much more so if not, should have permitted his wife to be used as an incubator for another man's child to satisfy that man's paternity. However, it does indicate that perhaps these ancients were somewhat less possessive and selfish than husbands today. When, in modern times, artificial insemination is resorted to, it is primarily to satisfy the woman's maternal instinct, and perhaps the husband's desire to build a family around her even if not of his own blood. The donor never sees the mother, nor he her, when the test tube method is employed, and except for the doctor, even the identity of the donor is kept secret. Of course there arises the possibility that if the same donor fathers two children of opposite sexes, it could lead to incest if the two met by chance and fell in love with each other.

As far as the Spartans go, we can ascribe the custom of the substitute husband to their poverty, or to the fact that the State compelled the practice for reasons of eugenics, as it adopted male children who could serve it as soldiers; if, however, the child did not pass the test of the health commission, it was, according to Richard Lewinsohn's **History of Sexual Customs,** " thrown on the infants' graveyard in the gorge of Taygetus." No wonder the population of Sparta declined and generally remained at a low level.

Among the Polynesians of the South Seas, the Marquesas were the only islands where polyandry was rampant. This was probably due to a surplus of the male population. Another reason might have been that male labour was very much needed, particularly as, according to Bengt Danielsson's **Love in the South Seas,** the necessity for building Marquesan dwellings on stone platforms "had with time degenerated into a competition to possess the largest and finest platform." This prestige rivalry seems a far-fetched reason, yet one has only to remind oneself of the custom of ' keeping up with the Joneses ' to realise that the farcical side of human pride is universal.

Again, these polyandrous customs were not as common among the ordinary people as among the chiefs' families. The women of the community, though it was a Patriarchal one, did not hold a subordinate position and therefore had more sexual freedom. Yet it was the first husband who wielded real power, even over the subsequent husbands who were more beholden to him than to their common wife. It was he who allocated work amongst the secondary husbands who lived in separate huts, and none of whom could, without his permission, exercise his conjugal rights on a particular night. Naturally enough, a sensible chief husband would have kept the secondary ones contented by sharing conjugal rights more or less proportionately with them, and thus ensuring a peaceful and ordered home life.

Polygyny among Ancient and Modern Races

The social structure of a community, and to a considerable extent, religious belief, together govern the form of marriage allowed by law within its midst. Polygyny existed, and still does, among a variety of totally different races and societies of varying cultures.

It was only in the sixth century A.D. that the Justinian Code banned polygamy from Europe, proof enough of its widespread existence at the time. At this stage, one must differentiate between polygamy and polyerotism. Polygamy implies a multiplicity of husbands or wives, while polyerotism is natural attraction to several men or women though it may or may not lead to fornication and adultery. It is obvious that though polygamy has vanished from Europe, or precisely because of this factor, polyerotism sways a considerable section of the populace of Western communities. Pre-marital relations or fornication, and extra-marital relations or adultery, are common enough, particularly the former, especially among the working classes who generally begin their love life earlier than the middle and upper classes among whom the adolescent boys and girls are busy with academic studies till at least their late teens. It is customary for most young people, particularly young men, to have carnal experience with several individuals when they are not ' going steady ' (horrible phrase) with a prospective marriage partner.

Among the Hebrews of old, polygyny was even enjoined by their religion. Under the *levirate*, a man was bound to marry his brother's widow if the deceased had left behind no son. This obligation had to be fulfilled even if the brother happened to be already married. Another Semitic race, the Arabs—and, as a matter of fact, all Mohammedans—also practise polygyny. The woman occupies a low status amongst them, and is treated like a piece of special property not to be exposed to the gaze of the outsider. That is why among orthodox Muslim women the veil has still not been discarded. To the husband, his several wives must be the vessels of his pleasure, for that and only that, is what they are said to have been created for. "Your wives are your tillage; go in therefore into your tillage in what manner soever ye will ", said Mohammed to his followers. However, the Mohammedans restrict themselves to four wives at a time, and a fifth woman can only be made a wife when one of the four existing wives has been divorced—a procedure, which, as we shall see in a later chapter, is a very simple one among Muslims.

Though, strangely enough, it does not seem to be generally known, among the Hindus, until but a few years ago, a man could have as many wives as he pleased. But polygyny is a custom that only the rich and privileged can afford; so that despite the legal and religious sanction, this practice was far from being popular. Even among the Mohammedans of India, generally only one wife seems to be the rule. However, this monogamous existence in communities that permit polygyny, is due to circumstances mostly, and, to a certain extent, to the influx of foreign, particularly Western ideas, so that socially polygyny is declassé even among the wealthy.

In primitive society, where chiefs, priests, and sorcerers, can practise polygyny to their hearts' content, the man lower down the social scale is often left with hardly any women to choose from. This leads to wife-lending. A married man will, in return for a gift, permit a young bachelor to sleep with one of his wives. This may sound astonishing at first, until one realises that among the Fiji Islanders, for example, the chiefs monopolise a few hundred women so that there are few left to go around. In such polygynous societies, the women get used to their inferior position, and, as among the Zulus, will even help their husband to find fresh wives. A chief's marriages are influenced by tribal politics. He generally marries a woman from every village, and when a wife from a particular village dies, a substitute is provided from the same clan, and each time a dowry, subscribed to by all the male members of the clan, goes with the bride.

The ' Sororate '

Primitive tribes are wont, like the Jews of old, and other races, to marry off the eldest daughter first. Among many North American aborigines, the husband of the eldest daughter automatically gains conjugal rights over all the other sisters of his wife, a custom known as the *sororate*. He can, and in practice often does, forfeit his claim over his sisters-in-law, or rather his *sororate* wives, alowing them to marry other men. However, they must have his express permission before doing so. Often it is to him, rather than to the parents, that the bride-price is paid.

The *sororate* also flourishes among Australian aborigines, Amazonian tribes, the Kaffirs of Africa, and the aborigines of Mozambique. In Mongolia, the precedent seems to have been established by the marriage of Ghengiz Khan to two sisters.

Henriques makes some thought-provoking observations on polygyny: " Because of Western tradition, with its emphasis on Christian marriage, there has been a tendency . . . to regard other forms of marriage as inferior. This was given a quasi-scientific boost in the nineteenth century when a stage of primal promiscuity was postulated from which man evolved through group marriage, polyandry, and polygamy to the blessed state of monogamy. Such theorising . . . is highly fallacious. To speak of evolution in forms of marriage is nonsense. Each type must be seen as part of a particular structure, fulfilling its necessary and proper function in the society in which it exists. One form does not *develop* into another. Nor is one form inferior to another. All are fulfilling the same purpose—satisfying the sexual, procreative, and familial needs of men . . . "

What Henriques does not seem to take cognizance of is that social structures are apt to change, sometimes after hundreds of years, and such changes are bound to bring about alterations in the laws governing such customs as marriage and divorce. The polygamous customs of pre-Christian and even early Christian Europe were eventually replaced by monogamy. Another classic case is that of polygyny among Hindus, which has very gradually come to be replaced by monogamy. Hence, to the present writer it does not seem erroneous to think of monogamy having 'evolved' from polygamous states of marriage. But, of course, one heartily agrees with Henriques in decrying the attitude of the monogamous societies which look down their noses at polygamous peoples.

In Britain, polygyny was present up to mediæval times, and this also applied to Ireland. Of course when polygamy did not suit a man's purse, recourse was freely had to fornication or temporary marriages. As a result, many illegitimate births occurred and the Anglo-Saxon synod of 786 A.D., declared that a bastard would not be legally entitled to inherit property. The attempt was not a conspicuous success, and in the tenth century, seven years' trial marriages became the vogue. While these trial marriages cannot be considered to have been polygynous, yet they did, in a sense, cater to man's polyerotic nature.

Ancient Babylon encouraged polygyny for purely practical reasons. Labour was needed for temple and palace construction, agricultural work, and for fighting the wars. Attempts at abortion were severely punished with whipping, and even an accident resulting in miscarriage brought the individual responsible for it a fine and perhaps forced labour for the monarch ! The family law of Babylonians classified the various wives and laid down clear rules of inheritance. However, here as elsewhere, these multiple wives could only be afforded by the wealthier classes, and the poor, as in other polygynous communities, did not take much advantage of the custom. It must have been hard enough for these wretches to support one wife and family.

Among the Zulu tribes, a man's wealth is reckoned by the number of wives he has. The more land a man possesses, the more wives he needs to sow and harvest it to feed the family. The Trobriand Islanders, though mostly monogamous, insist on plurality of wives higher up the social ladder. The headman of the village must always be a man of wealth and this means he must keep several wives. In most aboriginal tribes, the first wife is generally considered to be the true one. Her status is higher than that of subsequent wives. When a wife is captured from an alien tribe, it is more for the purpose of her helping out with the household work; for this reason, she is known as the work-wife, while the first one enjoys the prestige of being the love-wife. However, their positions are sometimes interchangeable, depending on the attractiveness of each, and the man's fancy.

Every sub-clan provides a wife for a chief, according to the decrees of custom, as we have already seen, and each wife, in the event of death, is replaced by another from the same sub-clan. Moreover, every chief inherits the widows of the preceding chief. Many of them having been similarly inherited by the predecessor when young, may be quite elderly or old, having been the property of successive chiefs. Carnal knowledge of them all is not obligatory, but the right to it remains with the current chief.

Tetragamy among
Mohammedans

The restriction of Mohammedans to four wives, a custom known as *tetragamy,* is said by Lewinsohn to have been interpolated into the Koran by the Kadis. Mohammed himself did touch upon the point once, but in a vague manner, when, following the Battle of Uhud in which many men were killed, he enjoined his followers to marry their widows, "'two, or three, or four of them'". He was obviously using just a figure of speech and not laying down the law as to the exact number of wives a man should marry, and he himself remained mono-gamous in his early days, later marrying no less than about fourteen wives.

One must bear in mind that even among the Muslims, monogamy is the ideal state of marriage, but polygyny is permitted as a very sensible concession to man's polyerotic tendency. Mohammed himself set an example in his early years when he was married to Khadija, his first wife, who was fifteen years older than him, and remained strictly faithful to her. It was only after her death, while he was in his mid-fifties, that sex became a preoccupation with him, and, with every Islamic victory over the enemies of his faith, he married a new wife either from the conquered people, or from the widows of his own soldiers.

Having considered the tetragamy of the Mussulman, let us cast a glance at other polygynous communities and the number of wives customary among them. Among the Polynesians, the number has been grossly exaggerated by foreigners, as, apart from exceptional cases, the average number seems to be just two. Hence the *punalua* marriage, *puna* meaning 'source' to symbolise the woman, and *lua* meaning 'two'.

The Polynesians did not resort to polygyny in sexual abandon, but rather for several good reasons: Social and political advantages accrued by marrying wives from different clans. The greater the number of wives and children, the easier and cheaper it was to entertain the many guests that chieftains often had staying with him. If one wife were barren, or produced only female children, another had to be resorted to for male heirs. However, the Polynesians were too well principled to discard the first wife because she had turned out to be barren and could not provide a male heir. Besides, it was practical to preserve good relations with her family.

The *sororate* or custom of several sisters being the wives of one man, also prevailed among the Polynesians, as it was considered that they would be able to adapt themselves more easily than wives obtained from different families. In addition to this practice, the *levirate* or practice of a man marrying his brother's widow, also existed among them, and a chief had perforce to marry the widows of his deceased brother.

Mohammed is said to have moaned often about the scourge that a multiplicity of wives constituted with their jealousy, bickerings, and intrigues; but among the care-free Polynesians, the situation was far pleasanter as division of labour eased each wife's burden and made her feel better disposed towards the others. However, the wives could, and one supposes often did gang up against their joint husband. Danielsson, however, maintains that such methods must have been " excellent correctives for the husband."

Why was polygyny a conspicuous failure among the Mormons of America ? Unlike the South Sea Islanders, the Mormons did not grasp the psychological and practical problems of the situation, and, therefore, failed to cope effectively with it. They packed their wives together in small houses, probably through economic necessity, and enjoined on them the necessity of sisterly love towards one another, not taking into account individual and feminine caprice. They also sometimes made the mistake of showing partiality to one wife or other, and failed to allot different tasks to each one. The Polynesians, on the other hand, gave each wife a separate hut or room, divided them according to each one's social status, and thus made each one's position clear from the start, so that there was no outcry for equality as each one knew her place. Most important of all, the labour was divided fairly amongst the lot. Each wife was visited, in turn, by the husband so that he could not be accused of practising favouritism.

Incestuous Love
and Marriage

The most conspicuous of all the taboos of primitive tribes, as we saw in Chapter 1, is the incest taboo resulting from the communal totem-feast at which the clan kills and consumes its clan-ancestor, the particular animal which is its totem. The analogy to the Œdipus Complex was explained at length. Œdipus, having killed his father Laïus, marries his mother Jocasta, and when he discovers his blood relationship to her, forfeits the prize he has won and gouges out his eyes by way of repentance. Similarly, the clansmen, having killed and eaten their totem ancestor, forego, as reparation for their crime, the right to marry their clan sisters of the same totem.

Ancients, other than the Greeks, did not have this intense dread of incest. The Hebrews resorted to incestuous coitus for the sake of progeny when a member of the opposite sex, save a blood-relation, was not available. After the destruction of Sodom and Gomorrah with brimstone and fire, and with Lot's wife turned into a pillar of salt because she turned around, in defiance of the Lord's injunction not to do so, to look at the holocaust, the bereaved Lot dwelt in a mountain cave with his two daughters:

> "And the firstborn said unto the younger, Our father is old and there is not a man in the earth to come in unto us after the manner of all the earth:
> Come, let us make our father drink wine, and we will lie with him, that we may preserve seed of our father.
> And they made their father drink wine that night: and the firstborn went in, and lay with her father . . . " (**Genesis,** 19: 31-33).

The next night, the younger daughter lies with her father, and the Old Testament tells us:

> "Thus were both the daughters of Lot with child by their father. And the firstborn bare a son, and called him Moab: the same is the father of the Moabites unto this day.
> And the younger, she also bare a son and called his name Ben-ammi: the same is the father of Ammon unto this day " (**Genesis,** 19. 36-38).

Apparently, Jehovah or *Yahaveh*, the god of the Hebrews, would not tolerate the terrible sin of sodomy, but certainly showed no wrath when incest was committed; however, those, one must remember, were yet pre-Freudian times, and the Electra Complex was awaiting to be discovered by this illustrious future son of Judaism.

Those who believe the Old Testament account of the creation of the world, and adhere to the tale of Adam and Eve as the first and only human beings created, from whom all mankind owes its descent, must also grant that, in that case, human progeny started with incest as Adam and Eve had but two sons, one or both of whom must have slept with the mother in the interest of perpetuating the species.

In the Egypt of the Pharaohs, at certain periods, incestuous marriages became fashionable. In certain royal dynasties, it was obligatory on the heir to the throne to marry his sister, referred to as the ' throne princess '. Thus the son of Sethi 1, *viz*, Rameses II of the Ramesside or Nineteenth Dynasty—who persecuted Moses and the Jews till the various plagues descended on his kingdom and he was forced to let Moses take his people out of slavery, across the Red Sea which obligingly opened before them, into the Promised Land as far as the waters of the Jordan—is supposed to have been married to his sister Nefretiri who shared the throne with him.

In the Hellenistic Age, too, this custom prevailed among Egyptian royalty. Thus the voluptuous Cleopatra, beloved, in turn, of Julius Cæsar and Mark Antony, occupied the throne with her brother Ptolemy of the Ptolemaic Dynasty, who was also her husband. The Ptolemaic Dynasty practised consanguineous marriage for almost three centuries, yet though, eugenically, inbreeding is not advisable, their dynasty did not suffer from marked degeneracy.

This prevalence of incestuous marriages in Egypt possibly had some connection with the worship of Isis and Osiris, as Lewinsohn explains: " . . . any family tree, divine or human, that traces its origin back to a pair of first ancestors, must assume incest between parents and children or between brothers and sisters. Cain and Abel had no other way of reproducing their kind." The last part of this statement bears out our own views, expressed but a few paragraphs before, regarding the Old Testament version of the creation of the world.

In ancient Persia (one must here emphasise that the Persians who ruled over a mighty empire were an Aryan race from whose midst sprang the prophet Zoroaster, and their *only living descendants* are the Parsis of India and the Iranis of Persia, sprung of the same race, who still practise Zoroastrianism; the modern non-Zoroastrian Persian, including the Shah of Persia, is of Semitic stock and observes the Islamic faith of Mohammed; he is a Persian, not racially, but by right of conquest dating back to about 800 A.D., by which time the real Persians had disintegrated and many were forced to flee to India before the oncoming Muslim hordes), consanguineous marriages were commonplace, and instances of kings marrying their own daughters are to be found in the Persian poet Firdaussi's **Shah Namah** or Book of Kings.

Among the ancient Hebrews, before the time of Moses, step-brother and step-sister could marry provided they had the same father but different mothers. Thus Sarah married her step-brother Abraham. Among Arabs, and Mohammedans in general, consanguineous marriages are forbidden, the prohibition extending very clearly to in-laws, such as a sister-in-law, a mother-in-law, or the widow of a brother or a son. Thus though the Arabs, too, are a Semitic race, their ban is the reverse of the Jewish practic of *Levirate* under which a Jew must marry his deceased brother's wife.

According to the American ethnologist, Lewis H. Morgan, the Iroquois tribe have a form of group consanguineous marriage. Members of respective generations are considered husbands and wives. The grandparents belong to one generation, the parents to the next, and the children to the third. In simpler language, brothers and sisters, as well as first cousins, may marry among themselves, but the line is drawn at a father marrying a daughter or an uncle marrying a niece.

Among the Polynesians, marriages were forbidden, in early times, between uncles and nieces, or parents and children. Yet on some of the islands the rule was flouted. In Hawaii, it was claimed that a chief could have no better marriage partner than his own sister—reminiscent of the custom among the Egyptian ruling dynasties. The offspring of such a union among the Polynesian hierarchy was considered to be a superior being referred to in divine terms and highly respected so that all who entered the child's presence had to bend low and touch the ground in humble prostration. The union between brother and sister was likened to a bow which was bent, and for that reason it was called a *pio,* the native term for a bow. It often happened that such a consanguineous relationship was combined with polygyny or polyandry.

Apart from Hawaii and Rarotonga, incest was little known in the islands of the South Seas. The incest taboo even applied to a ' name-brother ', *i.e.,* one who had thrown in his lot with a man without in any way being related to him. As they enjoyed all the rights and privileges of real brothers, they also came under the bans that applied to consanguineity. They therefore could not indulge in coitus with each other's wives.

The Christian Church, while presumably not opposed to the Adam and Eve theory and its inevitable implication of the two sons, or at least one, committing incest with Eve, the mother, viewed incest with the same horror as primitives. Yet it was rife among Christians right up to mediæval times. Thus Pope Alexander VI was accused of incest with his daughter, Lucrezia Borgia, and is said to have promptly blamed his son Cesare of having perpetrated the same crime with his sister, the aforementioned Lucrezia. It has also already been pointed out that other popes, too, were guilty of incest. A peculiar pheno-menon was that though the early Saxon Christians had refrained from forming marriage alliances with their first cousins, in the eleventh century the Church, carried away by its primitive horror of incest, expressly forbade the marriage of cousins of the second, or even third, degree.

Among North American Indians, polygyny was interspersed with incest, the reason for the former being a surplus of women owing to so many men getting killed in wars and skirmishes. Should, for some reason, the balance be disturbed and the men outnumber the women, no doubt polyandry would be resorted to, as, among primitive people, a state of non-marriage is unthinkable. Moreover, it was quite customary among the tribes of California and Omaha for a man to marry a niece or even an aunt. The wives sometimes favoured these arrangements, often even seduously encouraged them, on the grounds, no doubt, that the she-devil they knew would be easier to cope with than an alien they did not know.

Ghost Marriage
and ' Shamanism '

Perhaps the strangest marital custom is that of the ' Ghost Marriage ' among the Nuer tribe of Southern Sudan. The custom rests on a superstition that a grown man can find peace in death only if he has children to keep his memory alive on earth. Therefore, should a mature young man die before his marriage, a relative of his must, in his name, marry and beget children. If this is not done, the dead man's ghost will haunt his kith and kin, and bring evil fortune to them.

The relative who acts as a ' stand-in ' for the dead man, plays the role of an actual husband in household matters and conjugal relations, yet, legally, he is not the husband, and the children are considered to be the dead man's, the wife and mother being looked upon as the lawful married wife of a ghost !

Yet another weird custom is that of certain tribes of Siberia, such as the Yakut, Chuckchee, and Buryat, who practise a religion called *Shamanism*. The *shaman* is a kind of medium between this and the spirit world, and is generally given to epileptic fits while communing with *kelets* or spirits that combine in themselves the elements of good and evil. They are homosexual, and though of the spirit world, are said to espouse human beings, but only in homosexual relationships. This appears to be a cover for actual homosexuality, for we are told by Henriques that " . . . both men and women *shamans* enter into homosexual relationshops with humans . . . " Curiously enough, while permitting shamanic homosexuality, the ordinary form of homoerotism is severely disapproved in these same communities.

Child Marriages

Amongst different races in different lands, amongst primitives and the civilised alike, a curious custom exists: the marriage of children, sometimes even before their birth. Perhaps the most grievous type of child marriage is when a girl is betrothed to a man who is old enough to be her father.

Because in England at least one is used to girls and boys marrying generally in their late teens or early twenties, and very rarely in their early or mid-teens, one is apt to think that this is the custom in all Christian countries. However, the old Roman law which permitted marriage at twelve years of age for the girl, and fourteen for the boy, was accepted by the early Church and still prevails in parts of Europe. Modern legislation, spurred on by social consciousness, may have raised the age limit for marriage here and there, but the chief reason for this is the economic factor, particularly in industrial countries or those that are becoming gradually industrialised, where the high cost of living makes it difficult for a young man to start a family.

In mediæval times, ignoring the legal age of marriage, the Church performed *spousals de futuro*, which meant blessing future marital unions between persons not yet of marriageable age. Rattray Taylor tells us in **Sex in History** that " . . . the Church performed marriages on children . . . even on infants in arms. For instance, the youngest marriage in the Chester records is one between John Somerford, aged three, and Jane Brerton, aged two; the point of those early marriages was frequently to prevent an estate reverting to the crown under feudal law. For the marriage of those under seven, parental consent was necessary. But all such marriages could be declared void when the legal age was reached, provided copulation had not taken place. Conversely, copulation was also what converted spousals, technically, to marriage . . . "

The last sentence needs elaboration. The mediæval Church, with its horror of sexuality, had its own ecclesiastical courts which functioned apart from the civil courts, and sexual offences generally fell within the former's jurisdiction. Canon law did not, like civil law, seek to protct an individual coming to harm through others' misdeeds, but sought more to save him from his own weakness. Hence, it punished impurity of thought, and much more so, fornication. A couple who confessed to, or were caught in the act of, fornication for the first time, had to sign a contract to the effect that in case they fell into sin for the third time, they were to be considered as having wed each other from the date of the first act ! Presumably the second act was permissible. But the third act resulted in ' marriage by punishment'. Refusal to live as a married couple meant excommunication, and the ecclesiastical courts could even deprive the man of his civil rights and force him to public repentance by making him confess his sin, before fellow-citizens, enveloped in a white sheet.

The Church almost gained a stranglehold on secular law, and many of its absurd and sadistic measures were incorporated into civil law. It is, therefore, easy to understand that if fornicators could be forced to marry, those already betrothed, converted the betrothal into marriage by committing *copula carnalis*.

It was the upper classes of England who practised child marriage extensively, obviously to guard inheritance. Soon their example was followed by all classes. As the important factor was to avoid payment of feudal dues by means of child marriage, the custom became so widely prevalent that in Scotland such marriages were banned at the turn of the sixteenth into the seventeenth century. Child marriages at the ages of two and three were also in vogue in both France and Italy during the Renaissance, and these were consummated when the children reached puberty. Sometimes the daughters, while yet tender girls, were handed over to the families of their future husbands, probably to relieve the parental homes of an economic burden at least where the not so well-to-do were concerned.

Child marriage among savages is a commonplace occurrence. Sometimes, as in East Victoria, a boy is betrothed to several girls so that there would be less danger of his losing a wife through the girl's premature death; similarly, a girl would be wedded in her infancy to several boys. What is odd is that this kind of child marriage existed even among non-polygamous tribes. Presumably, on coming of age, only one of the several child husbands or wives was chosen, probably the first one to have been betrothed.

The most pernicious custom was that of marrying the girl to a mature man. Often the girl's upbringing was paid for by the future son-in-law so as to establish his claim over his future wife, and to relieve the parental home of financial worry. The custom could also have its amusing and convenient side. William J. Fielding narrates one such story in his **Strange Customs of Courtship and Marriage** : A Tasmanian was concerned about the attention being paid to his wife by a youth. The husband solved the problem by giving his child daughter in marriage to the youth so that, under the mother-in-law taboo, the young man had perforce to desist from his romantic ardour for his child bride's mother.

Child betrothals can also prevent marriages by elopement, and among tribes which discourage pre-nuptial relations, it also protects the girl's virginity. In Hawaii, the *hiapo* or children were often betrothed in their infancy, the two families exchanging gifts. The odd part of such marriages was not merely the marriage of a girl to a grown man, but also that of a boy to a grown woman. In the former case, the bridegroom might even relieve the parents of the responsibility of rearing their child, and entrust her walfare to trustworthy hands with implicit instructions to fatten the girl, as the Hawaiians relish plumpness in their women.

The Congo tribes find a child bride cheaper than an older one. Among the Trobrianders, according to Malinowski, betrothal in infancy is looked upon as marriage, and the designations of husband and wife are conferred on the children, even though, when the time for consummation arrives, another ceremony is performed. These people allow pre-marital experience so long as the affairs are conducted with propriety. This is tantamount to the pre-nuptial sexual lives of the young in modern civilisations where hypocrisy rules that you can do what you please so long as you are not found out.

India, of course, has been the country most notorious for her child marriages among the Hindus, the majority community. The *Vedas* or Holy Books give quite sensible reasons, in conformity with the religious ideas they propogated, for this ancient custom which continues only among the very backward sections of the Hindu community. The main reason is a religious one: A man, to gain happiness in the next world, had to leave behind, if possible, a long line of male descendants, and according to the *Rig Veda,* or Book of Hymns, an adopted son could not adequately act as a substitute. To quote Fielding who, in turn, cites another source: " . . . a Hindu man must marry and beget children to perform his funeral rites, lest his spirit wander uneasily in the waste places of the earth." The orthodox Hindu believes in reincarnation, but this doctrine makes it clear that a departed soul may not inhabit a fleshly abode again for many, sometimes countless, years, after the death of its previous body. Hence ' in the waste places ' would indicate the childless soul haunting the earth as a ' ghost '.

Hindus, like Christians, subscribe to belief in ' original sin ', so that they consider that every child is born in sin. But marriage, with its sacramental ritual—for, till recently, marriage among Hindus was a sacrament—is considered to get rid of this sin. Hence child marriage serves to regenerate the child.

The *Vedas* enjoin that a girl must marry before " her breasts swell." The *putra,* or son, saves his father from *puta* or hell, and child marriage facilitates the process of an early fatherhood. Thus it can be seen that child marriage among the Hindus was in keeping with the religious teachings of the people. However, Hinduism, being one of the oldest religions in the history of mankind, has a great deal of superstition clinging to it. Hence the *Vedas* confer doom on parents, or an elder brother, whose daughter and sister respectively, has not been given in marriage before the commencment of her menstrual period, and command that a Brahman who marries such a girl should be ostracised. Needless to say, the enlightened Hindus disregard these ancient counsels as being out of keeping with modern times.

The age of the bridegroom is prescribed by the Laws of Manu in proportion to the age of the bride. Thus he can be three times as old as the girl just under eight, but only two and a half times the age of a girl of twelve. Hence the absurdity of marrying a mere child to a man much older than her own father is minimised, though, we dare say, among the ignorant and avaricious, this law is probably waived aside in return for monetary compensations, which, with a people as disgracefully poor as the masses of India, cannot be ignored.

Fielding quotes Mahatma Ghandi as having said: " I loathe and detest child marriages." A rebel as ever, we are told that Ghandi maintained that the Hindu scriptures did not sanction child marriage, and if, unbeknown to him they did, they were wrong. Certainly, enlightened Hindus no longer carry on with the custom, just as when both religion and the law, till recently, permitted them an unlimited plurality of wives, even the wealthy ones amongst them generally remained monogamous.

The Zoroastrians of ancient Persia also seem to have prescribed to the notion that a man who left no issue was far lower in the scale than the man with children. They held the odd belief that heaven would shut her pearly gates before the childless man. Their descendants, the Parsis, certainly do not hold such weird beliefs, and are the most liberal-minded religionists one can find, subscribing mainly to the three excellent tenets of Zoroastrianism: Good thoughts, good words, good deeds, in token of which the Zoroastrian boy or girl, during the *navjote* or initiation ceremony just before puberty, dons a muslin garment over which is tied a specially woven *kusti* or sacred thread which must be tied three times round the waist as a constant reminder of the three precepts.

Parsis certainly have no child marriages amongst them, today, as such a custom was long abandoned, though it did exist in its last tottering stages, about three or four generations ago, and many a Parsi, in his late thirties or over, can recall his parents telling him stories of how his or so-and-so's grandparents were married as children, or even ' promised' to each other before birth.

Among the legendary Persians, incest was rife, particularly in the royal dynasties. Due to the endogamy of their early ancestors, the Parsis of India are inclined to decry marriages outside of the community, whose numbers, due to this short-sighted outlook, are fast dwindling, the whole community totalling less than one million. In the last two generations, exogamous marriages with Hindus, Muslims, and Christians, the latter mostly English or American, have taken place to a limited extent. But if a Parsi woman marries a non-Parsi, her children are not accepted into the community and are barred from the Zoroastrian fire-temple.

Descendants of yet another and early civilised branch of the Aryan family, and the first Aryans to build a mighty empire greatly feared in its time, the Parsis display the typical arrogance of those of Aryan descent—perhaps with a little more justification that Hitlerite Germany where lack of endogamy such as was strictly observed among the Parsis until recently, must have considerably diluted the Aryan blood—and proudly proclaim that to be a Parsi you must be born one. Proselytising is scorned by these modern Zoroastrians, despite their rapidly dwindling numbers. Marriage among first cousins is permitted but is not customary today, and of course, marriage between nearer degrees of blood kinship is strictly forbidden.

CHAPTER 6

MATCH-MAKING AND MARRIAGE RITES

The Match-Maker—Matrimonial Bureaux—'Mariage de Convenance'—Jewish 'Shadchan'—Japanese 'Nakaudo' and 'Naishōkiki'—Symbolic Relics of Matrimonial Customs : Rice-Throwing and Egg-Breaking—Fertility Rites—Symbolism of the Wedding Ring and Wedding Bells—Joining of Hands at Marriage Ceremony—A Beatnik Wedding in Southampton—Lad of Seventeen acts as 'Preacher'—Marriage Merry-go-Round—Relics of Bride-Capture in Ireland, Scotland, and Wales—Malthusian Doctrine obstructs Marriage—Blessing the Bridal Bed—The Three Tobias Nights—Symbolism of the Shoe thrown at the Bridal Couple—Painful Bridal Night—'Goblin' Wedding—Roman Marriage : The 'Confarreatio' and 'Usus'—'Patria Potestas' : Roman Patriarch's Right of Life and Death over Children—Sacerdotal Christian Marriage—Marriage Laws.

I N primitive and backward societies, marriage is, as we have seen, hemmed in with many taboos, most conspicuous of all being the incest taboo. Civilised communities, particularly in the West, give the individual considerable freedom in selecting a marriage partner. However, one must not imagine that the freedom is unlimited. Financial, class, and status values often prevent the path of true love from running smoothly, especially in the case of 'minors'.

One has only to read the columns of the daily Press to realise the plight of young lovers whose parents do not agree with their choice of a husband or a wife. Snobbery often has a lot to do with parental objection when the young attempt to transcend class barriers, and except for the aristocracy who, at least in England, have a monopoly of eccentricity and throwing caution to the winds—modern royalty generally excepted, which makes it far less glamorous than the old, autocratic, flamboyant royalty—bourgeois parental views often win the day. The conforming individual has generally to limit his or her selection to a particular class, creed—this applies especially to Roman Catholics—or race.

The romantic love which exists in modern civilisations, is, for the mature person, an individual affair, unless it happens to be a member of royalty not too far down in the line of succession to a throne, or in the case of the aristocracy, to a title. But in primitive society, a marriage is treated as an affair that concerns the family and even the clan as all in it are ' brothers ' and ' sisters '. Marital unions are not formed, as in the West, merely to meet the biological and material needs of a couple, but rather with a view to forging worthwhile links and relations which generally involve property. The entire manœuvre of bringing about a suitable partnership is often carried out with the precison of a battle plan.

The Match-Maker

The match-maker in civilised society has become something of a figure of fun; but in tribal society, he occupies an honourable place. He serves as an intermediary carrying out negotiations and ironing out differences with the consummate skill and delicacy of a seasoned professional. In Europe, the match-maker once played a far more dignified role than he does today, particularly among the peasant communities of such countries as Poland, Russia, and Germany.

Matrimonial bureaux are a flourishing trade in England, but they probably cater more for the middle-aged and those who, because of their manner of existence, have not the opportunity to make suitable contacts on their own. In tribal villages, the headman often officiates as the go-between, taking his instructions from the grandparents, or an uncle, rather than the parents. The same happens on the other side, so that the negotiations are carried on by the two intermediaries.

In **Love in Action,** Henriques informs us that in the Sikkim village of Lingthem, " All the real marriage negotiations are carried on between two *bek-bu* (between-men) representing each side. Any experienced and tactful man, with the exception of the spouse's father, who knows the correct things to say and the correct way to say them and has sufficient vocabulary of the *tong-bor* (elegant circumlocutions) may take this role . . . " After due discussion, the girl's *bek-bu* would confront her family with a proposal from the other side, which, at first, they would make a show of turning down, then ask the intermediary to make further inquiries about the boy's character, disposition, and labour worthiness. An astrologer would also be consulted to see whether the horoscopes of the prospective partners foretold harmonious relations between the pair.

From all this it must not be thought that romantic love is non-existent in primitive society. Owing to the greater freedom of pre-marital sexual practices, the intensity of ungratified romantic ardour may be missing—for it is the artificial restraints and bourgeois conventions of modern society that promote romanticism—but that it exists, there is no doubt. Lovers' suicide pacts occur as much among the aborigines of the Fiji Islands, the South Sea Isles, and the New Hebrides, as elsewhere. In Tibet, Siberia, and New Guinea, elopements often take place, and sometimes mock ones with the full connivance of the parents. This is sufficient evidence that romantic love stirs even the savage breast.

During Europe's Romantic Age, romance took on a commercial value, paradoxical as it may sound. The fashionable spas, such as Baden-Baden, which was then the Queen of them all, became disguised marriage marts, and parents who could afford it, travelled to them with their marriageable daughters in the hope of finding them suitable partners, one of whose main attributes had to be a fat bank balance.

The ball-room also became a hunting-ground, and balls were organised with regularity in the capitals and big cities of Europe. If, after the ball, many a heart was aching, there was many a heart also rejoicing. The coming-out balls of débutantes in London, and, till recently, the court presentations to the monarch, all served to show off the charms of the young on the threshold of life. In all societies, whether savage or civilised, dancing seems interlinked with sex. Ballroom dancing, of course, by bringing couples into close proximity, stimulates the sexual urge, and many a marriage is made, in a manner of speaking, to the tune of a waltz and the rhythm of dancing feet.

Just as in Europe the *mariage de convenance* or marriage of convenience, was, and probably still is, effected for political reasons, particularly in royal circles, so also among savages does the custom prevail. The Polynesians, it appears, are obsessed with the desire for purity of blood, and among their aristocracy mésalliances are carefully guarded against, especially where the daughters of the chiefs are concerned. As individualism is crushed in their society from an early age, and community interest is drilled into the minds of the young, there does not seem to be much difficulty in their adapting themselves to the spouses they are saddled with by their parents.

On the island of Mangareva, if marriages of members of the chieftain clans took place with commoners for several generations the progeny were treated as Ishmaelites in the same way as in the European morganatic marriages which did not confer royal or titular status on the noble's commoner wife or her children by him. Like the balls and social occasions in civilised society, which serve to parade *en masse* the attributes of young men and women, the Maoris of the South Seas and the Samoans had a custom called, by the former, *kai tamahine*, or mass courtship. During a festive season when there was not much work, the young men of a neighbouring village would visit the home of a prospective bride, and with dancing, music, and singing, exhibit their masculine charms. The game of love afforded much merriment with each suitor vying with the others for the fair one's attention. Casual coitus with other female members of the family was part of the fun, just as, no doubt, such promiscuous dalliance also plays a part in civilised society, particularly in the West.

The Jews of Europe have had, since mediæval times, right up to our own, the services of *shadchans* or professional match-makers. Their existence can be understood when one realises that the Jew lives in Christian Europe in an atmosphere of veiled hostility which is made obvious only when an outright racialist such as Hitler arises to proclaim it with bravado. Naturally, marriage into Christian families is, for the Jew, a problem, and endogamy becomes a necessity; besides, the Jews themselves very often prefer marital unions with members of their own race. Often it may happen that in some towns and villages, too many Jews have been wiped out in a purge such as the inhuman practices of the Nazis less than a quarter of a century ago.

The few Jews, thus isolated from other members of their race, find in the *shadchan* a convenient intermediary. Among Jews from Slav countries, the practice has been particularly rife, and they have taken it with them to the United States where it still exists, again because it is well known that in the New World, too, anti-Semitism covertly exists. It would seem that in America there are special matrimonial journals that cater for the lovelorn of all races, and it is also possible to procure a wife or a husband by mail order.

In Japan, the match-maker is called a *nakaudo*. He comes in once the *naishōkiki* or family ' spy ', mostly a woman, has found a suitable partner for a boy, and a meeting of the couple has been arranged with apparent and elaborate casualness. The *naishōkiki* not only arranges the match, but also supervises the marriage festivities and officiates at the wedding ceremony.

Following the French Revolution, there was a campaign for increasing the birth rate. Women walked the streets invoking their fellow citizenesses to give more children to their country. Henriques informs us that taking advantage of the State marriage policy, in Paris, one " Liardot founded the first marriage agency, under the name of *bureau de confiance*, combining it with a boarding house for daughters of marriageable age. The undertaking prospered so well that Liardot soon added a bi-weekly gazette entitled the *Indicateur des Mariages*. The agency itself gradually developed into a pleasure resort in which clients danced and gambled, and could make female acquaintances without any serious thought of marriage. M. Liardot's idea, however, caught on and out of it there developed a flourishing business branch of sex life."

Symbolic Relics of Matrimonial Customs

A review of matrimonial rites in various parts of the world and in different periods, presents an interesting cavalcade of pomp, pageantry, and circumstance. Weddings are generally public ceremonies through which due notice is, as it were, given to the community as a whole that henceforth a couple will be united to each other. All the aspects of duty and responsibility to the community which the latter values in a couple, are embodied, symbolically, in the various marriage rites. Through the wedding ceremony, society bestows its public approbation and its collective blessing on the union and its hoped-for fecundity.

The grain, generally rice, that the earth yields from her fecund womb, is strewn over the bridal pair in both East and West, though confetti has, to a large extent, replaced the rice in Western countries. Before the Russian Revolution, hops were sprinkled over the bride's head. In the Orient, the bride and bridegroom carry cocoanuts in their hands and an egg, held in a woman's hand, or a cocoanut, is ceremoniously made to encircle the bride's head three times before being broken at the feet of the bridal pair. These are obviously invocations to fertility. The Maronite sect of the Syrian Christians in the Lebanon, throws corn and raisins at the newly married couple, while the old Chinese custom was to place fruit and nuts in the corners of the bridal bed. These symbolic fertility rites are very poetically interpreted by Henriques:

" The symbolism of fertility in the use of seeds can be extended from the womb to material prosperity in general . . . It is a very good example of the duality of this type of symbol. The connection between the seed germinating in the earth and the sperm germinating as it were, in the womb, is obvious. In the same way, the idea of the seed growing in the earth symbolises the growth of prosperity, for in present society prosperity is equated with crops . . .

" Promotion of the woman's fertility and the achievement of material prosperity may depend upon the averting of evil. The symbolic offerings of grain, rice, fruit, and nuts, have also a proprietory function . . . "

Flowers—in beauty perhaps excelling all of nature's bounties—are the most decorative part of weddings the world over. Garlands, button-holes, bouquets, sprays, or a posy, are worn or carried. In the West, the bride's spray or bouquet often has orange-blossom or white lilies predominating, the former, a prolific bloom, symbolising fertility, the latter, virginal purity. The Crusaders are said to have introduced the orange-blossom from the Middle East for bedecking the bride with, no doubt having noted the Saracen custom of placing an orange-blossom crown on the bride's head. Thus in mediæval times, the Western bride, like her Eastern counterpart, wore a chaplet of orange-blossom over the veil covering her head, or sprigs of orange-blossom. The flower girls who strew flowers in the bride's path are meant not merely to smooth her path, but also to evoke fruitfulness.

The egg-breaking previously mentioned, is a custom still prevalent in India, Persia, Java, and other countries of the East. In Europe, about three centuries ago, the bridal pair would crunch them under their feet. Not only was fertility implied by this custom, but also the breaking of the bride's maidenhead. The egg has been replaced in many Western communities by articles of fragility such as china or glass. To this day, glasses or pots are broken in Germany, Scotland, Yorkshire, and Yugoslavia. Among Jews, either the *rabbi* or the groom breaks a glass at the wedding ceremonial. Among Serbs, the groom's father accompanies the bridal pair to the bed-chamber and drinks a toast to them, after which he shatters the glass on a window. Hearing the noise, the eavesdropping guests attempt to break an egg which has been placed in a sack. This symbolises the consummation of the marriage by the bride's defloration.

To sweeten and smooth the course of married love, the Spartans, Rhodesians, Bulgarians, and Rumanians, smear the door with honey. Morrocans smack their brides by way of asserting their authority. The commonest custom of all, of course, is the exchange of rings. Whether it has a phallic origin is hard to say with certainty, though the finger could be taken as symbolic of the phallus, and the ring of the vulvar entrance, the slipping on of the ring signifying sexual union. That the ring symbolises union is undoubted. Among the early Egyptians, the circle, as depicted in their hieroglyphics, represents eternity, and the wedding could thus signify everlasting unity in this life and the next.

Wedding rings are normally plain gold bands. Among Christians in Europe they do not appear to have been used till the ninth century A.D. In later mediæval times they were exchanged to solemnise the bond which was verbal. The ancient Romans used iron for their wedding rings. The Hebrew wedding rings were generally of gold, but silver, or even a baser metal, could be used. The exact origin of this token of unity seems lost in obscurity. One theory is that the ring evolved from the custom of marriage by capture when bracelets were used to fetter the captive bride. Thus a suitor in ancient Ireland would give his sweetheart a bracelet made of human hair. Whatever the origin, the ring is a very old symbol of conjugal unity, and in Greece have been found rings used for betrothal in 400 B.C. Among the Hebrews, the wedding ring was certainly symbolic for it was often too large to be worn round the finger.

Wedding bells in Christian society herald joy for the bridal pair, as well as a crisis in the life of society, for in the union, two families that are part of the community, have come together. From the newly married couple, it is hoped, will emerge a fresh branch, an off-shoot of the old ones sprung from the communal family tree. Just as at puberty, a religious ceremony, such as the Catholic first communion or the Zoroastrian *navjote*, welcomes the boy or girl into the life of the community, the marriage ceremony confers on the couple a share of the responsibility of maintaining the community and keeping it going by their own contribution towards its welfare.

The joining of hands during the wedding ceremony is an enchanting custom still to be found in many old communities of India, Burma, New Guinea, and among Christians. Among the Portuguese and in countries of Eastern Europe, the priest may bind the hands of the bridal pair with his stole. This custom also exists among Zoroastrians, and a Parsi *dastoor* or priest may also use a sacred thread for the purpose. In old China, the couple's hair was tied together.

In a nutshell, marriage is of all legal contracts the most important, as on it family life is built, and the fertility resulting from it helps perpetuate the community. As Malinowski avers. " . . . it focuses in a difficult personal relationship of two the interests of wider groups: of the progeny of their parents, of their kindred, and in fact of the whole community."

A Beatnik Wedding

For our first description of a wedding ceremony, we shall take a modern rite in a progressive and advanced society, *viz*, England, the locale being the port of Southampton, and the setting, the altar of the Church of the Merchant Seamen, so that when the nuptial rites of more barbarous and backward countries are unfolded, the shock they might otherwise engender will be cushioned, and the judgment of them will not be delivered with too superior an air.

On the very day that this chapter is being written, the *Daily Mail* (May 25, 1962) of London, carries an authentic but tongue-in-cheek account of a wedding, by its reporter, Bernard Jordan, an eye-witness, which we here tell mostly in his own words:

" The bride wore black. Black jeans and black pullover. The groom wore brown knee-high cowboy boots and a beard.

" The congregation, in beards and donkey-jackets, became a little restive as the ' preacher ', Kenneth Hinkins, 17, got half-way through the marriage ceremony . . .

" So he said: ' Okay, peasants, let's cut it out. You're man and wife '.

" A clarinet sounded a beat version of the *Wedding March* in the roofless and war-blitzed Church of Holyrood in High Street, Southampton.

" Violinist Barry Stallon, 19, kissed his ' bride ', art student Hilary Birkett, 16, and waved to the cheering beatnik guests.

" A young man with hair stretched in folds down to his shoulders, who was keeping watch for any sign of the police, shouted ' All clear '.

" Another mock wedding before the altar of the ' Church of the Merchant Seamen ', preserved as a garden of rest by the people of Southampton in memory of men who died at sea, was over.

" Ken Hinkins said: ' So far I've conducted about 15 weddings this year. I guess I ought to be a preacher, dad '.

" Later, the bride and groom said: ' We don't regard it as a mock marriage. We are man and wife.

" ' You don't have to go through the red tape of church services, permission from parents and all that rot to be man and wife.

" ' With all this talk of war and bombs falling life's going to be too short to worry about that sort of thing '."

Church ' red-tape ' can certainly be dispensed with as it is no longer mandatory. But what about a marriage certificate, and permission from the parents of the bride who is reported to be only sixteen ? She, however, is unconcerned:

" ' Of course my parents don't know we're married. They wouldn't agree I suppose . . . Even if my parents did agree to a wedding I couldn't go through all that rigmarole of wedding dresses and brides-maids.' "

The report reveals that the couple first got ' married ' six months ago and " ' this ceremony was just to show that we are still happy.' "

Reporter Bernard Jordan explains that the groom " has been ' married ' twice before in mock ceremonies, which he ended by just saying: ' I divorce thee ', three times."

Aparently the previous brides were sixteen and nineteen years of age. As a footnote be it added that the bride is reported as saying that she is a relative of the late Lord Birkett. Jordan's report is a social document that deserves to pass on to posterity as a sample of the ' beatnik ' youth of our day and age—the Nuclear Age when Thanatos exhibits his powers of chaos and diabolism, and the two Big Powers display their sado-masochistic glee at inventing and testing bigger, better, and ' cleaner ', weapons of mass destruction. We laugh with horrified fascination at tales of Nero fiddling while Rome was burning, but we ourselves seem going merrily to hell as we await the world's holocaust.

Marriage Merry-
go-Round

In his notable work, Henriques gives us fascinating glimpses into the strange wedding rites, old and new, of many lands. Among the Gaelic people of Wales, Ireland, and Scotland, the relics of marriage by capture remained in the shape of mock capture right up to the eighteenth century. The Welsh bridegroom would set out with a posse of his friends. Reaching the bride's home, he would ask for her to be handed to him just as among primitives, but she would be refused him. A scuffle, or a mockery of one, then ensued, in the midst of which the bride mounted the steed of one of her close relatives who galloped off with her, the bridegroom's posse giving them the chase and capturing the bride when exhaustion set in.

The odd marriage custom of bride and groom resorting to trans-vestitism, or dressing in the clothes of the opposite sex, has already been described elsewhere. Among the Masai tribe of East Africa, the bridegroom keeps on his wife's clothes for as long as a month. In eighteenth century Wales, the bride wore her husband's clothes for a period after the wedding. Eating and drinking are, of course, the usual concomitants of a wedding. But among some primitives eating from the same bowl or dish in itself constitutes the ritual that binds the pair. The Chinese of antiquity ate the sacrificial animal's flesh together and drank from two halves of the same melon. In traditional Japan, the couple drank wine from the same goblet, exchanging the cup no less than nine times. Among the Jews, the bridegroom or the *rabbi* smashed the cup after the pair had drunk from it. Similarly in the Russian Orthodox Church, the priest mixes wine with water and holds it out to the bridal pair who sip from it.

In ancient Greece and Israel, the custom of priests officiating at a wedding was irrevocably established. Thus among these people, and the descendants of most of them, marriage has been a sacrament as much as a contract, and a sacrificial offering was made or the blessing of God was invoked. In ancient Rome, ten witnesses had to be present at a Patrician wedding, in addition to three priests; some sects of Muslims insist on two, while the Zoroastrian Parsis must have five. For Christian contracts, two are sufficient.

In Russia, following the Revolution, church marriages were abolished in 1917 and civil registration took its place. In ancient Egypt, marriage by contract was permitted only to the upper classes, and not till 2000 B.C. did the lower classes win the same right. After the French Revolution, civil marriage before a registrar could be voluntarily effected, but later, in 1792, it became "the only legally valid form of marriage."

Malthusian Doctrine
obstructs Marriage

Owing to the Malthusian Doctrine that to prevent Europe from becoming over-populated and underfed (based on the theory that "human beings multiplied very much faster than the means of subsistence") young men should remain continent and not marry till the age of thirty, Austria, Southern Germany, and other countries which till the end of the eighteenth century had encouraged marriage, suddenly clamped down on it. In the Austria of Metternich, a person had to receive official sanction of marriage and this was denied him if the State discovered that he had no stable profession or trade, and no other certain means of living. Right up to the time of the 1914-18 war, this system prevailed and was, of course, used at times as a political weapon.

Lewinsohn asserts in his **History of Sexual Customs** that a Prussian army officer could not marry till he had attained his captaincy, the only exceptions being those with ample means. Unfortunately for the Malthusian Doctrine, its arguments proved fallacious, for ruthless prevention of marriage merely resulted in an increase in illegitimate births and in no wise did the population decrease as had been intended by the introduction of the system which necessitated a permit for marriage and infringed so callously on a citizen's personal liberty.

From Henriques we learn that amongst the Bantu Kavirondo, proof of consummation of the marriage has to be publicly made evident, and may ". . . . entail the performance of the initial act in front of the wedding guests . . . " Slavonic people, too, we are told, would send the bridal pair to bed before witnesses, as well as the Germans and the Swedes, until the eighteenth century. The latter would even insist on the bride and groom undressing before witnesses.

Right up to the Reformation, Christian Europe cared nought for sacramental marriage which in England was introduced by the Tudors. Marriage was a private contract between a man and a woman and the bond could be mutually sealed between them. While in Saxon times the father sold his daughter for the bridal price or *wed*, in Christian England, he still comes " to give the bride away." As among the Jews, the bridal pair sipped wine and ate the sops. At the conclusion of the bridal mass, the priest kissed the bridegroom by way of benediction, and this the groom passed on to his bride; hence originated the kiss at the altar. From Rattray Taylor's **Sex in History,** we learn that, at the termination of the ceremony, the wedding feast was actually eaten in the very body of the church which was not obstructed with pews. The same night, the father of the bride gave a ball in his house where the bridal pair remained for at least a week.

The most interesting part came on the wedding night when the newly wed pair got into bed. Their friends helped them to undress and in their night-gowns they sat in state in bed before the guests. Now entered a priest, or several, followed by acolytes with lighted censers from which rose incense. The bridal pair had to drink of the posset the priest offered them. He would then bless the bed, and sprinkle holy water on the pair while the acolytes censed the room so that the demons might flee. Presumably, the sexual act would attract them, unless, of course, they were aware that until the three *Tobias Nights* had passed, the bridal pair were not supposed to indulge in sexual intercourse. This benediction usually took place at midnight. The custom is still kept up in certain districts of Germany.

Tobias Nights

The Tobias Nights which extended the period of sexual abstinence from the one night prescribed by the Fourth Council in 398 A.D., to three nights, owe their name to the tale of Tobias in the Roman Catholic Bible or the *Vulgate* : The Median Sarah, daughter of Raguel, married to seven husbands, was widowed because the devil Asmodeus had slain them all. When Tobias asked Sarah's hand in marriage, Raguel feared the outcome. But the Angel Raphael made Tobias burn some liver and then tied Asmodeus in the desert. Tobias now approached Sarah and invoked her to join him in offering prayers to God to whom they would be united for three nights. Thus having forfeited three nights with Sarah in devotion to God, Tobias remained unharmed and the fourth night they spent as man and wife.

Strange as it may seem, right up to the last century, the tradition of the three Tobias nights is said to have been observed among some of the peasantry in Germany, Scotland, Switzerland, Brittainy, and Italy. For wholly different reasons, modern sexologists often advise a man not to rush into the brutal act of defloration but to take his time in initiating his bride, even if it means several nights of abstinence.

The fear of demons was a superstition that gave rise to quaint and charming customs, one of them being perhaps the source of the bridal veil, which, in remote days, was meant to keep the bride hidden from the sight of evil spirits. The Egyptians and the Chinese similarly veiled the bride, and in early Christian times, and still among the Jews and in the Orthodox Church, a canopy is held over the bridal couple so that no danger may descend on them. However, there are other quite logical reasons advanced for the origin of the bridal veil. Some say it is a symbol of humility and servitude, as in the case of nuns who are called the ' brides of Christ ', the lay bride thus wearing the symbol of her servitude to her future lord and master. It could, as suggested elsewhere, be a mere relic of ancient times when brides were captured and probably covered to conceal them from the view of the pursuers. Among some people, such as orthodox Mohammedans, the bridegroom first sees his wife when he parts her veil during the wedding ceremony. The canopy held over the bridal pair is the origin of the regimental custom of providing an archway of swords at a regimental wedding.

But evil spirits were said to infest not merely the air but also to rise from the nether world. So to protect the bride and groom from their magic spell, they were often carried into the church, the groom in Cyprus still being borne aloft on the crossed arms of his comrades. Even aboriginal tribes follow a similar custom. The red runner that covers the steps up a church or cathedral probably has its origin in this ancient practice of protecting the bridal pair from demons from above and below.

The shoe thrown at the bridal pair may signify battle between the opposite families as a relic of the custom of bride-capture. But most probably it goes deeper than that. In the book of Ruth, an ancient Jewish custom involving the use of the slipper is clearly indicated :

Boaz, a distant kinsman of the widowed Ruth's mother-in-law, Naomi, desires to make Ruth his bride, but a nearer kinsman has prior right to her. Therefore Boaz approaches him and urges him to buy a piece of land belonging to Naomi. " What day thou buyest the field of the land of Naomi, thou must buy it also of Ruth the Moabitess, the wife of the dead, to raising the name of the dead upon his inheritance " (Ruth, 4: 5). But the nearer kinsman does not wish to wed Ruth and instead urges Boaz to do so: " Now this was the manner in former time in Israel concerning redeeming and concerning changing, for to confirm all things, a man plucked off his shoe, and gave it to his neighbour: and this was a testimony in Israel " (Ruth, 4: 7). The near kinsman gives Boaz his shoe signifying that the latter has bought his right from him, and is now free to marry Ruth with that right. Might not the throwing of the shoe at the departing bride and groom symbolise that the bridegroom has been given the right to take her away from her parental home, or merely that the marriage contract has been fulfilled and the bride's family surrenders its right to her in favour of the bridegroom ?

Painful Bridal Night

In Love in the South Seas, Danielsson tells us of the wedding night of a bride in the Marquesas. It is more of an ordeal than a pleasurable night. The general festivity would terminate with the bridegroom giving the male guests a signal. His bride would stretch out before him with her head in his lap. The male guests would then troop in, one by one, the oldest and poorest heading the queue. Then came the chiefs, and last of all, the bridegroom. It is not to be wondered at that the bride was often chained to her bed for several days after the extraordinary sexual hospitality which tradition compelled her to extend. However, far from being considered degrading, it was a matter of honour and pride for a bride to copulate with as large a number of men as possible.

Fish, rice, and saké (wine made from rice) form an important part of the Japanese village wedding, the first two being the staple food of the villagers. After banquets at the homes of both bride and groom, the naishōkiki or match-maker and officiator at the wedding, takes the bridal pair into a hut where the marriage ceremony is gone through. Saké is poured into nine cups in three tiers atop one another. The groom first drinks from the smallest cup, then the bride. The fathers-in-law exchange drinks, and likewise the nakaudo and his wife. Then seaweed and cattlefish wrapped up in small packets are given to each of the three couples. This procedure is followed by some more fish, this time a dried one specially folded in a red and white paper and given to the groom's father. A banquet follows at which the bride is present but not the groom. At the tail end of the banquet, the ubiquitous fish and saké again appear and the bridegroom's father ceremoniously declares that the feast has ended.

Goblin Marriage

Among the Bánaro tribe of New Guinea, under the system of daughter-exchange, four couples normally get married together. The brides are confined to cells for nine months prior to the wedding, being fed on sago pudding all that time. As they emerge from their cells on the wedding day, cocoanuts are pelted at them and they are shoved into the river, emerging wherefrom they are arrayed in bridal attire. Dancing follows.

The wedding ritual starts in the evening. Each father-in-law must deflower his daughter-in-law. However, with modesty befitting an elderly man, he commissions his *mundu* or friend to officiate in his stead. Each bride's mother then entrusts her to the father-in-law who leads her to the goblins of Bánaro waiting in the Goblin Hall. Inside, the *mundu* or friend awaits the bride pretending to be a goblin. He takes the bride to where the bamboo pipes are stored, and there deflorates her. His task carried out, he hands the bride back to her father-in-law who returns her to her mother. He then goes to the Goblin Hall and takes his turn as *mundu* and deflowers the bride of the son of his own friend. Thus each father-in-law deflowers his friend's, but not his own, daughter-in-law. The bridegrooms, as can be seen, play hardly any part in all this. Their maternal uncles supervise them in a special hut. They may not marry their brides till such time as the girls bear their first infants.

When the first child is born, the husband denies being the father of the child to which he refers as a ' goblin-child '. The pretence is taken up by the mother who disclaims having had coitus with a goblin. Meanwhile, the husband having built a house, the mother and the goblin-child repair to it and family life begins. But the father-in-law can still claim his right to have sexual congress with the daughter-in-law at special times, when the Goblin Hall is again chosen as the locale.

Roman Marriage

Ancient Romans were uninhibited regarding sexual matters. As among primitives, a girl of twelve or a boy of fourteen were initiated into the mysteries of sex. This may have been for demographical reasons, as their campaigns necessitated fresh blood and they were eager to boost the birth rate. In those remote days, bride-purchase was usual, but if a man could procure a wife, somehow, without her father agreeing to it, and if he lived with her for a year, *usus* or custom made theirs a legal union. Thus the husband and father earned his *patria potestas* or patriarchal right under which he had the right of life and death over his offspring.

The Twelve Tables of 457-449 B.C., the very first historical record of Roman Law, forbade marital ties between patricians and plebeians. The *confarreatio* came, in course of time, to be the only form of marriage. It was of a sacramental nature and the ritual resembled Christian Communion, after which the union took place before the Pontifex Maximus and no less than ten witnesses. During the ritual, the bridal pair, as Lewinsohn tells us in **A History of Sexual Customs** "ate together a sacramental loaf of unleavened bread, the *panis farreus;* in doing this, they were eating the body of the god and were bound together in the god so long as they both lived."

The law forbidding marriages between patricians and plebeians was repealed but a few years after it was made, because a member of the Decemviri which had banned such marriages, one Appius Claudius, himself fell in love with a plebeian girl. Virginia, as she was called, was the daughter of an officer and engaged to a Tribune. Rather than permit her to become Claudius's mistress, her father, exercising his *patria potestas,* or patriarchal right of life and death over her, stabbed her in the Forum. In the army there was a hue and cry, and thus the hands of the patricians were forced into permitting mixed marriages in future.

The other strange custom of the Romans was wife-lending, which we have already encountered among primitives before. Wives were loaned by the Romans to their own or their wives' friends. Again, to quote from Lewinsohn: "Even such a pattern of Roman civic virtue as Cato the Younger ceded his wife, the equally respectable Marcia, to Hortensius, because Hortensius wanted to have children by her. Octavian's own first wife, Livia, had been passed on to him by Claudius, her former husband; this did not prevent her becoming Rome's first Empress and enjoying all the honours attendant on that rank."

Sacerdotal Christian Marriage

By the twelfth century, the dogma of the sacramental nature of marriage had gained sufficient ground, but it was only after the formation of the first post-Reformation Council, *viz,* the Council of Trent (1545-1563), that the Church declared that to be valid a marriage must be performed by a priest before witnesses. Even in Protestant countries such as England, sacerdotal nuptials became obligatory despite Luther's desire to place matrimonial affairs entirely under civil jurisdiction.

Civil marriage was made mandatory after the French Revolution by the Constitution of September 1791, and a religious ceremony by itself was no longer considered enough to make it valid. In course of time, in most countries of Europe, civil marriage became the accepted legal procedure. In the United States of America, however, the marriage is valid in law in either case, and the choice between a civil or a religious ceremony is left to the parties concerned, but if the sacerdotal procedure is preferred, a licence has to be obtained and in many states an interval of time must lapse after procuring it, before the marriage takes place.

The law in regard to marriage in England makes marriage valid whether it is civil or sacerdotal; but banns have to be put up in the latter case. Incestuous marital alliances are forbidden and the term 'incest' covers all kinds of relatives, including in-laws, and step relations. The Table of Prohibited Degrees drawn up by the Church of England in 1563 generally serves as a guide even though the Church itself has by now discarded the list. In the case of in-laws, the rule has become relaxed to cover certain degrees of relatives on the side of a deceased spouse, but not if she is divorced.

To make assurance doubly sure, polygamy is prohibited and punishable. The age-limit for marriage is sixteen which exceeds the age of puberty. Hence, if a girl happens to become pregnant before that age, or if the boy is under the age-limit, their child remains illegitimate and no measures can be taken against the boy for rape. Youngsters from the age of sixteen till the age of twenty-one, cannot marry without the consent of their parents. If they lie about their age and succeed in going through a form of marriage, civil or sacerdotal, the marriage is valid but not legal, and the boy can be convicted and sent to jail for a maximum of seven years. Anal intercourse between husband and wife is prohibited, though such a case can only come to light if one of the partners objects to it and seeks divorce for that particular reason, which is allowed by the law. For Jews and Quakers, there are special marriage laws.

While marriage is a universal institution, it is clear that it follows very varied patterns, always the outcome of a particular social and cultural mould. We may be shocked and overcome with feelings of revulsion at what we consider the 'peculiar' customs of other societies, but we must bear in mind that to them our marital customs may seem equally strange and unbelievable.

CHAPTER 7

ADULTERY AND SEXUAL MORES:

CLASSICAL TIMES TO THE RESTORATION

*Adultery : Not Moral but Property Offence among Hebrews—
Adultery in Classical Greece—' Hedone ' or Sensual Pleasure : Prime
Creed of the Greeks—Adultery among the Romans—Adulterous
Personalities of Rome's Imperial Age : Julius Cæsar, Mark Antony,
the Emperor Augustus, the Elder Julia, the Younger Julia, Caligula
the Sadist, Messalina the Nymphomaniac, Claudius the Incestuous,
Nero the Libertine, and Poppæa his Mother-Substitute—Adultery in
the Middle Ages—The Troubadours and their Baronial Ladies—
Mother Cult of the Virgin Mary—Golden Age of Chivalry also Age
of Debauchery—The Renaissance tolls Death-Knell of Hypocrisy—
Sexual Inhibitions discarded—The Reformation : Patrist Reaction—
Counter-Reformation outlaws Nudity from Art—Birth of the
fictitious Don Juan—Perversions of Sex Life in Roman Society—
Simultaneous Arrival of Renaissance and Reformation into England
—Henry VIII divorces Catherine of Aragon—Seventeenth Century
Morality and Biological Discoveries—Mores of the English
Restoration—Unbridled Debauchery—Libidinous and Frivolous Age.*

THE marital union of a pair is considered to confer on each
exclusive sexual possession of the other. In polygamous societies,
the exclusive rights extend over a number of marriage partners.

In patriarchal societies, the property-conscious male jealously
guards his right, though he permits himself the privilege of extra-
marital relations with other women while denying his wife the same
licence as he allows himself. However, the breaking of the marriage
vows is not confined to the man, as the female, too, often indulges
in extra-conjugal relations with other men.

In early Biblical and classical times, permissive adultery was not
rare when a wife had no male issue, or when sexual abandon was the
order of the day during Pagan festivities. Among some primitive
tribes of today—and even in certain advanced societies of classical
times—loaning wives to guests, as a mark of hospitality, has been
known to be customary.

Among the Hebrews of Biblical times, the commandment against adultery was unequivocal: "Thou shalt not commit adultery" (Exodus, 20: 14), and " . . . thou shalt not covet thy neighbour's wife . . . " (Exodus, 20: 17). These are reiterated in the fifth book of Moses (Deuteronomy, 5: 18, 21). The third book of Moses prescribes a severe penalty for the offence: "And the man that committeth adultery with another man's wife, even he that commiteth adultery with his neighbour's wife, the adulterer and the adulteress shall surely be put to death " (Leviticus, 20: 10).

The legal codes of the ancient Hebrews, derived from the Babylonian Laws of Hammurabi, were distinctly recondite in their interpretation of what constituted adultery. Being a patriarchal community, they jealously guarded the property right of a father or a husband over his daughter or wife, and, being endogamous, they also protected the honour of Israel. Thus, if a married Jew had an adulterous relationship with an unmarried woman who was *not* an Israelite, he committed no offence; but if the girl were a Hebrew, then the adulterer had violated her father's property right, and was guilty of having harmed him. Again, if a man, whether married or single, seduced a married woman, then both were considered to have trespassed on the cuckolded Israelite husband's property right, and, therefore, both paid with their lives.

Apart from infringement of the Israelite male's property right, a Hebrew could commit adultery to his heart's content. If a married man had extra-marital relations with a Hebrew or other girl who was not married and had no father alive, no offence had been committed, the adulterer's wife having no right of exclusive possession in the husband, as the status of the Jewish woman was an inferior one in the patriarchate. Hence men could keep as many concubines as they wished, and a barren wife often supplied her husband with one of her own handmaidens in the hope that the latter would provide him with issue.

These laws existed in the first half of the millennium before Christ. But after 500 B.C., there crept over the ancient world a sweeping change which made these earlier inhabitants of our planet develop a guilt complex regarding sex, and belief in the after-life, which, with time, became more and more of an obsession. This change of outlook worsened the position of the woman in Hebrew society, for the sex guilt was placed squarely, and unfairly, at her door. The penalty of stoning an adulteress to death was an indication of this unjust attitude.

It is obvious that the Hebrews of the Old Testament, even in the post-exile period, did not look upon adultery as a moral offence, and hence did not live fully up to the commandment forbidding it, except when it affected the property right of another male Israelite. But in the New Testament, with the coming of Christ, the moral issue became predominant, and he condemned even the motivation of the act:

" Ye have heard that it was said by them of old time, Thou shalt not commit adultery . . . But I say unto you, That whosoever looketh on a woman to lust after her hath committed adultery with her already in his heart " (**Matthew,** 5 : 27, 28).

Adultery in Classical Greece

In Homeric Greece, the two classical instances of adultery were those of Helen of Sparta, and Clytæmnestra. Helen was the wife of Menelaus, King of Sparta, but became enamoured of Paris, the handsome son of the King of Phrygia, with whom she eloped. This precipitated the Trojan wars in which Paris lost his life. When Troy had fallen, Menelaus took back the fair Helen who looked back with regret on the tragic romance which had wreaked so much havoc. In Homer's **Odyssey,** she is made to say: " I groaned for the blindness that Aphrodite gave me, when she led me thither from my dear native land, forsaking my child and my bridal chamber, and my husband, a man who lacked nothing, whether in wisdom or in comeliness."

Not Homer, but other Greek poets such as Lesches and Euripides, averred that after the fall of Troy, Menelaus had sought, with drawn sword, to avenge himself on Helen for her adultery. However, she, using her feminine wiles, exposed before his angry gaze her fair bosom, the sight of which so overcame him that he forgave her.

Clytæmnestra, immortalised in the **Oresteia** of Æschylus, was a far more treacherous adulteress, who, from love of Ægisthos, slew her noble husband, Agamemnon, on the night of his return home after a long absence. Electra, Agamemnon's faithful daughter, plotted the destruction of Clytæmnestra with her brother Orestes. It is after her that Sigmund Freud chose to name the Electra Complex when describing a daughter's inordinate love for her father with envy of, and desire to do away with, the mother.

Far more diverting were the adulteries of Alcibiades. Diogenes Laërtius, and Pherecrates, the comedian, are quoted by Hans Licht in his knowledgeable work, **Sexual Life in Ancient Greece,** as describing the bisexual Alcibiades in the following respective ways: " ' When a young man he separated men from their wives, and, later, wives from their husbands ' "; and, " ' Alcibiades, who was formerly no man, is now the man of all women.' " As Licht points out in a footnote, the latter description is evocative of that attributed by the historian Suetonius to Curio who called Julius Cæsar the wife of all men and the husband of all women.

The historians, Strabo and Clearchus, attributed adulterous orgies to Dionysius the Younger, ruler of Sicily. In his home town of Locris, Dionysius is said to have invited the women of the town, married and unmarried, to a banquet at which he stripped himself and them, making them chase doves that had been set free in the banqueting hall with their wings clipped. He then rolled in bed with them all performing obscene acts. The husbands and fathers of the women avenged themselves on Dionysius by capturing his wife and children and submitting them to similar gross acts of debauchery.

The Greek attitude to adultery seems to have been one of extremes, either deeply tragic and gloomy, as in the cases of Helen and Clytæmnestra, or wholly comical as in the instance of Alcibiades and Dionysius. What is important to bear in mind is that the prime creed of the ancient Greeks was *hedone* or sensual pleasure which was the source of the hedonistic cult of the later Victorians fathered by Walter Pater, the Oxford don, and carried to extremes by the brilliant, pleasure-loving Oscar Wilde. Corinth was famed for being the Mecca of adulterers, particularly every fourth year, when most roads to the Olympic Games led through the city. This was the reason married women could not attend the Olympics, and not because the participants performed in the nude, as girls were allowed to attend. Nudity was not a shame-cult with the Greeks. One can, of course, appreciate that Greek husbands did not wish the extra-marital attractions of Corinth to be dimmed by the presence of their wives.

One is amazed to learn from Richard Lewinsohn's **A History of Sexual Customs,** that even Plato, that devotee of truth, beauty, and goodness, who, in his later years, preached free love and sexual equality between male and female, was, at one time, in favour of a law being introduced " forbidding a married citizen to have sexual intercourse with any woman except his lawful wife." It was perhaps because his puritanical demand proved to be a cry in the wilderness that he subsequently eulogised the virtues of free love.

Adultery among
the Romans

Despite their severe laws against adultery, the ancient Romans' general attitude towards it was lenient enough. Wives would often overlook the adulterous relationships of their husbands, and even their parents sometimes encouraged them not to spy on their spouses' extra-marital indiscretions. Moreover, if a married Roman indulged in sensual pleasures with slaves or prostitutes, the affairs were not looked upon as being adulterous.

In many cases, wives even encouraged the liaisons of their husbands. Livia, the third wife of Julius Cæsar's grand-nephew, the Emperor Augustus—who, despite his lecheries, posed as a moralist and even banished Ovid, the bard, for his **Ars Amatoria,** a frank treatise on the art of love—went so far as to procure young plebeian girls for her husband, to keep him pleased as she was childless by him. She herself had indulged in adulterous relations with him while yet married to another. But she was not the first to do this. Her predecessor, Scribonia, Augustus's second wife, while yet tied to her first husband, had committed adultery with Augustus who was then the husband of Clodia whom he had deserted.

Most of the great personalities of the Imperial Age of Rome were adulterous. Julius Cæsar who, in his youth, had had a homosexual relationship with King Nicodemus, " . . . seduced many women of high rank ", as the historian, Suetonius, tells us, outside of his three marriages. He also had an affair with Cleopatra of Egypt, herself married to her brother Ptolemy. Likewise, Mark Antony, married to Augustus's sister, Octavia, went down in history as the lover of Cleopatra.

The elder Julia, daughter of Augustus by his second wife, Scribonia, romanced with one Sempronius Gracchus, a patrician, while married to her second husband, Agrippa. When asked why, despite her many adulteries, her five children resembled Agrippa, she coolly answered that she yielded to her lovers only when she knew that she had conceived a child by her own husband. On the death of Agrippa, a marriage of convenience for reasons of state was arranged for her with the future Emperor Tiberius, her step-cousin, the son of Augustus's third wife, Livia, by her first husband.

Needless to say, the marriage with the scholarly Tiberius was a failure and Julia continued to tread the adulterous path. Licht quotes Seneca as declaring of her: " ' She counted her lovers in scores. At night, she revelled through the city streets; she chose for the scene of her embraces the very forum and the platform from which her father had promulgated his law against adultery. She made daily rendezvous at the statue of Marsyas, for she had now turned from adulteress to whore, and permitted herself any licence with unknown lovers.' "

Eventually, Julia's own father, Augustus, disgusted with her debaucheries, reported her to the Senate and she was banished, and even male slaves could not approach her without special permission from Rome.

Like mother like daughter, and the elder Julia's daughter, the younger Julia, had also to be banished for adultery. Yet Augustus himself, though procuring their exile because of their lustful ways, could not himself forego his own lusts, and, in his later years, developed a fondness for virgins, many of whom his own third wife, Livia, mother of Tiberius, procured for him as mentioned before.

Caius Cæsar, better known under his nickname, Caligula, who succeeded Tiberius as Emperor, was the libidinous grandson of the elder Julia, his father being Germanicus, Tiberius's nephew and grandson of Livia, so that he had the blood of both the Julii and the Claudii, which made him the vilest, cruellest, most debauched, and unbalanced of all the Julio-Claudian House. A sexual degenerate, Caligula had incestuous relations with his own sister, and debauched women of all ranks, high and low, while for wife he had Cæsonia, a woman who matched him in his sensual and dissolute ways. He also indulged in homosexual affairs.

Caligula's paternal uncle, Claudius, a scholarly and cultured man, was chosen by the Roman soldiers to succeed the pathological profligate who had been murdered by some officers. Claudius had a passion for women, but, as a change from the others, had no homosexual predilections. After divorcing two wives, he married Valeria Messalina, the daughter of a cousin, a veritable nymphomaniac to which obsessive craving for men is often applied the name, 'the Messalina Urge' after her gluttonous appetite for men.

Messalina emulated prostitutes and spent some of her nights in a brothel or *lupanar,* with a plate outside her cell, in the name of ' Lysisca ', where she tasted meretricious love in the embraces of men from the streets. When she went so far as to marry another man in public and even present him with her dowry, Claudius finally had her executed. He then fell in love with his own niece, Agrippina II, his brother Germanicus's daughter and sister of the murdered Caligula.

The incest prohibition was conveniently overcome by Claudius persuading some senators to move the Senate to declare such a marriage of public importance. Unfortunately, Claudius had a son, Britannicus, by the executed Messalina, and it is suspected that Agrippina II contrived the murder of Claudius so that her son Nero by her previous husband, Cn. Domitius Ahenobarbus, grandson of Mark Antony through the latter's daughter, Antonia I, could succeed Claudius before the latter could name Britannicus as his heir.

Nero, as is well known, was a psychopath with a hereditary taint. His mother, the ambitious Agrippina II, was a libertine who had had illicit affairs galore; his father, Cn. Domitius Ahenobarbus, descended of the line of Mark Antony, was known for his extreme sadism which had taken such forms as driving his chariot over a child on the *Via Appia* or the Appian Way, and killing a freedman of his because the latter would not drink as much as he was ordered to, as we learn from Otto Kiefer's fascinating study of early Rome, **Sexual Life in Ancient Rome,** in which the author declares: " . . . We can understand why Nero's father, when congratulated on the birth of his son, replied that any child of his by Agrippina must be another monster and a curse to the state."

The father's prophecy was certainly fulfilled with a vengeance. Nero turned out to be a tyrant and a sensual debauchee with distinct bisexual tendencies. He married, first, his step-sister Octavia. Before murdering, out of fear of rivalry, his step-brother Britannicus, who was three years his junior, Nero is reputed to have had homoerotic relations with him, as with other men, such as the actor Paris. He is also said to have contracted a homosexual ' marriage '.

Dressed as a slave, Nero wandered through streets and brothels on his libidinous way. One of his favourite companions was Otho, a future Emperor, who was married to a self-willed, cunning, but beautiful young woman, Sabina Poppæa, who, as Tacitus, the historian, declared, " made a pretence of modesty and a practice of sensuality."

By alternately abandoning herself with, and withholding herself from, Nero, the ambitious Poppæa made him eager to possess her as his wife. Otho was sent away to govern the Roman province of Lusitania, and Poppæa was installed as mistress till such time as Nero could get rid of his wife Octavia, and his mother, the domineering Agrippina, towards whom, it has been maintained, he bore an undercurrent of incestuous affection.

As Poppæa had similar traits to Agrippina's, and was, moreover, older than Nero, no doubt he identified her with his mother for whom his ambivalent incestuous affection or fear turned to disgust, so that, secure in having found a mother-substitute in Poppæa, he had Agrippina murdered. When his wife, Octavia, could not be persuaded to consent to a divorce, she was accused of adultery with a flute-player. But even torture would not make her servants accuse their mistress of adultery. Later, she was falsely accused of having had adulterous relations with Agrippina's murderer, and was sent into exile where she was foully murdered.

So Poppæa became empress at last, but for a mere three years after which she died during pregnancy, the death being due, it was rumoured, to a kick from Nero after the burning of Rome when he was becoming more and more unstable. In the final analysis, Nero was a frustrated poet who, instead of sublimating his impulses into creative channels, diverted them to grossly perverse ends.

Adultery in the Middle Ages

In the Middle or Dark Ages, both fornication and adultery were common even among the higher clergy, including many occupants of the papal throne. Sergius III managed to have the fruit of his adultery, his bastard son, succeed him. Pope Leo VIII died in the very act of adultery. John XII, deposed in 963, was tried on various charges including incest and adultery. Balthasar Cossa confessed to adulterous and other grievous acts before the Council of Constance which tried him. As Chamberlain to Boniface IX, he had used his brother's wife as his own mistress.

Adultery concealed itself under a knightly cloak in mediæval times. Lewinsohn makes apt observations on the moral codes of the period : " . . . The entire feudal system depended on the fidelity of the vassal to his liege lord, and family life on a marital fidelity which left no place for other relationships. But the elaboration of the conception of fidelity brought with it as its corollary the elevation of infidelity into a fine art.

" An act of infidelity was no disgrace, always provided that one preserved the forms of polite society and was prepared to draw the sword and if necessary (this was not often the case) to die for one's heart's passion. The art of adultery used the same terminology as

the official code of morals: honour, purity, virtue, loyalty, were part
of the regular vocabulary of the heroes who seduced other men's
wives. Any knight who contented himself with wedding a maiden
before having himself grown practised in adultery and carried off
several trophies of the chase was unworthy of his spurs. Adultery
was a social diversion among the upper classes. A knight had to have
'a lady' whom he worshipped, to whom he devoted himself, and the
lady had to be married, if possible to a husband of a slightly higher
rank than the lover, for in knightly love the eye was always turned
upwards. Everything was pure, delicate, and noble—*honi soit qui
mal y pense.*

"... Church and State alike tolerated the adulterous relationship between the young knight and the baronial lady. A cavalier
might even bring religion into his affairs of the heart. It was the thing
to choose a celestial patroness, and the usual practice, incredible
though it sounds, was to invoke the Virgin Mary to patronise the
liaison and soften the lady's heart towards her suppliant ... Never
before, however, had mankind committed such blasphemy as to make
the Virgin the patroness of organised adultery—for the knightly *minne*
service, divested of its romantic trappings, was just that."

Among the knights, were many poets who called themselves
troubadours, and composed love lyrics for their baronial ladies, who
were, invariably, the wives of feudal lords. This daring movement—
for, in the past, writing a love song for a married woman was an
offence for which the extreme penalty could be death—started in
Provençal at the commencement of the twelfth century, and spread
all over Northern France, Germany, and England Most historians
agree with Lewinsohn in deeming the relationship between baronial
lady and knight, which came to be known as *donnoi,* to have been
wholly adulterous. Yet there are some writers who uphold the claim
of the troubadours themselves that theirs was 'pure desire' un-
mingled with fleshly intent. They support their theory with the
argument that though many of the troubadours did speak in their
verses of undressing their lady-love and caressing her naked body,
yet they made no mention of fulfilment of sexual desire, or of illegitimate children springing from such unions. But such omissions are
easily explained by the fact that as it was a romantic age of dissimula-
tion, unsavoury details, such as illegitimate births, were concealed under
the cloak of gallantry. Besides, as the woman was already married,
such children could pass off as the offspring of the actual marriage
without anyone being the wiser.

It was about the middle of the twelfth century that these same
romantic troubadours, who had elected the Virgin Mary as their
patroness, founded the Feast of the Immaculate Conception. This
is advanced as a reason for believing that the troubadours were
afflicted with a mother-fixation and were matrists, some of them even
being homosexual. However, a mother-fixation, as in the case of

Nero, often results in a man falling in love with a woman resembling his mother and thus serving as a substitute; this is yet another pointer to adulterous relationships between 'mother-fixated' troubadours and baronial ladies who were mother-substitutes. While no doubt there were exceptons when no intimacy occurred, we must disclaim the theory that adultery was not committed with the admired woman because, representing as she did the mother-figure, the troubadours were overcome by dread of incest, and were thus impotent with the woman they idealised, a theory that even Freud, with most of whose deductions the present writer is inclined to agree, advances in connection with those suffering from mother-fixation.

These undoubtedly matrist troubadours no doubt influenced even patrists with their advocacy of gentleness and chivalry towards women, thus leaving their mark on patrist behaviour patterns, so that, as G. Rattray Taylor points out in his **Sex in History,** " even its opponents must concede that it produced a highly civilised effect upon the behaviour of feudal chivalry.   Deluded by Christian redactions of the ancient Celtic legends, we have come to think of the Celtic heroes, such as King Arthur, as paragons of gentleness and honour, and we extend the delusion to cover the knights who lived during the period of the Crusades.   In point of fact, they were, as Prof. Hearnshaw says, ' a horde of sanctified savages, whose abominations scandalised even the Byzantines and whose ferocities horrified the very Turks themselves.' "

The thirteenth century, known as the Golden Age of Chivalry, was, actually, a time when debauchery flourished. Arriving at Marseilles, Richard I of England discovered that his own knights had squandered the funds meant for the particular campaign on revelry with prostitutes !   One would not be far wrong in claiming that the thirteenth century marked the end of the Middle Ages when men were hamstrung with sets of rules that were supposed to be divinely inspired, a mediæval superstition.

Renaissance tolls Death-Knell of Hypocrisy

The Renaissance, as it flowered, tolled the death-knell of prudery and hypocrisy.   Individuality, so long suppressed, came into its own. Men rediscovered the Greek ideal of the Body Beautiful and the guilt-culture that had suppressed sex died a natural death.   An efflorescence of creative art—nurtured, no doubt, by the new sexual freedom—burst upon the Christian world.   The movement, starting in Italy in the second half of the thirteenth century, was, obviously, a recrudescence of matrist principles.   The mass violence that had permeated the mediæval air with its sado-masochism, was now replaced by individual violence.

An extreme example of individual licence was the priest Niccolo de' Pelegati who celebrated his first mass after committing murder, towards the tail end of the fifteenth century. Subsequently, he formed a bigamous marital alliance with two women and committed more murders. Rape, adultery, and incest were three of the varieties of crimes perpetrated by one Sigismondo Malatesta, the head of a leading Italian family. Young noblemen, rather than risk adultery and consequent death at the hands of the cuckolded husbands, found a way out by breaking into a convent to rape the nuns who had no such men to defend their honour.

Duelling gained popularity because a cuckolded husband's right to demand satisfaction from his wife's betrayer was indisputable. Sexual inhibitions having been discarded, the new age assumed mores that were not compatible with Christian teaching. The Renaissance was a period when authority was openly flouted, and the Christian Church, extremely authoritarian, found its dogmas receiving but little respect. A priest, Pietro Leon of Valcamonica, fornicated with almost four hundred nuns placed in his care, seduced women in the confessional, and punished resistance with torture. Pope Leo X openly denied the existence of God, while Pope Alexander VI, born Rodrigo Borgia, held obscene orgies. He and his daughter, Lucrezia, once watched with relish two mares mate with stallions in a courtyard inside the papal palace. He confessed to having committed incest with Lucrezia, and also accused his son Cesare of fraternal incest with her.

Not heroic deeds as in the days of the Romantic Movement, but sexual virility was the gauge of a man's worth during the Renaissance. Sex was freely spoken of, and Guilio Aretino, leading poet and pornographer of his age, wrote: " . . . What is the harm if we see how a man mounts a woman ? My opinion is that we ought to carry representations of that instrument which Mother Nature has given us for our self-preservation, hung round our necks and clasped on our caps."

The Reformation which followed the Renaissance, was, of course, a patrist reaction to the contempt for authority and to the dogmas of the Church which harboured licentious men within its hierarchy. Luther, Calvin, and their followers who broke away from the Church, were looked upon as sex-fiends because they advocated marriage for the clergy and permitted divorce, thus reverting to the marriage law of the Old Testament. When the Reformation had deluged almost half of Europe, Rome, backed by the Emperor Charles V, reiterated its dogmas through the Council of Trent which sat in Trent and Bologna for almost eighteen years, from 1545-1563. It was the Council of Trent that, as we know, made marriage sacerdotal, and celibacy compulsory for the entire clergy.

The Counter-Reformation, following the decision of the Council of Trent, outlawed nudity from visual art. Paradoxically, Charles V was very fond of Titian's nude Venuses of which he had quite a collection, and his son, Phillip II, relieved the gloom of his study in the Escorial with nudes. However, the new prudery affected Michelangelo's 'Last Judgment' on the wall behind the altar of the Sistine Chapel. When his seven years of labour on it had ended, he having painted all the figures in the nude, including Christ and the Virgin, Pope Paul IV, on his accession in 1555, ordered the destruction of the fresco. However, there was an outcry against the proposed vandalism, and the Pope compromised by entrusting one of Michelangelo's pupils, Daniele de Volterra, to clothe the bare figures in the gigantic fresco. Daniele gave them billowing apparel, and for his trouble was nicknamed *Il Braghettone*: the Breeches-maker. As a sidelight, it is pertinent to mention that Pope Paul IV, as Cardinal Giampietro Carafa, had been the head of the notorious Inquisition.

Though Michelangelo was the worst sufferer from the prudery that the Council of Trent let loose in the Vatican, it was not long before there was a resurgence of the nudity cult that the Counter-Reformation had tried to crush. Guido Reni, Caraveggio, Francesco Albani, and above all, Rubens, continued to portray the beauty of the contours and tints of the naked flesh.

It was in this period that Gabriel Telléz, or Tirso de Molina, invented a literary figure that has gripped the imagination of romantics ever since: Don Juan. Set in the Middle Ages, 'The Mocker of Seville and the Guest of Stone' first performed in 1630, as we learn from Lewinsohn, portrayed a profligate who seduces a society belle and two ordinary girls. He then looks for a fourth victim. Eventually he gets his deserts when the ghost of Dona Anna's father whom he has murdered, appears to carry him down to hell for his lechery and his cynicism. The original name of the anti-hero was Don Juan Tenorio of which the first two alone seem to have been retained with the years.

Sex-life took a curious turn at this stage. Perversions manifested themselves in high Roman society. Incest seems to have been the commonest of them all. The incestuous doings of the Borgias, father, son, and daughter, have already been mentioned. In 1599, Roman society was shocked by the trial of Beatrice Cenci who had killed her father, Francesco, because he had committed incest and then shut her up. The girl was found guilty and executed. As heterosexual relationships of an unlawful nature evoked too much attention, and Church and State watched out for irregularities, homosexual relationships blossomed. Lesbian love was called *donna con donna*, and, according to Brantome, was greatly prevalent not only in Italy but also in France and Spain. Catharine de Medici, who mothered three kings of France, was said to have introduced it in France.

One of Catharine's sons was the future Henry III of France. Till the age of twenty-three, he was inordinately interested in girls, and later became completely homoerotic. A daughter of hers, Margo, who married the king of Navarre, the future Henri IV of France, was a nymphomaniac. Catharine herself was a metatropist who delighted in sadistic acts, the cruellest of which was the Massacre of St.

Bartholomew's Eve of which she is credited to have been the real author.

In Spain, the most pious of courts, reigned Philip II who was married to Catharine de Medici's daughter. Their son, Don Carlos, revealed an incestuous affection for his mother. He, too, like his maternal grandmother, was a sadist and delighted in tormenting females. His step-brother, Philip III, was a profligate who is said to have fathered almost three dozen bastards. By a quirk of fate, his son, Philip IV, turned out to be a zealot who favoured Spartan living and made the Spanish court take on the air of a mausoleum.

The Renaissance and the Reformation were ushered into England almost simultaneously to facilitate, as has been explained elsewhere, the divorce of Henry VIII from Catherine of Aragon. The Tudor period in England was her golden age. The English of those days were a merry, hearty, robust people who swore and drank and whored after the pattern of the much-married King Hal. Roughly at the time of the Counter-Reformation on the Continent, across the Channel reigned Queen Elizabeth I, Henry's daughter by Anne Boleyn. Despite her highly publicised romances with several courtiers, including Raleigh and Essex, she has been suspected of having been a genuine hermaphrodite. By remaining unmarried throughout her life and all through her long reign, she earned the name of the Virgin Queen, not a misnomer as it may today appear to be, if one takes the term ' virgin ' to mean *virgo* in the Latin sense which was applied to any spinster irrespective of whether she had had carnal knowledge or not, and not as we use it today to mean *virgo intacta*, a carnally uninitiated woman.

Seventeenth Century Morality and Biological Discoveries

Surprising though it may sound, till the middle of the seventeenth century, human birth had remained, more or less, a mysterious process. Copulation, and the exact nature of fecundation and gestation, were only vaguely comprehended. The average person was, naturally, interested in knowing whether the sex of a child could be determined and which was the best time to ensure fecundation. Theologians, however, were more interested in attempting to fathom at what stage the soul enters the embryo. With no biological justification whatever, Thomas Aquinas had, in mediæval times, proclaimed that, in the case of a male embryo, the soul came to dwell in the fœtus forty days after conception, while a female embryo would remain soulless till the eightieth day after conception. Hence an abortion, by whatever weird and crude means then prevailing, though not permitted by the Church, did not seem as heinous where a still soulless embryo was concerned.

The second half of the seventeenth century provided some of the important answers to the many sex riddles that had existed till then. Both Aristotle of the pre-Christian era, and Aquinas, had agreed on a bi-seminal theory expressing it in vastly different terms.   They imagined that just as man contributed his semen, so also woman contributed a similar fertilising element.   Descartes formulated the theory, observing: "The semina of the two sexes mingle and act as yeast, each on the other." This was a comparison to beer-brewing in which the froth from beer could serve as yeast for future beer.

The bi-seminal theory was refuted by William Harvey whose name is associated in medicine with the discovery of blood circulation.   This English Physician-in-Ordinary to the Stuart Kings, maintained the principle of *ovism,* explaining that the *ovum* or egg was a principle of reproduction to be found among all living creatures.   When he made his pronouncement, which took all by surprise, he was already over seventy, and soon ended on the scaffold with the execution of Charles I with whom he had gone into voluntary exile.   Next, an Italian scientist, and then a Dutch anatomist called Reynier de Graaf, revealed the changes that occur in animals' *ova* after fertilisation.   Hence the covering that encloses the maturing egg and bursts before the ripened egg leaves the ovary, is known as the *Graafian follicle.*

Not much later, a Dutch optician, Leeuwenhoek of Delft, brought, in November 1677, to the Royal Society of London, the world's leading scientific association, his observations on the nature of semen which he had examined through microscopes.   Being brought for examination the semen of a sick man by a student, Ham, he had discovered the *spermatozoön,* invisible to the naked eye, but thousands of which could be detected through the microscope.   Encouraged by the Society to continue his investigations, Leeuwenhoek submitted a paper with drawings of *spermatozoa,* dead and alive.   The Royal Society published the paper in 1678.   The existence of the male and female principles having been discovered, their precise roles in fertilisation still remained unknown.   A controversy raged between the animalculists who asserted that the male principle was the original source of life, and the ovists who gave the female principle paramountcy.   Not till two hundred years later, in 1877, did a Swiss biologist, H. Fiol, observe the entry of the sperm into the ovum of a starfish, and the fusion of male and female cells became clear except to the most sceptical.

Both Church and State did not, as before, place obstacles in the way of biological research.   However, in the seventeenth century their main interest was to raise the birth rate.   As Lewinsohn tells us, in England and France, both industrialised countries, demographic theories came into being, and remained unrefuted until the end of the next century.   "Put shortly," says Lewinsohn, "they amounted to the proposition that density of population was decisive for a country's wealth.   The more people, the better.   A dense population was not the result of economic well-being, but the precondition for it.   One need not therefore fear to bring children into the world, or to admit foreigners; immigration was better than emigration . . . The important factor was not the circumstances of the individual family, but the national wealth, and this was increased by a higher birth rate. The larger the families, the larger the labour force; the more one could export, the more money would come in. *Ergo,* producing children meant making the country richer.

"Who profited by the wealth, the whole population or only a small upper class, was an aspect of the question with which the theoreticians of population did not concern themselves, or only in passing, for it was a dangerous one. The age concerned itself little with social problems . . . "

As, despite the old Poor Law, large families often found themselves in difficulties, these were solved by sending children to work, even down the pits. So the troubles of large families, were the nation's gain in labour force. This policy, later called mercantilism, had been practised by Colbert in France, and Cromwell in England, but it remained for Sir William Petty, one of the founders of the Royal Society, to formulate it. A surgeon by calling, lecturer in natural history and music, this accomplished, versatile man drew from his observations of life the theory that the individual's fate counts for little as against the general welfare of a nation, and claimed that these "general phenomena affecting the entire people . . . were calculable." What is today called 'population policy', he named 'political arithmetic'.

Johann Peter Sussmilch, his best pupil, a German pastor, published his investigation of population policy in 1741, in the course of which he observed that the human population tends to increase except during wars and natural plagues, and this increase is good for the welfare of communities. About fifty years later, the clergyman, Malthus, debunked this theory and warned that should the human race keep on multiplying, famine would overtake and ravage them.

Mores of Seventeenth Century
English Restoration

The seventeenth century in England, known as the Restoration, was particularly noted for the immorality of its life, a natural reaction to the patrist authoritarianism, hypocrisy, and guilt-ridden codes of the Puritans. On the Continent, the Roman Catholic Church, in attempting to counter the Reformation, had itself become authoritarian and the Puritan zest for stern rule coresponded to the dogmas of the Church, particularly the dogma of papal infallibility.

In England, with the restoration of the Stuarts to the throne, lust and sensuality held full sway under Charles II. Alas, the English could never impart charm and refinement to their corruption as could the French, better versed in elegance and wit. Cynicism and frivolity were the outstanding features of Restoration society. The historian, Macaulay, observed:

"Unbridled debauchery, the natural consequence of unnatural severity, was the prevailing fashion in those days, involving, of course,

the moral degradation of women . . . Any lady of the court exhibiting
her white throat and bosom at balls and parties, distinguishing
herself by quick and appropriate repartee, flirting with chamberlains
and captains of the Guard, singing ambiguous songs with an ambiguous
expression in her eyes, slipping occasionally into a page's dress to
perform some mischievous prank—had more chance of being worshipped by a devoted circle of admirers, of being honoured by the
Royal attention, of marrying some rich and distinguished nobleman,
than Johanna Grey or Lucy Hutchinson would ever have had."

It was Charles II, the liberator of his people from oppressive
Puritanism, who, with his languid and dandical ways, his flippancy,
and above all his libertine habits, set the pace for the morals and
manners of the Restoration, leaving his indelible impress on the era.
He paraded his mistresses openly, three achieving everlasting fame or
notoriety, whichever way one chooses to look at it, these being the
Duchess of Portsmouth, Lady Castlemaine, and the orange-seller-
turned-actress, Nell Gwyn. Indeed, with what degree of veracity one
does not know, he is reputed to have uttered among his last words,
the solicitation, " Let not poor Nellie starve ", to which a verse of
Algernon Swinburne in his **Poems and Ballads** would seem to testify:

> " Our Lady of Pity thou wast : and to thee
>   All England, whose sons are the sons of the sea,
>   Give thanks, and will hear not if history snarls
>   When the name of the friend of her sailors is spoken :
>   And thy lover she cannot but love—by the token
>   That thy name was the last on the lips of King Charles."

Men and women of the Restoration were outspoken in sexual
matters. Libidinous conversation was the vogue. Men dilated on the
physical charms of their paramours, and women, too, expanded on the
virile qualities of their lovers with lengthy and frank physical details.
According to Dr. Iwan (or Ivan) Bloch's comprehensive study of
English morals through the ages, entitled **Sexual Life in England,**
" Men sometimes handed over their wives to their friends to make what
use they liked of them, as Mr. Cooke did to Sir William Baron." Bloch
quotes the *Mémoires* of the Comte de Grammont as his source.

As was to be expected in such a frivolous age, confinement and
childbirth were treated as matters not worth making a fuss over. Pepys
recorded that he was told by one Captain Ferrers that at a ball " a
maid of honour had dropped a baby while dancing." Taine wrote
of its having been wrapped into a handkerchief and carried away to
the King, and also mentioned—which is hard to swallow—that Charles
II dissected the body and made lewd jokes.

In no other epoch did the shoddy manners and mores of the upper
circles infect the lower strata as virulently as during the Restoration.
This was probably due to the fact that members of higher circles
mingled more freely with the populace than they had done in the past,

mostly, one would presume, to sample low living and to give their lecheries greater scope. The modern craze for 'slumming' is but a hollow echo of such times. Ladies of the court went out disguised as ordinary women, and, no doubt, tasted the joys of 'raw flesh'. Even the Queen is reported to have donned the habit of a peasant and mixed with fairground characters. Bloch quotes Bishop Burnet's testimony from the Comte de Grammont's *Mémoires*:

"The court in those days took part in the most licentious masquerades. King and Queen, ladies and courtiers, went about in disguise, entered the houses of unknown people and danced there, making bad jokes. It was not easy for them to be recognised by such as did not know the secret. They were carried about in common hired chairs, and the Queen was once lost by her chairmen . . . She was left all alone . . . In the end she had to drive to Whitehall in a hired coach."

Society women, in disguise, often frequented taverns and dispensed freely with their kisses while carousing. They even went without their gallants to brothels to taste the wines. It would not be surprising if occasionally there was a Messalina among them. These convivial times foreshadowed the effervescence of the more refined though no less debauched period of Georgian Bucks and Regency Rakes.

CHAPTER 8

DEBAUCHERY IN THE ROCOCO
AND GEORGIAN ERA

Europe's Age of Gallantry—Royal Adultery on a Grand Scale—
Actresses appear on the Scene—Group and Individual Idiosyncrasies
—The Order of Sodomites—De Sade and his Sadistic Orgies—' Back
to Nature' Sex Morality of Rousseau—The Infantile Masochistic
Fancies of Rousseau—Sexuality under Napoleon—Romances of the
Little Dictator—Love Life in Eighteenth Century England—Georgian
Rakes—Brothels Galore—Europe's First Gentleman : George IV—
Beau Brummell, the Dandy—Regency Bucks—End of a Colourful
Era.

THE eighteenth century is often referred to as the Age of Gallantry
in Europe. It seems more fitting to recall it as the age which
produced rococo or highly ornamental furniture between the years
1730-80, for the manners of the times were as flamboyant as the furniture, and the morals equally outlandish.

A plethora of royal adultery on a grand scale broke out in this
period all over Europe. Czar Peter I of Russia banished his first wife
to a nunnery, and cohabited with a Lithuanian girl named Martha
Skavronskaya for ten years, having discovered her working as a servant in the house of a Baltic Protestant Pastor. When he married her
and she was baptised as a member of the Orthodox Church, she came
to be known as Catherine. This nymphomaniac committed adultery
with a brother of her husband's former mistress who was promptly
put to death by the infuriated Czar. Catherine survived Peter I by
two years, ascending the throne after his death. It took literally a
regiment of men to sate this woman's sexual hunger.

In France, no royal mistress could sit on the throne which was,
traditionally, only for a consort who came of a ruling house. The
mistress of the king was called *maîtresse-en-titre*, and while her liaison
with the monarch lasted, there were no other regular mistresses. Into
this category fell Madame de Maintenon, Madame de Montespan,

and La Vallière, mistresses of Louis XIV at varied times. Louis XV's mistresses were Madame Pompadour and Du Barry. The social standing of such women was high, and often their influence over the monarch, so that they were sought after by diplomats and others seeking royal favours. As Lewinsohn remarks, in his **History of Sexual Customs,** there was now added to the traditional nobility, a *noblesse de lit,* or literally, bed-nobility.

Before these women could worm their way into the king's heart, they generally made their way to court by marrying a titled man. Thus Du Barry, the milliner, married a count, and the Pompadour a nobleman from the country. Maintenon was the wife of a poet accepted in royal circles. Apart from married women, mistresses were recruited also from the Queen's ladies-in-waiting. From the ranks of these came Madame de Montespan, and La Vallière, as well as one of the English King Charles II's mistresses, Louise Reneé de Kéroualle, the future Duchess of Portsmonth and rival of Nell Gwyn.

Apart from one regular mistress, the monarchs and princes indulged in casual amours lasting from one night to several weeks, with courtesans who were sneaked into their bedrooms without the knowledge of the reigning consort or the favourite mistress.

The eighteenth century in Europe produced a figure whose name has come to be associated with romanticism as much as the fictitious Don Juan's: Giacomo Girolamo Casanova di Seingalt, more usually known as plain Casanova. He had no fixed profession and seems to have tried his hand at various occupations. His main interest in life, however, was the perpetual romantic quest of a satyr. His *Mémoires* read like the outpourings of a highly imaginative mind, so outré and grotesque are some of the situations. However, it would appear that they were not faked and bear the light of investigation.

Casanova was primarily an exhibitionist. He delighted in making love to a woman while being watched by another. Moreover, he also seemed to get out of himself as it were and watch his own performances, so vividly does he describe them. This was probably due to a Narcissistic trait not uncommon in such men. He once seduced two nuns, Armelline and Emilie, by inviting them to an oyster supper when he plied them with champagne and oysters, making the room so hot that they had to divest themselves of part of their habits. Then he got them to play a game of one removing with her own mouth an oyster in the other's, during which he deliberately slipped an oyster into each one's corset so that both were forced to strip. On another occasion, two girls, Veronique and Annette, were his collaborators. While having intercourse with the short-sighted Annette, he feasted his eyes on Veronique who had started to bare her physical charms bit by bit. When he had satisfied himself for the fourth time with Annette, he switched over to Veronique. On yet another occasion, he practised various coital postures with two girls, Hedwig and Helen, in the presence of both.

Men are given to boasting that they can get a woman without having to pay for her 'bounty'. Casanova, on the other hand, preferred buying them. This was probably to satisfy a subconscious urge to humiliate them and prove his own superiority. Obviously it was a quirk of character, for most men with a pronounced Narcissus Complex prefer to think that they can conquer a woman with their own manly charms. In addition to being an exhibitionist, he was also a *voyeur*, a not unusual combination, and, one would say, quite complementary, for one who likes to demonstrate his skill will also be eager to watch another's, or perhaps even his own in a mirror suitably placed.

The latter half of the seventeenth century, and the entire eighteenth century in Europe were also notable for another innovation. For the first time in two thousand years, women appeared on the stage as actresses. Even in the days of antiquity, except in mimes in which women of doubtful reputation participated by undraping themselves in an ancient form of strip-tease, all women's parts in drama were taken by males who were mere striplings or sometimes castrated youths. From Greek times, till Shakespeare's days, it was the same practice. Men appeared even in opera disguised in women's roles and singing falsetto when, at the commencement of the seventeenth century, opera gained popularity. In earlier times, Italy had supplied *castrati* or castrated males to all Europe for singing soprano parts in the church choirs.

It can well be imagined that actresses became the rage in society circles and young men pursued them with zest from the eighteenth century onwards, though the trend for women in drama had begun to set in from the previous century, Nell Gwyn herself having been an actress of sorts. The stage thus provided a new hunting ground for recruits for the romantic life of the gay blades of different countries, and particularly for casual royal romances. For the nocturnal revels got up by Louis XV in his deer park, more and more actresses, dancers, and singers, were collected. It became a theatrical tradition for the chorus girls, the members of the *corps de ballet*, and the opera girls, particularly those who took part in crowd scenes, to make themselves available to the wealthier members of the audience. In the reign of Louis XIV, two ballerinas leaped to prominence on the strength of their royal romances: Camargo and Barberina. The former was a Belgian and listed the Duc de Richelieu and the Comte de Clarmont among her lovers. The other was Barberina Campanini, an Italian.

Barberina was famed for her beauty which was noticeable even in the grotesque dances that led to her fame. According to Lewinsohn, "French aristocrats and English lords fought duels for her." The patronage of Frederick the Great enhanced her reputation. He engaged her for the Berlin opera, and in Berlin and Potsdam society she came to occupy a very high social status, Frederick the Great being her regular visitor who was distraught when she married Cocceji, the

Grand Chancellor, and went with him to Silesia. Her marriage, like Camargo's, ended disastrously, and the rest of the days of both women were spent in charitable work. Barberina actually opened a convent for noblewomen over which she presided, and for her services was made Countess of Barschau by Frederick William II. Her conquest of Frederick the Great was all the more remarkable as he is said to have been primarily homosexual, though, undoubtedly, there must have been a heterosexual strain in what was probably a bisexual nature, to have made him become so captivated by her charms. The third famous ballerina of the time, was Marie Sallé who was a Lesbian.

Actresses followed the dancers into the royal beds. The Duc d'Orleans, the Regent of France, had an affair with one who bore him a son who later became Archbishop of Cambrai. Clairon, the tragedienne, who starred in Voltaire's plays, had three royal lovers: the Duc de Luxembourg, the Marquis de Bissy, and the Prince de Soubise. Singers were not far behind their theatrical colleagues of the ballet and the drama; one of them, Sophie Arnould, had a tremendous romance with the Comte de Brancas. "Nevertheless," observes Lewinsohn, "stage folk remained a pariah caste. The Church denied them the sacraments and a resting place in consecrated ground: they were buried in the sinners' cemetery outside the town. No exception was made, even for Adrienne Lecouvreur, mistress of Count Maurice of Saxony." In France, this may have been due to the attitude of the Roman Catholic Church. The Church of England at least seems to have been far more reasonable, for Nell Gwyn lies in the crypt of London's St. Martin-in-the-Fields near Trafalgar Square.

Group and Individual
Idiosyncrasies

In the Rococo Age, the absurdly overwhelming value that had been accorded to virility during the Renaissance, died a natural death. A man's worth was no longer measured by his performances in bed. Nor were the men of this age less virile than those of previous times. The Duc de Bourbon, Louis XV's Premier, after the monarch's first night with his bride, the King of Poland's daughter, reported as was the custom, the consummation of the marriage, adding that the royal bridegroom had " bestowed on her seven proofs of his affection."

Despite the normal heterosexual robustness of the age, eccentricity and aberrations, group and individual, came markedly to the fore.

' The Order of Sodomites ' created a furore in the reign of Louis XIV. As homosexuality was strictly taboo, it had been practised but covertly. Prominent members of the aristocracy, such as Prince Conti, the Duc de Gramont, and the Marquis de Béran, had banded themselves together under the Order, their guiding spirit being the Italian composer, Jean-Baptiste Lully, who had been born in Florence, and was the Director of the court theatre as well as opera. Louis XIV took

measures to suppress homosexuality after this, but, no doubt, it went
underground. No longer deemed a perversion but a mere deflection
from the norm of sexuality in our age, it was then considered an
abnormality. Yet in the England of the eighteenth century it was
extremely fashionable despite the law against it which still prevails
notwithstanding the Wolfenden Committee Report which strongly
recommended its abolition, almost five years ago, in September 1957,
to be precise.

Individual idiosyncrasy of a truly perverted and repulsive nature
was displayed by Donatien Alphonse François de Sade who was born
in 1740. This was the man who gave to the language of pathology
and modern parlance the term ' sadism ', aptly named after him to
describe acute forms of man's inherent aggressive urge in sexual relations, when, in later years, *algolagnia* or the pleasure principle in pain,
was thoroughly analysed by experts such as Krafft-Ebing. De Sade
was brought up by an uncle, an *Abbé*, who could boast of two mistresses. By the age of twenty-four, married to a girl whose sister he
preferred, he bought a country retreat which he used as the scene of
his brand of perversion.

In 1767, broke out the Keller scandal. One of De Sade's victims,
Rose Keller, reported him to the authorities with the help of one
Madame Jouette with whom she had taken refuge. Rose Keller alleged
that after being forced to remove all her clothes, she had been forcibly
tied to a bed, face downwards, De Sade gripping her waist firmly with
his knees, while he flagellated her posterior with whips and canes, and
inflicted knife wounds all over her body, into which he poured hot
sealing wax. As she begged for mercy, not having made her Easter
confession, the monster threatened to kill her unless she gave in to
him. Despite De Sade's confession to part of the charge, in which
he admitted having used a whip of knotted cord on the poor girl, and
a surgeon's testimony as to the wounds, De Sade was able to buy his
freedom. About five years later, visiting a brothel in Marseilles, he
indulged in an orgy with the inmates, during which he fed the women
on chocolates mixed with cantharides extracted from the Spanish fly.
Two of the women died of poisoning, while one jumped out of a
window and suffered injuries.

De Sade fled to Italy to escape the death sentence which was
passed on him in his absence. However, he ventured to return to Paris
where he was arrested in 1777, and, the death sentence of the Aix
Court being, after a lot of intrigue, quashed, he was merely imprisoned.
In the Bastille, he sought an outlet for his perverted instincts by writing
pornographic novels such as ' Justine ' and ' Juliette ' its sequel. The
heroine of the first novel, unlike her sister who is the heroine of the
sequel, suffers untold agonies of torture in trying to defend her honour,
including an attempt by a surgeon to vivisect her and assaults from
monks in a cloister. Eventually, she falls into the hands of a vicious
sex-murderer who likes hacking off women's heads with a sabre, and,

escaping this fate, is condemned to death for being his accomplice in mass-murders, the final piece of sadistic irony.

De Sade was released from the Bastille in 1790 when all those imprisoned " without the due process of law " were given their liberty by the National Assembly. The next year, his ' Justine ' was published. His final downfall came when he wrote ' Zoé and His Hundred Acolytes '. In it he portrayed two women, who, being but thinly disguised, were obvious caricatures of Madame Tallien an over-sexed woman of the *Directoire*—the period of transition from the French Revolution to the Napoleonic dictatorship—and Joséphine Beauharnais, who was a Creole from Martinique called Joséphine Tascher de la Pagerie, and had married the Vicomte de Beauharnais, guillotined in 1794. The widow, after sampling many lovers, became the mistress of the Vicomte de Barras, but the prize was snatched away from her when Madame Tallien, while yet married, became the Vicomte's favourite mistress. Joséphine, a gentle but cunning creature, contented herself with an artillery general of Corsican origin: Napoleon Buonaparte. De Sade was audacious enough to send his parody to Napoleon when he was First Consul of France. This brought about his arrest, not, ostensibly, for the cruel parody, but for his earlier work, ' Juliette '. He was sent to an institution for insane criminals at Carenton where he died in 1814.

Individual idiosyncrasies, such as those of the Comte de Sade, when highlighted, often lead to imitation by groups of those in search of fresh experience or those already predisposed towards them. Thus in 1795, Grimode de la Reynière, a gourmet, opened in the Palais Royal a dining club called *Diner des Mystificateurs*, where love-potions and drugged wines were served.

' Back to Nature '
Sex Morality

The Age of Gallantry, it is significant, was the age of royal mistresses. The high-born could afford to caper around with their polyerotic love affairs. The low-born, which formed the great majority of the populace, could afford no such luxury. Thus it was only natural that the laxity of the morals of aristocratic circles caused a feeling of discontent and envy lower down the social ladder, even affecting the intellectuals. The latter, however, like the middle classes in every society, were too genteel, too dependent on the patronage of the nobility, to advocate open revolt. They were too content to fall back on the idea that enlightenment in the sense of better education, and propaganda of the literary variety, would bring about a change in the structure of society.

In older times, sex guilt was placed squarely on the woman as the seductress. In the eighteenth century, blossomed the *romans de mœurs* in which the lover was well-born and did the seducing, the low-born woman becoming his victim. Thus sex guilt became transferred to him. This idea was the theme of many a literary work for which the trend was set by the Abbé Prévost's famed ' Manon Lescaut ', which appeared in 1731. Ex-soldier and friar, Prévost lived in England where his novel was rivalled by Samuel Richardson's ' Pamela, or Virtue Rewarded ', which was classed as the finest erotic novel of the time, telling as it did the adventures of a working class girl who preserved her chastity despite many temptations. Richardson's ' Clarissa ', later gained him even more fame; even Rousseau and Goethe are said to have been inspired by his ideas.

The aristocracy claimed the privilege of licentiousness for themselves, but on their minions they inflicted severe laws to limit their chances of leading an equally immoral existence. In France, so many women of good breeding took to prostitution that they constituted a threat to its common practitioners. To influence the sexual mores of the times, strong voices were needed to make positive suggestions for reform. This need was answered by Jean-Jacques Rousseau, born in Geneva, and brought up in a Calvinist atmosphere. In his first novel, *La Nouvelle Héloïse*, or ' The New Héloïse ', he preached morality without openly attacking the propertied classes though he regarded such private ownership as the prime cause of the evils that infested the social structure. His sex morality, in essence, was that there was a law of nature that would bring together a man and a woman to share the joys of sexuality and to build a family if they kept themselves uncorrupted. This lofty idea was modified in his next novel, ' Emile ', in which he stoutly claimed that individuals could not be changed while institutions remained stagnant in their morass of evil. The book was banned in France, and Rousseau fled to Switzerland, and, later, to Holland.

Yet this same Rousseau, as his **Confessions** reveal, was not inherently disposed to follow his own lofty sex creed. His mother having died a few days after he was born, he developed a longing for a mother-substitute. Left in the hands of an uncle, the latter sent him to the house of a clergyman who was looked after by an elderly spinster called Mademoiselle Lambercier. Rousseau had at last found a mother. Any chastisement from her was welcomed, and he derived a great thrill at her slightest touch.

Grown up, Rousseau led a solitary sexual existence, masturbating for relief with Mlle. Lambercier as his imaginary partner. It can be seen that he was clearly a *gerontophile*, *i.e.*, a man attracted by older women. But even a woman of thirty-five as against his twenty-one years, one Madame de Warens, merely disgusted him when she initiated him into the secrets of heterosexual love. Yet she became his mistress, or rather, his mother-substitute. Later, he seemed to derive greater pleasure from the caresses of Madame de Larnage who was many years his senior. Prostitutes and society women alike left him cold. The following extracts from Rousseau's **Confessions** make it clear that not only was he a *gerontophile,* but also a masochist wishing to suffer pain at the hands of older women, in his case as a result of childhood chastisement which obviously caused a form of infantalism bordering on arrested development of sexuality:

" It was because Mlle. Lambercier had a motherly affection for me that she sometimes exerted a maternal affection which meant . . . the usual punishment of infants.

" . . . when at last she pulled me across her knees, I found that the reality was far less serious than the anticipation of it. What is even more strange is the fact that this punishment, coup for coup, blow for blow, greatly stimulated my affection for her who inflicted it.

" Thus . . . I ceaselessly sought, by further acts of naughtiness, to earn some more of the same kind of correction.

" A large degree of sensual gratfication had arrived with the sting and the shame of being bared to the punishing pain, then to the rod which followed. Each experience, therefore, left me with a desire which was far greater than the fear of another infliction . . .

" I devoured with my eyes every attractive woman. But I never sought the usual act of sexual intercourse, though I was attracted even to torment by their charms. In the deeps of my mind I transformed them all into so many Mademoiselles Lambercier ! I pictured myself lying over their laps, being chastised in the same manner !

" Even on reaching marriageable age, this perverse yearning still persisted, driving me near to madness—or depravity . . .

" As soon as I was old enough to realise what they were, I took a very strong aversion to prostitutes and to courtesans of any kind . . .

" . . . during my irresistable erotic passions, and in my yearning fancies while I committed extravagant acts on myself, I imagined I was having the aid of the opposite sex—the Mademoiselles Lambercier I longed for. Ignobly in these ways I passed through puberty, filled with sexuality without seeking, or even wishing for any other satisfaction than that which the Mademoiselle Lambercier had so innocently and unsuspectingly afforded me.

" It was thus, too, when I became a man, my childish desire far outweighing the natural order of sexual satisfaction. It is this abnormality, added to my natural timidity, which has always barred me from being enterprising with women . . . "

Sexuality under
Napoleon

Napoleon Buonaparte was the dictator of a Police State. Yet he bothered himself but little with the sex lives of his subjects. The wise measure of medical inspection for prostitutes was introduced in his time by Dubois, the Paris Prefect of Police. Napoleon gave his soldiers a great deal of sexual liberty, one might even say licence, and even more of it to his officers. The soldiery roamed the streets of Paris like libertines and had to be checked from time to time, but no such control was exercised over the officers.

Once in power, as is well known, Napoleon was openly and ruthlessly adulterous. He discarded women like worn-out gloves when he tired of them, which might be in a night, or a week, or a month or more, as his fancy dictated. He made advances to married women and forced them to his will when their husbands were abroad on missions according to his contrivance. Women, too, were often anxious enough to submit to him once he had reached eminence. He boasted unreservedly of his conquests over women, and even narrated his romantic episodes in detail before his intimates. The list of his amours is a long one, but the tragedy of his love life was that women were not drawn to him by any conspicuous sex appeal, but rather because of his exalted position, and he was probably aware of this at least subconciously. Lewinsohn observes that throughout his life he had to have a woman spend the night with him, and gives a fitting explanation for Napoleon's sexual ardour: " Precisely because the gods had not created him a woman's darling, he was anxious to prove his manhood in women's estimation and in his own . . . "

Though promiscuity was his ruling passion, Napoleon has been recorded as having been faithful in his own way, to three women: his first wife, Joséphine de Beauharnais, Marie Louise of Habsburg, and Marie Walewska, the Polish countess, whom he stole from her elderly husband. It is even suspected that he committed incest with his sister Pauline who was younger than him by eleven years. Of all these women, Marie Walewska was the one who influenced him most. His disastrous Russian campaign was due to her instigation to liberate Poland from Russian domination. She bore him a son, while Joséphine remained childless by him throughout their marriage though she had three children from her previous marital venture.

For the sake of a legitimate heir, Napoleon divorced his first wife. A marriage was arranged between him and the Austrian Emperor's daughter, Marie Louise, a seventeen year old girl. When he married her, she was a virgin, but in later years she bothered little about chastity, and even had an illegitimate child by a lover while Napoleon was in exile, the lover being Adam von Neipperg who had been sent as her escort by the Viennese court, which heaped honours on him even after the episode.

Love Life in Eighteenth Century England

The spirit of the seventeenth century Restoration glided into the eighteenth century England of the Georgian Rakes, and later, the Regency Bucks. In the previous century, the Stuarts had travelled a great deal in France and brought back with them a taste for French manners and morals, which, as we have seen, infected English society from the moment Charles II returned from exile in France. and the licentious period of the Restoration commenced. This Francophilia continued in the jolly, roistering lives of the upper classes of England in Georgian days. However, there was more elegance and refinement than in the rambunctious century that had gone before. Thus royalty no longer visited the town brothels, but, following the example of the French, maintained such establishments for the use of their own circle. The *bonhomie* of the Restoration died out and class distinction became sharper. It was in this time that snobbery, so much a part of English life even today, began to be cultivated deliberately.

Near St James's Palace, sprang up brothels that were frequented by courtiers and were so expensive that the lower orders stayed away from them. We shall not here dilate on the English brothel life of the period as it will be dealt with fully in a later chapter. Frivolous conversation became the height of fashion and gossips predominated in society, the demi-reps providing them with choice morsels. Even the Parliamentarian, Charles James Fox, before becoming a Minister, visited the brothel off St. James's, and in this connection Bloch makes an interesting observation: " . . . It is remarkable that so long as this man lived the life of a libertine he was respected for his justice and uprightness and for his true patriotism. But when he devoted himself entirely to politics, he renounced his debaucheries and his virtues at the same time. This is a very interesting psychological manifestation. For the virtues and faults of the individual have a very close connection with his or her sexual life. If the former are to be understood, the latter must be taken into account, and what applies to the individual applies likewise to society. The sexual life of a society, with its various symptoms, is always a true reflection of the culture of the age." Dr. Ivan Bloch's **Sexual Life in England,** in which this passage occurs, provides a fascinating panorama of English sexual mores through the ages.

A special feature of the Georgian period were the masquerades or fancy-dress balls for which buildings such as the Pantheon and Almack's were erected. As can be imagined, these revels were conducive to immorality and were condemned by the Bishop of London and others. While the *bon ton* drove to these masquerades in their carriages, there were often crushes in the streets, and the mobs would surround the carriages with flaming torches in their hands, shouting obscenities the while. Madame Cornelys, a German Tyrolean and daughter of an actor, arranged many such fancy-dress balls. The Soho masquerades she devised went on for a score of years.

Courtesans found ready entry into social circles. Of these, the most prominent was the actress Anna Bellamy who collected around her a scintillating group of actors, including the great Garrick and Chesterfield, statesmen, and intellectuals. She was the illegitimate daughter of Lord Tyrawley, a roué, and like her father she was herself very lascivious. Kitty Fisher, yet another courtesan, more renowned for her beauty than her wit or sparkle as was Anna Bellamy, placed a very high price on her charms, charging no less than a hundred guineas for a night. When the then Duke of York gave her only fifty pounds after a night of bliss, she refused to have him as a future client, and had the banknote made the ingredient of a tartlet which she forthwith consumed.

The famous Beau Nash once kept a mistress called Fanny Murray who acquired quite a reputation for herself for a whole decade in the second quarter of the century. She changed her lovers often enough and John Wilkes dedicated his ' Essay on Woman ' to her, expanding in it on her sexual pyrotechnics. A veritable *femme fatale* was Martha Ray who seemed to inspire an amazing depth of affection in a young preacher, Hackman, who, after years of being turned down by her, shot her as she was leaving a theatre. Fanny Barton, the actress, who had found her way into society with the help of two brothel-keepers, had a surprise visit from a Creole lover on her bridal night to the conductor Abington.

A female counterpart of Rousseau, inasmuch as she, too, was a *gerontophile,* was the Covent Garden actress, Mrs. Harlowe, who had affaires galore with elderly or old men. Another actress, Harriet Wilson, numbered among her lovers the highest nobles in the land, such as the Duke of Argyle and the Duke of Wellington. She started her dizzy career when only fifteen by becoming the mistress of Lord Craven.

One may perhaps truly say that the greatest English romance of the eighteenth century was the love affair of Emma, Lady Hamilton, and Lord Nelson who was responsible for the defeat of Napoleon Born in 1761, Emma started life as a nursery-maid in the home of a physician. She then worked for a greengrocer, and later for a wealthy woman in whose library she acquired a smattering of culture that, along with her beauty and intrinsic charm, would stand her in good stead in her amazing career of rags to riches.

When one of her relatives was pressganged into becoming a sailor, she pleaded for his release with the Captain, John Willet Payne, paying him the price in kind. Her first real lover, according to Bloch, was Sir Henry Featherston. He kept her as his mistress first in Sussex, then at London, where he forsook her, and where, at the time, lived Dr. Graham who ran an establishment called ' The Temple of Health '. He chose her as a living proof of his theories on health. She was immediately noticed and served as a model for artists and sculptors, and her face and figure adorned may *objets d'art*.

A connoisseur of art, Sir Charles Grenville, soon took her under his wing and installed her as his mistress. By him she had two sons and a daughter, she posing as their ' aunt '. Respectability walked into her life when Sir Charles's uncle, Sir William Hamilton, British Ambassador at the Court of Naples, a pronounced epicurean who had made Italy his home, finding his nephew in pecuniary distress, took advantage of the situation and made Emma, Lady Hamilton, taking her with him to Italy.

In Italy, Lady Hamilton became the bosom friend of Caroline, Queen of Naples and a nymphomaniac to boot, as well as a Lesbian, who conceived for Emma a great passion.   Marriage did not put an end to Emma's love affairs.   In 1798, when she was almost thirty-six, began the supreme love affair of her life—the romance with Nelson. Two years later, a sort of *ménage a trois* was set up by the trio, in Piccadilly.   Another two years, and Emma, having borne Nelson a son, found herself widowed.   She then moved to Clarges Street off Piccadilly, where the house in which she set up residence, still stands.   After the birth of a daughter, Nelson allowed her an annual income.   In 1805, however, the romance ended cruelly in Nelson's sudden death at Trafalgar, where, before the end, like Charles II in relation to his mistress, Nell Gwyn, he requested his physician and friend, Hardy, to " Take care of my poor Lady Hamilton ! "

From then on, Emma went from bad to worse, suffered imprisonment in the debtors' jail in 1813, and about two years later breathed her last in poverty at Calais.   This rags to riches story would be imperfect if one were not to mention that Lady Hamilton introduced the *tableaux vivants,* or plastic poses, which have survived her into our own times.

Georgian Rakes and Regency Bucks

The Georgian Rakes and Regency Bucks were not exactly Don Juans.   The Latin lover's romantic adventures are motivated by sensuality pure and simple.   The English Beaux were little concerned with passion.   Their approach to love affairs was cold and calculated, and motivated by a power complex that found satisfaction in a romantic conquest.   Such was the rake who was the ' hero ' of Richardson's novel, ' Clarissa '.   Taine thus described the rake: " What a character ! How very English !   . . . Unyielding pride, the desire to subjugate others, the provocative love of battle, the need for ascendency, these are his predominant features.   Sensuality is but of secondary importance . . . Pride, nothing but limitless, insatiable, absurd pride is the main, the only, the central motive of his whole being . . . He is generally a jolly and witty talker but his humour is only an outward symptom; he is coarse and immoral, he jests like a hangman, harshly and cruelly, over the evil deeds he has committed, or is about to commit . . . In France libertines were but frivolous fellows, whereas here they were mean brutes.   Knavery had poisoned their love."

Visits to brothels were commonplace in the life of the Georgian Rake. One of the sons of Lord Milton, after a sumptuous banquet in a brothel and voluptuous revels with several of the inmates, shot himself. The Duke of Queensbury lived only for sexual pleasure, his appetite for the outré growing with age. He was nicknamed 'Lord Piccadilly' or 'Old Q'. His death bed was littered with love letters as a fitting end to a life devoted to sexual eccentricities. Another British libertine was Baltimore who carried around with him a harem of eight women on his travels.

Intellectuals and writers did not lag behind the aristocracy. Charles James Fox, in his earlier years, was given to over-indulgence in wine and women. Samuel Foote, actor and poet, did not lag far behind. Lord Byron had the reputation of being an English Don Juan. But he was, from all accounts, more pursued than pursuing, being personable and attractive to women. His marriage to Annabella Milbanke broke up when she divorced him for a reason that was kept secret. After that, she accused him of having committed incest with his sister, Mrs. Augusta Leigh. Poems published after Byron's death and purported to be his, but not actually written by him, reveal that he was addicted to pæderasty or anal intercourse with women. The secret reason for the divorce, it was whispered, was that he had forced this mode of coitus on his wife while she was pregnant. According to Moll, the sexologist, Byron was also a homosexual.

The last of the Georgian monarchs was George IV, perhaps the greatest rake and debauchee of them all. Born in 1762, George IV was described as 'the First Gentleman of Europe'. Thackeray was scornful of him and declared in his work, **The Four Georges :** "But this George himself, what was he ? I look through his whole life and recognise but a bow and a grin. I try to take him to pieces, and find silk stockings, padding, stays, a coat with frogs and a fur collar, a star and blue ribbon, a handkerchief prodigiously scented, one of Truefit's nutty brown wigs reeking with oil, a set of teeth, a huge black stock, underwaistcoats, more underwaistcoats, and then nothing." Carlton House was the residence of England's First Fop as one may rightly call him, though he had a considerable rival for such a title in his friend and companion, the impeccable George 'Beau' Brummell, whose years of triumph lasted from 1799 till 1814, during which time he sparkled like a jewel at Carlton House and no social gathering was considered a perfect success unless he graced it with his immediate presence.

Bloch declares: "The women made a god of Brummell; the famous courtesan, Henrietta Wilson, speaks passionately of him in her memoirs." Brummell came to rather an unhappy end. He incurred gambling debts which ruined him, and even his one-time friend, the Prince Regent, would do nothing for him. In 1816, he left England. With the death of George IV in 1830, the era of the Regency Bucks came to an end. Brummell, who typified the age, was appointed Consul at Caen by William IV, but had the position taken away from him later. So passed away, in the early nineteenth century, the gay, gallivanting blades of the Regency who had preened themselves like peacocks, and with them died the effervescence and colour that England was not to know again in the same measure.

CHAPTER 9

VICTORIAN PRUDERY, AND PENALTIES
FOR ADULTERY

*The Age of Hypocrisy—Puritanism returns to England—Evangelical
Campaign against Gaiety and Pleasure—Patrist Period of Restrictive
Movements—Sexual Obsession as an Undercurrent of Prudery—The
Nineteenth Century on the Continent : Budoir Diplomacy—European
Women come out of their Shells—George Sand : Transvestite and
Lesbian ?—The Romances of George Sand—Europe's Romantic Age
—Growth of the Bourgeois—Wind of Prudery blows from England
to the Continent—Louis Napoleon and the Empress Eugénie—The
Paintings of Courbet, Manet, and Ingres, meet with Eugénie's Dis-
approval—Flaubert and Beaudelaire prosecuted for Obscenity—
Dumas, ' Camille ', and the ' demi-monde '—The Second Empire
and Païva—Punishment of Adultery through the Ages—Flogging and
Stoning of Adulteress—Drowning of Adulterous Partners—Greek
' Ass-Rider '—Death and Castration among Romans for Adultery—
Punishment for False Testimony against Adulterers—Ritualistic and
Orgiastic Adultery.*

WITH the passing of the Georgians, started the long reign of
Queen Victoria following the short one of William IV.
Puritanism returned to England in new guise, and hypocrisy
dominated the stuffy age of antimacassars, aspidistras, and mutton
chop sleeves and whiskers. The merry, hearty English became a
straightlaced, straitjacketed people, acquiring, in the process, many
inhibitions that still cling to them. The revelries at the Ranelagh and
Vauxhall Gardens came to an end, being replaced by genteel garden
parties and harmless and dull pastimes. The gay clubs of the Georgians
donned a serene gloom; even the legs of tables and chairs were covered
up in the interests of decency, and family life assumed importance, a
striking example being set in this direction by the Queen and her
consort, Prince Albert.

The demi-reps were now a little less hectic and were called
cocottes, many of them still being accepted in refined circles. A strong
gust of prudery blew over the land, but eroticism did not blow away

140

with it; it merely went underground. The monogamous Victorian home became highly respectable, but those who wanted a real fling, and could afford it, could take a channel steamer to Paris. Women could no longer flaunt, under their skirts, the long, often frilly and tantalising pantalettes of the Romantic Age of gallants. Their skirts had underlayers of other skirts and their legs were neither to be seen nor talked about. Prudery, Richard Lewinsohn explains in **A History of Sexual Customs,** went so far that women would not let themselves be thoroughly inspected even by physicians, but indicated on dummies, specially set up for the purpose, the spots where they felt pain ! The sex restrictions, it has been revealed by recent investigations into Victorian eroticism, led to an increase of masturbation among the young. Lewinsohn tells us: " . . . The phenomenon had been known of old, and from the end of the eighteenth century onwards doctors and teachers occupied themselves with it very seriously. Most of them regarded it as a pathological habit, to be attacked by drastic methods. In Victorian England, industry interested itself in the problem and produced its own answers. Cages were manufactured which were fitted over a boy's genitals at night and carefully locked; some, for better protection, had spikes sticking out of them."

Licence and restriction both tend to breed prostitution, and thus, the extreme restraints of the Victorian era gave an impetus to the oldest profession which will be elaborated upon in a subsequent chapter. Says G. Rattray Taylor in his **Sex in History :** " Victorian insistence upon the appearance of respectability without the reality has gained England a name for hypocrisy. In no field was this more marked than that of prostitution. It has been said that Victorian morality was based upon a vast system of prostitution: it has been noted that the Victorians were careful to create a supply of prostitutes by making it impossible for those who had once erred ever to recover their respectability."

The *cocottes* had, of course, to assume the airs of respectable women. Thus Dr. Ivan Bloch, in his **Sexual Life in England,** quotes a visitor to Covent Garden Theatre: " ' The short intervals we spent in the saloon. The saloon was full of prostitutes whose clothes revealed more than they concealed, but whose behaviour, on the contrary, did not in any way betray their calling. A meaning look from a man is answered by the lady concerned with the handing over of a card giving her name and address and containing a tenderly worded invitation. The girls carry the cards in their bosoms, and they therefore convey some of the perfume of their bodies. The offer of the cards is carried out with perfect courtesy and good will . . . It is a curious fact that English families, mothers and daughters as well as fathers and sons, move among these pretty ladies quite naturally, apparently unconcerned with their presence and activities."

In the first half of the Victorian era, the music-hall had an unsavoury reputation. Men of the upper crust visited these halls " for supper and song " often after a visit to the theatre. The songs were mostly smutty and slangy, with titles such as " My Woman is a Rummy Whore " and " The Coal Hole Companion ". These same music-halls burlesqued even sacred institutions right up to the 'seventies. Scandalous divorce cases and Church ritual were shamelessly parodied in such music-hall taverns as the 'Coal Hole '.

Sexual anxieties brought into being a veritable Evangelical campaign not merely to wipe out sexual indulgence, but also to smother with a wet blanket most forms of pleasure. The Vauxhall and Apollo Gardens, and the Temple of Flora, scenes of mirth, merriment, and abandon, closed down. Sunday observance became stricter and stricter and Sabbatinical prudery still manifests itself when even the Duke of Edinburgh is criticised. for playing polo on a Sunday. Theatres became emptier, even games such as archery and football were indulged in with less frequency, and social intercourse became hemmed in with curious conventions. Immorality had to shoulder the blame for everyday calamities. Thus Taylor remarks: " But if this general condemnation of pleasure reminds us of the Puritans, there were also aspects of Evangelican morality which seem almost mediæval . . . political and economic ills were attributed not to defects of government or to poor harvests, but to the immorality of man's behaviour."

The Victorian Age was a patrist period *par excellence*. The Victorian paterfamilias led the restrictive movement. Spontaneous impulses met with short shrift. The idea of original sin was revived, and children taught that they were " naturally depraved creatures ". The pains of childbirth could not be alleviated with the use of anæsthetics, because Victorians looked upon them as God-given to wash away Eve's guilt. When Simpson attempted the use of chloroform for women in childbirth towards the middle of the century, he was ruthlessly criticised. However, in 1853, the Queen herself decided to put chloroform to the test for one of her pregnancies, and the controversy subsided.

As can be imagined, in a strongly patrist period such as this, women occupied a very low status, even though a Queen sat on the throne. But Victorian morality, with its overwhelming hypocrisy, made woman a pure vessel rather than the source of original sin as she had been looked upon in mediæval times. Hence sex, which was unmentionable, and regarded as an animal function, was not to be enjoyed by her but to be used merely for procreation. The ban on marrying a dead brother's widow having been repealed, the Victorians reintroduced it, and it was not repealed till the end of the first decade of the present century.

Private societies for the suppression of vice sprang up like mushrooms. The foremost of these was the Proclamation Society, which brought down the evangelican axe on ' licentious publications' and free speech in general. Among works that the Society succeeded in having banned were Shelley's ' Queen Mab' and ' Œdipus Tyrannus', and Palmer's ' Principles of Nature'. Tom Paine, author of ' The Rights of Man' and ' Age of Reason', had to flee from England, and later from France, and go to America. The patrist attacks came from such men as the Duke of Wellington, a score of peers, and bishops as well. Even the language of the Bible had to be 'reformed'. Ordinary speech also came under fire. One had to say 'perspire' instead of 'sweat', 'accouchement' instead of 'pregnancy'.

Sexual and excretary functions had to be glossed over in both speech and writing. Here, the Victorians carried their prudery to excess, for even the mediæval Patrists and the early Puritans had not introduced such taboos. This extreme movement gave the English language a new word: to 'Bowdlerise'. Bowdler and Plumptre were two men who defended the theatre when the purist reformers condemned it for its grossness. They maintained that the theatre was an art form that could be elevated by emending the gross language used by many playwrights. Says Taylor: " It was not in a spirit of fanatical intolerance that they emended Shakespeare and revised 'Robinson Crusoe'; it was with the loving care of a jeweller polishing and cutting a jewel. Bowdler confined himself to deletion; Plumptre did not hesitate to rewrite. It was not merely sexual irregularity which aroused his sensibilities: he deleted even references to romantic love. Since he ruthlessly excised all murders and indeed all reprehensible characters, he successfully removed the element of conflict upon which the drama depends . . . "

The Victorians, with their verbal sensitiveness, due, of course, to an undercurrent of sexual obsession which they sought to repress, were the first to introduce laws against obscenity; yet, despite, or rather on account of this, they produced, surreptitiously, a fund of pornography. Under the Act of 1857, some of the most important works of the age, and subsequent periods of English history, came to be outlawed: Havelock Ellis's 'Psychology of Sex', James Joyce's 'Ulysses', and in the 'twenties of the present century, D. H. Lawrence's 'Lady Chatterley's Lover', as well as Radcliffe Hall's 'Well of Loneliness'. Victorian sado-masochistic pornography sold under the counter, and its greatest purveyor was Edward Sellon, author of 'The Romance of Lust'. One cannot but agree with Taylor when he declares: " The fact is, the institution of a system of censorship, while it fails to eliminate pornography, effectively eliminates the serious literary work which attempts to approach subjects realistically . . Victorian insistence upon the appearance of respectability without the reality has gained England a name for hypocrisy . . . "

The Nineteenth Century on the Continent: Budoir Diplomacy

On the Continent, the death of Napoleon altered the pattern of morality in Europe. The Bourbon Government abolished divorce, and the remarriage of divorced persons was annulled in 1816. Divorce was not reintroduced until 1884. Separation was permitted, but this meant that the partners could not remarry. Despite the law, however, a great deal of licence was permitted to the average man so long as he conducted himself with obedience to the State, under the vigilant eye of the secret police.

Prince Clemens von Metternich was the man who set the pace for the morality of Europe in the early part of the nineteenth century. Budoir diplomacy became popular under him. Though having a family of seven and married to a woman of an esteemed family, Metternich did not live with his wife. This suited his promiscuous nature, but he was careful to conduct romantic liaisons only with titled women and those whom he could use politically. Even during Napoleon's lifetime, he had been the Dictator's sister's lover, while he acted as Austrian Ambassador in Paris. At the time of the Congress of Vienna, his current favourite was the Duchess of Sagan. As an indication of the police-mindedness of the era, even Metternich himself was spied upon by the Police, and his love affairs were reported in secret documents.

The Vienna of Metternich's time became the world's love mart. Her prostitutes are said to have numbered no less than 20,000, and to have carried their trade abroad when called upon to do so. The penalty for procuration was so insignificant as not to deter the pimps from doing a roaring trade. The Police's first informant in their spying activities was Henriette Rothman, " queen of the prostitutes ", as Lewinsohn calls her. He goes on to say: " It was useless denouncing her; she was impregnable, because she was herself informer No. 1 for the police." One of these Viennese prostitutes had the reputation of wishing to conserve her virginity and for this reason offered her customers the delights of the flesh in every way except the normal. Venereal diseases were rampant in the gay capital, and one out of every four births was illegitimate in 1811, rising to one out of every two by 1847.

Duels, not with swords, but with pistols, were still a part of European life. Bourgeois values were responsible for this as more and more of the *nouveaux riches* joined the ranks of the middle classes and sought to imitate the customs of the earlier Romantic Age. Adultery often resulted in such duels, Pushkin, the romantic Russian poet, being one of the victims.

While in England the Victorian era, almost from start to finish, remained patrist, in Europe matrist principles prevailed at least until the middle of the century. While the Victorian woman was suppressed in her time, in Europe the female started to assert herself. There was almost a wave of female masculinisation. In England, it was represented by a very small section of ' blue stockings ', but in Europe it flourished because women became increasingly the lure of the male, and began to assert their autonomy. Thus in Mainz in Germany, Caroline Michaelis, a daughter of a scholar, became popular with the Cubists who supported the Revolution, and was hunted from pillar to post. Subsequently she married Wilhelm Schlegal, and, later, divorcing him, married Schelling, the philosopher. She also did a certain amount of writing. Another woman in Wilhelm Schlegel's life was Madame de Staël, authoress of 'Corinne'. She was an intellectual who ranked poets and scholars among her friends, and was looked upon as a herald of the German romantic movement as Lewinsohn tells us.

Another famous woman of this period was Aurore Dudevant who, under her pseudonym of George Sand, achieved both fame and notoriety. She was a transvestite habitually dressed in men's clothes. Descended, from her father's side, of aristocratic forbears, her mother, on her own account, was a singer and gypsy. Born Dupin, after a conventional convent upbringing she married Dudevant while yet only eighteen. By this rich baron she had a daughter. While married, she had three lovers, the influence of the third sending her to Paris in search of excitement. Here she took to writing and worked hard so as to be economically independent of her lovers whom she changed frequently. A domineering woman, she demanded the same role in sexual life, and hence her romances were generally tempestuous ones. She never seemed to find satisfaction in her singular romances. After an affair with Alfred de Musset with whom she lived for a while in Venice, she complained of his impotency and had an affair with his doctor when he fell iill.

The greatest and best known of George Sand's romances was with the composer, Chopin, who was in his late twenties while she was in her mid-thirties. It lasted almost a decade, during which she wore him out completely. Among others, she was courted by Prosper Mérimée of 'Carmen' fame, but neither found satisfaction in the experience. Only Franz Liszt resisted her witchery, as he already had a mistress, the Countess d'Agoult, who had deserted her husband for the musician. George Sand's male attire, her smoking of cigars, her domineering ways, her friendships with women, and her dissatisfaction with all her male lovers, probably concealed a strong masculine streak. She even wrote love letters to an actress who was already married and mistress of the poet, Alfred de Vigny. Though she never seems to have openly indulged in Lesbianism, it is more than possible that only in homoeroticism, playing the dominant role, could she perhaps have found sexual bliss.

At this time, in the Bernese Oberland, a forerunner of companionate marriage, with the full consent of the parents of young couples, flourished. In Germany, too, considerable freedom existed for the young, and Stendhal compared these natural and healthy practices to the conventions and artificial restraints of French society to the detriment of the latter, in his work, **De l'Amour.** Pre-marital intercourse was recommended by him as the best method of choosing a partner for life. Some years later, a young Frenchman, then unknown, wrote a book in which he, too, suggested anatomical and physiological study of the female form, not in theory but in practice, the work corruscating with witty aphorisms. The young man was Honoré de Balzac, later to become one of the pillars of French literature.

Europe's Romantic Age

The nineteenth century, particularly the early part of it, was undoubtetdly Europe's Romantic Age. Love flourished to the tune of violins and the lilt of dancing feet. Free love was appreciated by a certain section, but the *petit bourgeois* clung to their provincial and suburban conventions. *La vie Bohème,* or the Bohemian life, was all very well for poets, artists, Thespians, and their ilk; it would not do for *their* sons and daughters. Match-making raged in these circles. To encourage this, there were regular balls, either private or got up by social clubs and other such institutions. The Court opera house and the Court theatre held weekly dances in Berlin. The fashionable spa of Baden-Baden was filled with marriageable daughters escorted by their adoring mothers.

Gracious and colourful was the period of the Waltz, and many partners who first met in the dance, often became life partners. Property-consciousness was at its height, and a girl simply had to make a good match, though, compared to her mother's time, she had more freedom of choice and was generally consulted in the matter.

There is little doubt that the Waltz influenced romantic love on the Continent. The dances previously popular, such as the Polka, required lightning footwork, and the couples had had to gallop through their paces. The physical contact between partners had been limited, but now it became an embrace with the man placing one arm round the girl's waist. Romantics of the previous generation, now grown middle-aged or old, fumed at these new dances, among whose detractors were Musset and Byron, both having outlived their hot-blooded youth.

Reports relative to the sexual habits of nations are not by any means the monopoly of the twentieth century. Over a hundred years ago, in the fifth decade of the Romantic Age, a German investigated the sexual lives of a hundred married couples. His revelations were surprising. He claimed that only fifteen of the marriages had been truly happy ones, thirty-six had been only moderately so, and almost fifty had been unhappy. Only one of the marriages had adhered to the vow of absolute fidelity, proving that adultery was rampant. Germany had, of course, allowed dissolution of marriage, unlike the French who had abolished the former liberal practice. When brothels were abolished in Berlin in 1844, street prostitution took a turn for the worse, and Berlin's streets became studded with prostitutes for many decades to come.

The wind of prudery blowing from England did not leave Europe completely unaffected. It was of course laughed at and derided, but as in the later Victorian era Britain's position as a major power was undisputed and did not appear as short-lived as it turned out to be, in France in particular there was a certain amount of aping of English ways. Napoleon III, great-nephew of the first Napoleon, had an

English mistress, the actress Henriette Howard, or Elizabeth Anne Harryet, to give her her real name, who lived in the palace of Saint-Cloud while he was President of the Republic. She had financed his propaganda before he came to power, the money coming from a wealthy lover, a Guards officer. Suitably rewarded, Henriette had to part from her lover when he had won his chief objective, and he even entrusted to her the care of his children by another mistress.

In defiance of the old political tradition of a marriage of convenience, Napoleon III chose as his bride Eugénie de Montijo, daughter of an Irish wine merchant of Malaga, and sister of the Duchess of Alba, posing the while as a democrat who would consider the title of *parvenu* a proud one in a democratic age. To the surprise of all the dissenters, Eugénie kept her bearing as Empress and with Louis Napoleon presided over a scintillating court. This woman who had once been the paramour of Stendhal and Mérimée, remained faithful to her marriage vows though Napoleon himself was far from loyal. Her moral influence was much stronger than her spouse's.

Turning over a new leaf made Eugénie something of a prude. Hence Victorian prudery across the Channel found its echo, however feeble, in the French court. Eugénie disapproved of the artist Courbet's paintings and they were not accepted for exhibition at the Paris World Exhibition of 1855. Manet was accorded the same treatment when he sent his famous *Le Bain* or 'The Bath'. Similarly, Eugénie frowned on Ingres's 'The Turkish Bath' which Louis Napoleon had bought. As in Victorian England, in France too, Venuses and Adonises went out of fashion, being replaced by draped figures or animal sculpture. In the *Place de l'Opéra*, the sculptor Jean-Baptiste Carpeaux's creation of a group of nude dancers, aroused a storm of protest. Iconoclasts even splashed it with ink one night. While a controversy raged as to which spot to remove it to, the War of 1870 broke out, the building of the Opera House was halted, and by the time it was resumed, values in art had, fortunately, altered, and the work of Carpeaux remains in the *Place de l'Opéra* to this day.

As in England, the long arm of prudery reached out to grasp literature as well within its iron fist. Even the bourgeois Flaubert was prosecuted for his novel, 'Madame Bovary', because he had dared to depict a woman of the provinces committing adultery. He got away with mere censure, but the poet Beaudelaire had to pay a fine for his poems, *Fleurs du Mal*. Authors of lesser renown, were sent to prison. Alexander Dumas *fils*, son of the well-known Dumas famed for 'The Count of Monte Cristo', and 'The Three Musketeers', was, like his father, looked upon "as an apostle of morals of puritanical severity, who wrote not in order to tickle his public with lubricious themes and epigrammatic *bon-mots* but to strengthen family life and emancipate the institution of marriage from the bonds of money and the errors of the Romantic Movement", as Lewinsohn declares citing Gustave Lanson's 'History of French Literature'.

The younger Dumas's *La Dame aux Camélias* achieved instantaneous fame when published in 1848. Four years later, it delighted theatre audiences, and Verdi used it as the libretto for his opera, 'La Traviata', the following year. Its theme of the consumptive courtesan who gives up her bourgeois lover to save his family's honour, has remained a perennial favourite. Great actresses have played the role on stage and screen, in our own time Edwige Feuillere on the stage, and the fabulous Ala Nazimova and Norma Talmadge on the silent screen, and about a generation ago, the great Garbo in the talkie version.

It was in 1855, while at the height of his success, that Dumas *fils* invented the term *demi-monde*. He, however, applied it only to the half-world of women who lived between the meretricious prostitutes and the well-bred girls who had resisted the lure of sex. Says Lewinsohn, again citing Lanson: " Society is stronger than the individual, and the woman who offends against the moral laws of society ends by damaging herself. The Romantic writers failed to realise this, and Dumas, the anti-Romantic, tried to bring this simple truth home again to his contemporaries . . . His moral was, at bottom, good Victorianism. A discreet lapse from marital loyalty may be overlooked, but defiance of the institution of marriage, never ! The *demi-monde*, Dumas explains in the foreword to the bitter comedy which bears this title, begins where the legal wife stops: it ends where the legal wife begins. It is separated from honest women by public scandals; from courtesans by money."

The *demi-mondaine* belonged more to the period of the Second Empire than to Dumas's world, when women thought twice before breaking up a marriage for the sake of romance. It was a world from which the duel had faded away or was beginning to. In the Second Empire, such women ran literary salons, were seen openly in public with literary figures, and often lived as mistresses to but one lover who supported them in good style. Symbolising the morals of her age, lived in Paris, during the Second Empire, the famed Païva, or Thérèse Villoing. She started her adventurous career as the wife of a tailor in her home town. On becoming a mother, she fled her humdrum existence, and was next heard of in Constantinople, then Vienna, and finally Berlin. Her star rose when she found herself in Paris.

Sitting alone on the *Champs Elysées*, one day, she was approached by Henri Herz, the Austrian pianist, and Arsene Houssaye, a writer. She cohabited with Herz for several years, during which time she ran a salon that rivalled the salons of George Sand and the Countess d'Agoult. When Herz went to tour America, she started off on her own with the help of Jules Lecomte, the lover of Marie Louise, and the poet, Théophile Gautier. In London she found an admirer in Lord Stanley, and his purse helped her to solve her financial problems. With the death of her tailor husband, she married the Marquis de Païva, who later returned home to Portugal.

The next lover to be ensnared in her net was a Prussian Count, eleven years her junior. She followed him to Berlin after rejecting him, when she discovered that he had inherited a fortune. Returning to Paris, Païva still carried on with her meretricious trade, ranking among her cronies such men as Taine the philosopher, Eugene Delacroix the painter, and Saint-Beuve the literary giant.

The Prussian Count, Guido Henckel von Donnersmarck, helped Païva to achieve her life's ambition: to possess a palace of splendour all her own. Lewinsohn tells us that it took ten years to build, and was situated on the *Champs Elysées* opposite the very bench where Herz had befriended her. The building boasted of an onyx staircase, and a bathroom that Théophile Gautier described as " Fit for a sultana out of the Thousand and One Nights ! " In 1870, she married her count when he was a little over forty, and she fifty-two.

The first decade of the present century saw a revival of colour and splendour in both Europe and England. Victoria's son, the Prince of Wales, who was a gay blade, sat on the throne at the turn of the century as Edward VII. But in the next decade, the lights over Europe were dimmed, the violins wailed sad tunes beside the Danube, and the holocaust of the 1914-18 War burst upon the world, representing the birth pangs of the new social order that was to be born soon after.

Punishment of Adultery
through the Ages

In ancient times, adultery was dealt with harshly, the cruellest of punishments being meted out to the lovers. In patriarchal societies, such as the Hebrews, the woman was singled out for the brunt of the suffering. Nowadays, adultery is the common cause of divorce.

Among the Pueblos of New Mexico, the Zuni tribe which believes in peace and sobriety, adultery is regarded with equanimity. A wife's infidelity does not perturb the husband though it may lead to his seeking a divorce. The question of violence does not arise at all. This tolerance of the wife's infidelity may be due to the fact that theirs is a matrilineal society. In the dour Dobu tribe, adultery is common. As we saw in an earlier chapter, the Dobuan couple live, in alternate years, in each other's village. Adultery generally takes place within the forbidden degrees of clan sisters and brothers. Discovery results in endless childish quarrels between husband and wife, but nothing more.

Islam was, originally at least, both Religion and State, so that the Koran lays down laws which pertain to both religious and secular matters. The punishment for adultery is severe: George Allgrove in his intriguing work, **Love in the East,** quotes the following passage from the Koran: " The adulteress and the adulterer, flog each of them with a hundred stripes, and let not pity for them detain you from obedience to Allah, if you believe in Allah and the Last Day, and let a party of believers witness their chastisement."

But Islamic law guards against false accusations of adultery, by laying down that accusers must always furnish four witnesses of the act. Should a husband catch his wife *in flagrante delicto*, he must testify against her no less than four times, and the fifth time he must ask that the curse of God may descend on him should he be lying. However, the wife can escape the penalty by denying four times that she has foregone her chastity, and the fifth time call on Allah's wrath to loose itself on her if her denial is a lie. These oaths were probably introduced as deterrents, for a Mohammedan would think twice before defying the Koran. Among Muslims, as amongst Hebrews, both Semitic races, adultery is looked upon as depriving a husband of his property rights more than anything else.

In ancient Greece, particularly in Athens, it was common for a husband to kill the man who had cuckolded him. If not the husband, then the State itself inflicted death on the seducer of another man's wife. A woman caught in the act of adultery had to forego personal adornments such as jewellery, and was also forbidden to enter the temples. If she defied the rule and appeared in public wearing her ornaments, the first man to encounter her could strip her of her adornments as well as her clothes, and administer a beating without, however, crippling or killing her. The main thing was to humiliate her and make her unhappy.

Pimps, whether male or female, were more severely dealt with as it was considered that they brought together for lustful purposes persons who of their own accord would be shy or reluctant to give way to their natural lusts. The penalty for procurers was death. There were also purely localised punishments that differed from place to place. Thus, according to Plutarch, an adulteress was forcibly taken to the market place and stood upon a particular stone where all and sundry could gaze on her with looks of disapproval, after which she was placed on an ass and had to ride through the streets to complete her ignominy. Finally, she was again placed on the stone of shame and called the dishonourable name, ' Ass-rider ', which was synonymous with ' adulteress ' and stuck to her all her life.

In yet another part of Greece, Elis, adulterers were led through the city in bonds for no less than three days. As if that were not enough, they were deprived of civil rights for the rest of their earthly existence. Adulteresses had to stand on a stone in the market place for eleven days, sans girdle and in a flimsy vest so that, for greater shame, their nakedness was exposed to the gaze of the passers-by.

Roman law was even harsher with an adulteress. She could be condemned to death by a family council at which the wronged husband would be present. However, one does not imagine this drastic measure being taken except in very rare cases, for Romulus did give a husband the right to divorce an unfaithful wife.

There seems to have been no statutory penalty for adultery in ancient Rome. The husband had the power to mete out the punishment as he deemed fit, or to call a family council to decide the woman's fate. The severest penalty was death, but the adulteress might be spared her life and banished from hearth and home. The adulterer, too, was not always killed by an irate husband who had been cuckolded. He might be castrated or flogged. He could also be turned over to the servants of the husband's household and these, according to Kiefer, " inflicted sexual dishonour on the adulterer ", such dishonour generally consisting of forced sodomy being performed on the man to shame his manhood.

The Emperor Augustus first introduced a statutory penalty for adultery. This mostly consisted of deprivation of property rights and banishment. The lower classes could be submitted to corporal punishment. Under the *Lex Julia de adulteriis* of Augustus, an adulteress lost her dowry, half of it going to the husband, the other half to the State. Later emperors introduced severer measures. Under Constantius, it was decreed that one guilty of adultery should either be drowned or burnt inside a sack. Justinian's decree was more humane: adulteresses were sent to nunneries.

Roman society being patriarchal, while a husband could kill or repudiate a wife for her adultery, she herself had no such rights against him for the same offence on his part. However, if his adultery had been committed with a married woman, one presumes that the latter's husband would take action against him to the point of killing or castrating him.

Under the Laws of Hammurabi in ancient Babylon, an unfaithful wife could be thrown into the river. If she and her lover were discovered *in flagrante*, they were bound together and cast into the river. If, however, they were suspected, but not caught red-handed in the act, they were flung into the river unbound so that Providence could judge them. But to swim back alive from the Euphrates or the Tigris, was no mean task. If, on the other hand, the wife caught her husband in the act of adultery, she had but two alternatives: to leave him, or to receive a compensation from him, mostly financial, one would think.

Even in pre-Mosaic days, adultery was frowned upon among the Hebrews. The suspected adulteress had to submit to a bizarre ordeal: Her husband would take her to the temple with " a tenth of an ephar of barley meal ", as William Graham Cole informs us in his erudite work, **Sex and Love in the Bible.** The priest would then fill an earthen vessel with water and mix it with dust from the tabernacle floor, unbind the woman's hair, " and place in her hands . . . the cereal offering of jealousy." The woman, after invoking Yahweh, was made to drink the water mixed with the dust, known as ' the water of bitterness '. If, as a result, her belly did not swell, she was considered innocent; if it did swell, it was proof of her adultery.

Just as in Islam, the other Semitic faith, if a woman were falsely accused of adultery, those who testified against her had to die. This is illustrated by the Old Testament tale of Susannah whose honour two elders attempted to violate while she was in her bath. Failing, they falsely accused her of unchastity.   When their lie was exposed, they paid for it with the forfeiture of their lives.   Rubens, Tintoretto, and Rembrandt, have depicted the incident in their respective paintings.

In ancient Britain, from the reign of Ethelbert to that of Canute, the law punished a husband's adultery with a fine, but it was not a ground on which a wife could claim a divorce.   The fine, as among the Hebrews and the Muslims, was for depriving some other woman's husband of his property right, so that, we presume, if the man had committed adultery with a single woman whose father was not living, the fine could not be imposed.   Again, these patrists punished adultery in a woman far more severely, as a matter of fact, with downright cruelty, for her nose and ears were often cut off.

In the Mediæval Ages, the penances prescribed by Bede and Theodore for breaking the prohibitions on sexuality outside of the marriage bond, were very stern.   Fornication was considered bad enough, but adultery worse still.   In seventeenth century England, the Puritans punished fornication with imprisonment up to three months, but for adultery the penalty was death.   Rattray Taylor cites the case of an old man of eighty-nine being put to death for adultery in 1653. Recalcitrant juries that refused to bring in verdicts of guilty, were dismissed.   Death apart, adulterers were submitted to public humiliation by being " fastened to the wall in iron collars, or jougs " in churches.

Though puritanical thought found its echoes in the Victorian era, be it said to the credit of these prudes of a later age, that when an attempt was made to reintroduce the death penalty for adultery, the measure was thrown out.   In both 1856 and 1857, motions to this effect were introduced by reactionaries in Parliament, but they were, fortunately, defeated.

Is artificial insemination a form of adultery?   The Roman Catholic Church equates the two, for it considers that the marriage union merely entitles the couple to perform natural acts conducive to the birth of a child, but it does not confer on them the right to have a child by artificial means, which is, in their opinion, tantamount to depriving God of his prerogative.   As adultery constitutes a criminal offence in America, if the Roman Catholic view prevailed, then artificial insemination would also be looked upon as a criminal act for fostering adultery.   But, apart from the Roman Catholic community and sympathisers with the Church's view, the law itself does not consider artificial insemination to be criminal.   Incidentally, the Kinsey Report revealed that in the United States of America, forty per cent. of the married men had had extra-marital experience with single or married women.

Ritualistic and Orgiastic Adultery

Adultery in the guise of a communal or religious rite, or as an orgiastic phenomenon in the form of festivals, has been tolerated, and often encouraged, in the most civilised societies. In the case of orgies, particularly in the old Pagan days, they may have been a curative measure for repressions affording bottled-up emotions an easy outlet.

In ancient India, many a presiding temple deity was, at one time, credited with the power of curing barrenness. Abbé Dubois, who travelled extensively in India, gives one such example in his book, **Hindu Manners, Customs, and Ceremonies:** Barren women would visit the Tirupati temple in the Carnatic to seek fertility of the god Venkateswara or Vishnu the Preserver, one of the gods of the Hindu Trinity. The priests would then visit the women in the temple by night and copulate with them. " The following morning ", says Henriques citing the Abbé Dubois, " these detestable hypocrites, pretending complete ignorance of what has passed, make due enquiries into all the details; and after having congratulated the women upon the reception they met with from the gods, receive the gifts . . . Fully convinced that the god has deigned to have intercourse with them, the poor creatures return home enchanted, flattering themselves that they will soon procure for their husbands the honour of paternity . . . "

Fertility through divine grace was also a belief of early Christianity. Mediæval churches were filled with offerings of phallic emblems. R. Payne Knight describes, in his **Remains of the Worship of Priapus,** how, in the last quarter of the eighteenth century, a relic of the big toe of St. Cosmo was exhibited at the feast of St. Cosmo and Damian at Isernia near Naples. Women pilgrims placed in the church offerings of wax phalli. Similarly, the ancient Roman ceremony of defloration on the bridal night by the stone phallus of the god Tutunus was an invocation to the god of fertility.

As among the ancient Spartans, the Tallensi tribe of North Ghana permit a sterile or impotent man the right to let his wife have coitus with a lover in the hope of her conceiving a child by him. The lover may be a stranger, or even a clan brother of the wife, or a friend of the husband. There is a formal introduction to the elders of the tribe and a sacrificial fowl is offered. The lover's intercourse with the woman continues during her pregnancy and right up to the birth of the child, which the lawful husband treats as his own. Thus social approval sanctifies what is nothing less than adultery. The actual father must never consider the child as his own, nor claim any kind of kinship with it.

Spring and harvest festivals exist the world over. In pagan times, even civilised races such as the Greeks and the Romans revelled in seasonal festivals which deteriorated into veritable sexual orgies that will be dealt with in a later chapter.

Among primitives, there is the genuine belief that the fecundity of nature can, by a kind of magic, be helped by imitative human copulation. Thus, according to H. Bancroft's **The Native Races of the Pacific States of North America,** the Pepele Indians remained continent for a few days before seed-sowing time. On the day of the planting, selected couples would copulate at the very moment that the seed was put into the ground. This is a ritualistic custom and not merely an excuse for adultery and fornication. Similarly, among the Peruvians, at harvest time a race was organised between men and women. The men would chase the women and perform coitus with those with whom they caught up.

To mark the coming of Spring or *Vasant,* India has her *holi* festival during which even in modern Hindu society in big cities, members of the community wear the oldest clothes and spray one another with rainbow-hued liquids. Among them, the horseplay is merely a relic of bygone practices. But among primitives, in certain parts of Northern India, it seems to be an orgiastic festival starting on the first full moon in Spring. Ancient Hindus were certainly far from hypocritical about their sexual practices, as is evidenced by erotic temple sculpture, their ancient sex treatises, and the erotic nature of their idols.

CHAPTER 10

PROSTITUTION THROUGH THE AGES

Organised Societies breed Prostitution—Temple Prostitution—Obligatory Prostitution in ancient Babylon—A Priest takes the god Marduk's Place in ' Sacred ' Copulation—Sacrifice of Woman's Hair rather than her Chastity—Islam and Christianity halt Temple Prostitution—Practice of Temple Prostitution in Classical Greece and India—The Temple Dancers of South India—Dowry from Earnings of Prostitution—' Hieroduli ' or Temple Prostitutes in Roman Colony—Greek ' Hetæræ '—Altars and Temples in Honour of ' Hetæræ '—Aphrodite Porne: Goddess of Prostitutes—Renowned ' Hetæræ : Phryne, Thaïs, Aspasia—Roman Prostitution—' Meretrices ' and ' Lupanaria '—' Ambulatrices ' or Street-walkers— Christian Era riddled with Prostitutes—Empress Theodora banishes Harlots—Church sponsors Brothels after the Crusades—' Bagnios ' and Houses of Women : Mixed Bathing—The Renaissance revives Joy of Living—Death of Mediæval Guilt-Culture—Traffic in Human Flesh and its Progress.

PROSTITUTION is as old as the history of mankind. There has been no epoch in recorded history when it has been unmentioned. However, in primitive societies that encourage pre-marital experience, the need for it is more or less superfluous. Many tribal communities, such as the Polynesians, remained uncontaminated by the commercial factor in sexual relations till contact with ' civilised ' men who came to their shores infected them. Polygamy, by catering to the human being's polyerotic urge, diminishes the ranks of prostitutes, but does not do away with them, as not all polygamous communities encourage pre-marital promiscuity.

In The Symphony of Sex by ' Sardi ', it is declared : " Organised societies, with their restrictions on promiscuity and adultery, and more particularly those with monogamous standards, make sexuality a highly complicated problem and thus become the breeding-grounds of prostitution. Hence, to preserve, at one end, codes of morality involving marriage and family life, at the other end is bred immorality. Prostitution serves a definite need where ' free love ' is hard to procure and where hypocritical standards govern men's lives . . . " Even

St. Augustine was forced to admit: " Banish prostitutes from society
and you reduce society to chaos through unsatisfied lust."

Temple Prostitution

' Sacred ' prostitution is the outcome of treating sex as a holy
mystery with a divine significance. In ancient times, coitus was considered to be imbued with magical properties. Hence the worship of
the phallus among such civilisations of old as those of Rome, Greece,
and Arya-varta, the old India, where the *yoni* or vagina was also
venerated to a limited extent. As we know, the phallus served as a
talisman among both the early Greeks and the Romans. It is, therefore, not to be wondered at that among the ancients dedication of
virginity, or of virility, as in the case of eunuch priests, was considered
a sacred act.

Prior to Christianity, God was not a humanised figure but rather
a being of quasi-human origin, with, of course, power over the
generative force. Hence the primitive belief that a spirit entered the
woman's body through an orifice to facilitate conception. In animistic
religions which believed that spirits inhabited trees or streams, a
woman would enter a river or stand under a tree, and invoke the god
of the tree or the river to fertilise her. Thus every conception was
regarded as virginal, and human birth as a divine act, and these ideas
persist even in sophisticated societies though the role of the human
father has long since been established.

In this connection, G. Rattray Taylor makes a most illuminating
statement in his **Sex in History**: " While this idea obtains, *all* births
are virgin births, in the sense that no man, but a god, is responsible
for them. In a later phase, folk-memories of this persist, and culture-
heroes often claim to be descended from the union of a woman and
a god, usually the moon. Genghis Khan made this claim; and Isiah
was made by his translators to assert that the Messiah who was to save
Israel would be born in a similar manner. Later, Christ was credited
with virginal birth not because it was thought miraculous—it was not
—but because it was the standard way of claiming importance."

Taylor goes on to explain that in classical times, the term ' virgin '
did not have its present connotation. A *virgo*, among the Romans,
was any unmarried woman, irrespective of whether she had had carnal
knowledge or not. If she had not known any man carnally, she was
differentiated from other virgins by being called *virgo intacta, i.e., a*
spinster whose hymen was still intact. " It was, one may say, a
psychological virginity which was meant ", says Taylor. " It was the
married woman who had sold her independence, who had lost her
virginity. Moreover, to sleep with a god was held actually to *restore*
virginity, as Philo and Plutarch record (Cf. Donne's ' Nor even chaste.

except thou ravish me '. This idea was also implicit in the conception of the brides of Christ.) "

In Chapter 1, it was explained how, through belief in the mystical or divine nature of woman's fecundity, started the cults of fertility or mother-goddesses such as the Cretan Rhea, the Phœnician Astarte, the Phrygian Cybele, the Persian Anaïtis, the Cappadocian Ma, the Egyptian Isis, and the Babylonian Ishtar. Apart from her mother aspect, Ishtar also had another facet: that of the harlot. It was primarily the matriarchal societies of Southern Europe, and of Eastern Mediterannean countries such as Asia Minor and Egypt, that gave rise to the worship of the mother-goddess and temple prostitution.

Three millenniums before Christ, temple prostitution was firmly rooted among the Oriental empires, the most advanced and civilised races of the time. Moreover, both male and female prostitution existed side by side, and temples derived a large amount of revenue from the trade. Semitic people in particular practised such temple prostitution, but it was not confined to them, for among the earliest practitioners were the Sumerians who worshipped Ishtar, and had three categories of harlots: the *kizrate,* the *senhate,* and the *harimâte.* However, then as now, prostitutes were despised and reviled, and young men were advised not to marry them. While the priestesses were held in high esteem, the prostitutes were treated as outcasts and not even permitted to rear their own children, these being brought up by adoptive or foster parents, the penalty for prying into their paternity being death.

This contemptuous attitude towards harlots is somewhat difficult to reconcile with the practice of ' obligatory prostitution ', as recorded by the historian Herodotus, that obtained in Babylon in the mid-fifth century A.D., after the Persian conquest: In the Babylonian temple of Mylitta, the Assyrian Venus, every female born in Babylonia had to give herself to a stranger at least once in her lifetime. Women of breeding would arrive in carriages with an entourage. Every woman had to sit within the precincts of the temple or in the sacred enclosure wearing wreaths made of strings. Passages were marked out with strings, and along these walked the men to select their partners. A woman, once seated, could not leave the temple without having sexual relations with a stranger. Once selected, the stranger would throw into her lap a silver coin with the words: " Mylitta prosper thee." The pair would then repair beyond the holy precincts.

No woman could reject any man who threw her a silver coin of any size, for the coin, once thrown, was sacred. This form of temporary prostitution was supposed to appease Mylitta, and once a woman had given herself, she could return again to the bosom of her family. According to Herodotus, " Such of the women who are ugly have to stay a long time before they can fulfil the law. Some have waited three or four years in the precinct . . . "

Yet another form of temple prostitution in old Babylon was described by Herodotus. In the *Etemenanki* or Tower of Babylon, was a shrine furnished with a vast bed near which stood a table made of gold. Every night a woman, but not the same one, would sleep in the room, presumably as the bride of the god Marduk whose place was, one gathers, taken by the high priest or some exalted personage after the pattern of the Indian custom described in the previous chapter.

Documents from the reign of the Chaldean king, Nebuchadnezzar II, who lived many centuries before Herodotus, testify to the fact that prostitution was a flourishing trade in Mesopotamia. The wealthy citizens of Babylon were wont to send their female slaves to brothels from which they, the masters, derived enormous profits. Homosexual prostitutes also plied their trade. Even the temple of Ishtar had a special section devoted to male prostitution, under sacred supervision, the head of it being the *ukkurum*, a priest high up in the temple hierarchy.

Temple prostitution never quite disappeared among the Hebrews. There were both male and female prostitutes euphemistically called 'saints': *gedisim* and *gedesot*. However, there was not much trade for them in the temples, and they had to resort to the villages where they were treated with contempt, particularly the male prostitutes who were called 'curs' or dogs.

In later times, right up to the days of the Ottoman Empire, harems came to be in vogue, especially in the palaces. Babylon has been described in the Old Testament as a cesspool of vice, but one must bear in mind that these accounts come from politically inimical sources. Babylon was, in actuality, an extremely well-organised state, and the Laws of Hammurabi laid down a family system that is an example even to the modern world, both East and West. " The system was at pains to strengthen the individual family," says Lewinsohn, " to protect the interests of the issue, to strike a balance in sex-life between liberty and obligation; and it accorded to women rights for which they are still fighting today in many countries. In brief, in spite of certain aberrations, Babylon did good service in this field, as in many others, and moralists have reason to pay homage to this maligned city."

The obligatory prostitution of Babylon was also a practice that prevailed in Cyprus and Phœnicia. What may seem to us today barbaric practices were probably due to the sagacity of the ancients who realised the dangers of too much in-breeding, and therefore encouraged exogamous sexual relations outside the marriage tie with utter strangers. This was probably the origin of exogamy itself.

The statements of Herodotus regarding the Babylonian cult of Mylitta and of Lucian concerning the Phœnician service to Aphrodite that prevailed in Byblos, the modern Jebeil, are borne out by the Epistle of Jeremy in the Book of Baruch (6, 43) which declares: " The (Chaldean) women also with cords about them, sitting in the ways, burning bran for perfume: but if any of them drawn by some that passeth by, lie with him she reproacheth her fellow that she was not thought of as worthy as herself, nor her cord broken."

In Cyprus, in the cities of Aphrodite-Astarte at Paphos and Amathos, religious prostitution was common. Strabo also tells us of a similar custom among the Armenians who practised the cult of Anaïtis, in whose service young male and female slaves were made to prostitute themselves. What is more, even well-born maidens had to do likewise and the law ordained that they could not marry till they had thus served the goddess.

Hair growth and fecundity are often closely associated. Hence the sacrifice of a woman's hair often took the place of surrender of chastity to a temple god. Thus in Byblos in Syria, whose inhabitants believed that it was within their boundaries that Adonis was killed by a boar, according to Lucian's *De Syria dea,* women had to shave their heads when the death of Adonis was annually commemorated, the shaving being accompanied with lamentations and the beating of breasts. If they did not wish to lose their crowning glory, they had to prostitute themselves for a day in the market to unknown men, their earnings being offered to the temple of Aphrodite.

A similar custom existed in ancient Egypt which had a temple whose presiding deity was a nymph goddess who was a mermaid. Near the temple was a pool filled with sacred fish, and here the women had to offer their hair in lieu of their chastity. The maidens of Megara also had to sacrifice their hair at the tomb of Iphinœ, and every Argive woman had similarly to offer her hair to the goddess Athene before her marriage. In Delos, both young men and women had to make an offering of their hair in the sanctuary of Artemis.

This ' heathen ' practice of hair sacrifice was even absorbed by the Christians; hence nuns shave their heads on becoming the brides of Christ, and the pagan superstition is cleverly explained away with the lofty excuse that the nuns are thus surrendering their pride to the Virgin Mary as a thanksgiving for recovery from illness.

Christianity and Islam put an end to sacred prostitution such as flourished in the Eastern Mediterannean area. Yet right up to the last century, a survival of it remained in Tanta, which lay between Alexandria and Cairo. During the celebrations of the Feast of Ahmed al-Bedawi, hundreds of women, married and single, would collect in special tents where they gave themselves to strangers in fulfilment of a sacred vow.

The Old Testament furnishes evidence that sacred prostitution was practised by the ancient Israelites: " They sacrifice upon the tops of the mountains, and burn incense upon the hills, under oaks and poplars and elms . . . therefore your daughters shall commit whoredom, and your spouses shall commit adultery . . . and they sacrifice with harlots . . . though thou, Israel, play the harlot, yet let not Judah offend . . . " (Hosea, 4: 13-15).

Temple Prostitution in Classical
Greece and India

The Cult of Aphrodite popularised temple prostitution in
Classical Greece, particularly in that hotbed of vice: Corinth. Here
the religious ceremony of *pannychis* (a term later applied to harlots
themselves) was celebrated with lecherous abandon by the Corinthian
prostitutes. As we know, a thousand hetæræ were housed in
the temple of Aphrodite, over ten thousand in the time of Augustus
according to Strabo. Singularly enough, these ' priestesses ' of Aphrodite were held in some esteem and even Pindar wrote his Olympian
Ode in praise of them, as well as a hymn which they sang and danced
to.

Demosthenes's nephew, the historian Demorches, records that in
Athens the temples of Aphrodite were dedicated to Lamia and Lenæa,
two hetæræ. In Abydos, a temple was dedicated to Aphrodite
because a hetæra had caused the conquerors' guards to be drunk " with
love and wine ", and had then stolen the keys to the citadel and passed
them on to the authorities who forthwith attacked the guards and won
liberty for the besieged city.

In Dravidian India, temple prostitution was encouraged in the
person of the *devadasi* (literally ' servant of god ') who, through song
and dance, took part in temple ritual and public ceremonies of a quasi-
religious nature. According to the traveller, the Abbé Dubois, the
moment their religious duty had been performed, the *devadasis* would
" . . . open their cells of infamy, and frequently convert the temple
into a stew." This is most probably an exaggeration. These temple
dancers are still to be found in the temples of South India, but while
a *devadasi* often lives in concubinage with a man, or several men in
turns, she is no common prostitute.

These female ' servants of God ' are skilled in the highly evolved
dance technique of Bharata Natyam, a ' prayer through dance ' performed in the South Indian temples of Shiva. In **Indian Dancing,**
Serozh Dadachanji and Ram Gopal assert in relation to this particular
form and its practitioners:

" It is a highly specialised science with a traditional background
and rigid codes and conventions. For many centuries it has been
performed only by certain peasant families in the district of Tanjore,
these inheritors of the craft being known as *nattuvans*. Until recently,
the chief exponents of Bharata Natyam were *devadasis*, or temple
girls, specifically dedicated to the task of dancing for the gods. The
temple dancer, acquiring her professional knowledge from her
nattuvan, often forms with him a life-long alliance seldom broken by
either party. The institution of the *devadasi* and her offering of
prayer through the dance medium has its roots in religion, as it is
clear from the nature of the vocation . . . "

In the Deccan, or Maharashtra, on the Mid-Western coast of India, the god Khandoba has both male and female devotees, the former being called *vaghya*, the latter *murli*. At the *dussehra* festival when all animals and moving vehicles are decorated with flowers and garlands especially made of the *gulgota* or marigolds, Khandoba is worshipped in public processions in company with the god Ekvira. The male prostitution of Syrian temples has its equivalent in this part of India. Castrated or neutral eunuchs, generally in female attire, perform the rites of the goddesses Huligammer and Chaturshringe, the temple of the latter being perched atop a hill at Poona where lived the mighty Maharatha warrior, Shivaji, who gallantly fought the Mogul invaders when they ruled over Northern India. The eunuch priests collect in large numbers at the time of the *dussehra* celebrations and indulge in gaiety and religious ritual at one and the same time.

It is clear from their similar practices that in Dravidian India, before the advent of the Aryan invaders from whom are descended the modern Hindus (the term ' Hindu ' is a corruption of the name of the river Indus which is also the origin of the present name of ancient Arya-varta: India, though the river is now no longer part of the new India but, being in Sind, part of Pakistan), there was a traffic of ideas and customs with the countries of Syria and Asia Minor. It is pertinent that these ancient cultures were matrilineal, and in parts of South India, where live many of the descendants of the aboriginal Dravidians, both temple prostitution and matrilineal customs still prevail.

When the land of the Dravidians was taken over by the Aryans and became Arya-varta, prostitution also found favour among these new invaders. Hans Licht, in his **Sexual Life in Ancient Greece**, declares: " Anyone who . . . does not regard Greco-Oriental temple prostitution with sympathy, should remind himself that also among the ancient Indians, who must be reckoned next to the Greeks, or perhaps even their equal, as the most cultivated people in the world, quite similar institutions have arisen . . . "

Licht also quotes from the novel of a Dane, Karl Gjellerup, titled *Der Pilger Kamanita*: " ' My native place Ujjeni is famous throughout India for its gaiety and noisy joy in life . . . in particular the hetaeræ of Ujjeni enjoy an extraordinary reputation. From the famous hetaeræ, who live in palaces, found temples for the gods . . . and in whose reception-halls one finds poets and artists, actors, distinguished foreigners, and indeed, often princes, down to common harlots, all exhibit healthy, strong-limbed beauty and indescribable grace. At the great festivities, shows and pageants, they form the chief ornaments of the streets . . . In cochineal-red dresses, with fragrant garlands in their hands, redolent of perfumes and sparkling with diamonds, you see them, then, O brother, sitting on the splendid seats allotted them, or passing along the streets with amorous looks, exciting gestures, and laughing words of banter, everywhere fanning to a bright flame the sensual glow of those who desire enjoyment . . . Honoured

by the king, adored by the people, sung of by the poets, they are
called the varied crown of flowers of Ujjeni . . . "

Dowry from Earnings
of Prostitution

In the Greco-Oriental world, Aphrodite, the goddess of love in
her various guises of Astarte, Cybele, Anaïtis, Isis, Ma, or Ishtar, did
not merely preside over lovers but even commanded them to indulge
in fleshly joys. Thus earning a dowry by means of prostitution became
not merely a practical measure but also a sacred duty. Among the
Lydians, it was a common custom for every unmarried woman to
collect a dowry in this manner.

In the temple of Venus Erycina on Mount Eryx in Sicily, a Roman
colony, the service of *hieroduli* or temple girls who were prostitutes,
prevailed right up to the beginning of the first millennium A.D. The
Romans gave the temples and the *hieroduli* their protection, contributing large amounts to their treasuries, and garrisoning a couple of
hundred soldiers as potential customers.

Among tribes and races which have the custom of defloration by
someone other than the bridegroom, the dowry is often earned by
prostitution so that defloration is effected by a stranger. The aborigines of Nicaragua and Guatemala, as well as the Natchez of Louisiana
in the United States, follow this practice. In olden times, Cyprians
and Phœnicians observed the custom as much as the Lydians.

Greek Hetæræ

Aphrodite was a goddess with many facets. As Aphrodite Hetæra,
she was the patron goddess of harlots; as Aphrodite Peribaso, she
was the goddess or love who walked the streets; as Aphrodite
Trymalitis, she was the goddess who 'bored through', and finally as
Aphrodte Porne she was the Prostitute goddess. She thus gave divine
sanction to love among the Greeks, and for that reason the Greek
prostitutes were not despised. They were called hetæræ which meant
'friends' or 'life-partners', a euphemism not entirely hypocritical as
was proved by the good treatment accorded them.

Ruder names existed, too, and it is interesting to make a brief
survey of these: 'she-wolf' obviously referred to the harlot's covet-
ousness; 'the shut-in' to her confinement in a brothel; 'dice' to the
fact that men used them as if they were dice thrown in a game or a
gamble; 'foals of Aphrodite' for obvious reasons, and 'bedroom
articles' for use in bed.

BROTHELS AND STREET-WALKERS: The women in the brothels
were not called hetæræ but by Greek equivalents of the term 'whore'.
These belonged to the lowest order of prostitutes. Admission to the

brothels was about one *obol* or three halfpence. In addition, a 'gift' had to be made to the woman selected according to the demands made on her. The price could range from *drachmæ*, one of these being equal to nine pence, to *staters*, one being equal to a pound. A special official collected the prostitution tax from every brothel. This was paid from the earnings of the women. Even the prices were officially fixed by the *ogoranomi* or price-fixing officials who were under the supervision of the *astynomoi* or city officials who controlled public decency.

Street-walkers stood midway between the women in the brothels and the hetæræ. They infested harbours and lively streets leading to them. As in modern times, their customers would accompany them to their lodgings, or rooms rented especially for their 'business', or public baths, taverns, and inns. Often dark corners and doorways, and even the shades of monuments, were used for 'open-air' prostitution.

HETÆRÆ: The Greeks bestowed on their hetæræ, as distinct from the street-walkers and the inmates of brothels, an enviable social status. Houses were often named after them, and even their statues sometimes stood side by side in the temples with those of respected generals and politicians. Licht quotes Helbig as saying: "'Many of them are distinguished by refined education and a wit quick at repartee; they know how to fascinate the most distinguished personalities of their time—generals, statesmen, men of letters and artists, and how to keep their affection; they illustrate in the manner indicated a mixed existence of fine intellectual and sensual pleasures, to which the majority of the Greeks at that time paid homage. In the life of almost every more important personality, prominent in the history of Hellenism, the influence of well-known hetæræ can be found . . . '"

Even altars and temples were erected in honour of those hetæræ who had had affairs with prominent men. The maritime city of Corinth swarmed with Aphrodite Porne's disciples. Pindar, as we know, composed both an ode and a hymn in honour of 'the priestesses of venal love' when the rich Xenophon of Corinth won a double victory at the Olympic Games of 464 B.C. Such notable writers as Lucian and Machon extolled the hetæræ in Greek literature. Many excerpts from the latter have been preserved by Athenæus, as well as details from other works dealing with the lives of these devotees of pleasure and love. On the stage, the female parts were played by men, yet many a hetæra was the central character of the plays, mostly comedies.

Of all the hetæræ thus immortalised, the most ruthless and power-greedy was Thaïs, the central character of a play by Menander. She is said to have been the mistress of the bisexual Alexander the Great. When in 331 B.C., this highly strung youth defeated the Persians and their king Darius took flight, he entered the Persian capital of Persepolis where he held a sumptuous banquet to which thronged

numberless hetæræ, chief among them being Thais. When a steady
flow of wine had been imbibed and spirits ran high, Thaïs reminded
Alexander of the destruction by the Persian king, Xerxes, of part of
the Athenian Acropolis, and instigated him to crown his victory with
the sweet taste of revenge by burning the royal palace of the once
mighty Persian kings. To the tune of flutes, pipes, and drunken songs,
Alexander and his drunken soldiers marched out, led by Thaïs, to
the palace of the kings of the Achæmenide Dynasty.

Like a barbarian intoxicated with wine and victory, Alexander
hurled a torch at the magnificent palace of Persepolis with its winged
bulls with human faces supporting columns that seemed to balance the
fairy palace in the air. Thais, proud, no doubt, of having swayed the
will of the young conqueror, threw the second brand, the bibulous
young men following suit, so that in a few hours the pyre had consumed the dwelling place of the once mighty rulers of a great empire.
Thaïs, after the death of Alexander, went on to mount a throne herself
as the consort of Ptolemy I, king of Egypt.

Phryne of Thespiæ was yet another hetæra whose fame has rung
down the corridors of time. We know how, when tried on a serious
charge, she escaped the death penalty due to the presence of mind of
the orator Hypercides who was defending her. Remembering perhaps
how Helen of old had won her husband Menelaus's forgiveness, Hypercides suddenly exposed the lovely Phryne's breasts before the court,
and thus won her acquittal.

Phryne normally concealed her private parts with a tight *chiton*,
but at the festival of Poseidon she threw off all her draperies, let down
her hair, and went into the sea naked before the gaze of all, inspiring
the painter Apelles to do his famous ' Aphrodite rising from the Sea ',
while Praxiteles, the sculptor, took her for his model when he fashioned
his Aphrodite of Cnidus.

Praxiteles would not tell Phryne which of his works were his prime
favourites. So she invented a ruse and sent him a servant, one day,
to say that his studio had caught fire. Praxiteles at one expressed
anxiety at losing his ' Satyr ' and his ' Eros '. Subsequently, he made
a gift of ' Eros ' to Phryne, which she, in turn, dedicated to the temple
of the god of love in her home town of Thespiæ, whose inhabitants
commissioned Praxiteles to do a statue of Phryne which, as noted
before, stood at Delphi between the statues of King Archidamus and
Philippus.

Phryne's wit was as renowned as her beauty. When she lost
a wager because she could not arouse the erotic ardour of the philosopher Xenocrates to the extent of making him lose his self control, she
refused to pay up, declaring that she had taken the wager to move a
man of flesh and blood, not an insensate statue. These stories concerning Phryne reveal how privileged a position the Greek hetæra held
in the community.

Another hetæra who has left her mark on time, was Aspasia, to marry whom Pericles, the statesman, divorced his wife. Plato and Socrates were among Aspasia's guests and her influence over Pericles was so strong that Plutarch attributes to her the war between Athens and Samos as it involved her native town of Miletus. So famed were her qualities of mind, body, and heart, that the younger Cyrus of Persia named Milto, his mistress, after Aspasia. When he marched against his brother, Ataxerxes, she went on the campaign as part of his entourage, and when he was killed in 401 B.C., she fell captive into the hands of his brother but succeeded in charming him, too, and not only him, but his son Darius as well. This spelt the end of her social and political caperings, for Ataxerxes spared her only on condition that she became a priestess of Anaïtis.

Thus it will be seen that the hetæræ were not only the playthings of philosophers, artists, writers, and kings, but also wielded great influence over them, their works, and their lives. As their name suggested, they were the ' companions ' of men along with the boys and youths for whom the Greeks had an equal love. The Greek wife, on the other hand, was relegated to the home and child-bearing, and her social position was not as happy as that of the hetæra. However, though revered and pampered, these love-priestesses were also the butt of many jokes and epigrams. Thus Aristophanes makes a character declare in ' Plutus ': " And they say of the hetæræ of Corinth that if a poor man longs for their love they pay no attention to him, but that if he is rich they turn their buttocks towards him." Again when sailors were robbed by some hetæræ, an epigram was invented to the effect that these corsairs of Aphrodite and their ships were to be avoided, " for they are more dangerous than the sirens."

Advice given by an old procuress to hetæræ in a poem of Propertius is unfolded by Licht in an amusing vein: " Above all, says the procuress, you must not pay any heed to the laws of modesty. You must act as if you still had other lovers: that keeps a man in suspense and goads on his jealousy . . . take care always to show him traces of bites on your neck and breast, which will cause him to believe that they have been made by another lover . . . Also, do not reject people of the lower classes, such as soldiers or sailors; even though the hand is rough, remember that it brings money to you. And as to slaves, if only they come with money in their pockets, you ought not to scorn them . . . What do you get from a poet, who praises you heavens-high with his verses, but cannot make you any presents? As long as your blood is lively and your face free from wrinkles, make use of the opportunity and of that youth of yours, which vanishes so quickly."

Among those who consorted with hetæræ were many famous men in all walks of life. Aristotle, the philosopher, had a son by a hetæra called Herpyllis, and Plato had an affair with Archeanassa. Apart from Aspasia, Pericles took as mistress a woman called Elpinike, the

sister of one Cimon, with whom she had committed incest, and who
was not permitted to return from exile unless he consented to Elpinike's liaison with Pericles. Harpalus, appointed governor of Babylon
by Alexander the Great, fell in love with a hetæra called Pythonike
who sponged mercilessly on his ill-gotten gains. Yet he gave her a
wonderful burial accompanied by choral songs. He later sought the
hetæra Glycera to take the place of the dead woman. Sappho, the
Lesbian, had a brother, Charaxus of Mitilene, who was enamoured of
a hetæra known as Doricha and called ' Rhodopis ' by Herodotus.

Roman Prostitution

Among the early Romans, prostitution was a down-to-earth
business. If a man failed to find sexual satisfaction with his wife, he
resorted to a prostitute. Prostitution was thus looked upon as a
necessity which safeguarded the sanctity of married life by affording
a man sexual outlet without his lusting after other men's wives or
daughters. The Romans did not cloak prostitution with a holy mantle
as did the Greeks, though, of course, many such women did find favour
in the eyes of rulers and patricians who helped to elevate them socially.

The euphemism of the Greeks who preferred to refer to the higher
class prostitute as a companion, was eschewed by the forthright
Romans who called a whore a *meretrix* or one who earned her living
through her profession. Though many nicknames were applied to
these *meretrices*, pet names were hardly ever used, the best known
among the few that did exist being Catallus's Ipsitilla or ' little lady '.
Thus the brothel—one of which at least was to be found in every
provincial city—was known as a *lupanar* or the den of the she-wolf,
or a *fornica*. But to visit the *lupanaria* or brothels, and to associate
with a whore, was not considered improper. Kiefer's quotation, in his
Sexual Life in Ancient Rome, of a passage from Cicero's speech
for Cælius, testifies to this:

" ' If there is anyone who thinks young men should be forbidden
to make love, even to prostitutes, he is certainly a man of stern
righteousness . . . but he is out of touch not only with the free life
of today, but even with the code and concessions which our fathers
accepted. For when was that not customary ? When was it blamed ?
When was it not allowed ? When was it not lawful to do what is
a lawful privilege ? ' "

Even Cato, a stern moralist, did not frown on young men
visiting *lupanaria,* for Horace is quoted by Kiefer as reporting:
" ' Once, when a noble left a brothel, Blessed be thou, quoth the wisdom
of Cato: for when their veins are swelling with gross lust, young men
should drop in there, rather than grind some husband's private mill.' "

One must differentiate between the *meretrix* and the free-loving
woman of the patrician class, or the slave or freewoman who carried
on a liaison outside of marriage. Such affairs were not considered

degraded, and the well-born women who openly indulged in free love were often well educated and refined. They stood between the mater-familas or *matrons* and the *meretrix*, in the same way as did the *demi-mondaine* of the later society of Alexander Dumas *fils'* time.

While the *meretrix* was purely mercenary, these free-loving women accepted no money, at least not in a business way, from their lovers. Because of this, they were not included in the official register of pros-titutes kept by the ædiles. In the reign of Tiberius, in the first century A.D., a decree had been passed disallowing a woman whose husband, father, or grandsire, had been a Roman knight, from selling her body for lewd purposes. If such women were prosecuted for prostitution, they could be punished with fines or with banishment.

In Rome, the most notorious brothel area was the Suburra quarter in the second district, between the Cælian and Esquiline Hills. There were brothels also in the vicinity of the Circus Maximus, outside the city walls, and in the Vicus Patricius. The owner of a brothel was known as a *leno* if he were a male, or a *lena* were she a female. Most of the prostitutes were slave girls. Men returning from the bloody games at the Circus Maximus obviously fell easy prey to the harlots and bawds waiting for them.

The street-walkers were called by various names which Kiefer gives us: *ambulatrices* or 'strollers', *notiliæ* or 'night moths', *bustuariæ* who served the double purpose of professional mourners and soothers inside the cemeteries, and, finally, the *diobolariæ* or the twopenny harlots, the lowest grade of all. It is not to be wondered at that these women found patrons among the young men, for the female population was seventeen per cent. less than the male, and hence even if all the young men wished to marry, they could not.

Though association with a prostitute was not frowned upon, and no young man suffered disrepute because of it, a freeborn man could not marry a *lena* or procuress, nor a *lenone lenaue manumissa* or the freed slave of a bawd. Yet, curiously, a *leno* or procurer could attain citizenship of Rome. This preferment conferred on the male shows that Roman laws were patriarchal. In the reign of Caligula, a tax was introduced on *meretrices*. Roman prostitutes were not allowed to dress as other women; they were compelled to wear the male toga over their garments to sort them out from their more respectable sisters and the *matronæ* or matrons.

The ancient pleasures of Pompeii are still evidenced by the remains of the House of the Vetti, a luxury brothel. Frescoes of lovers are to be found in the main rooms, particularly the reception room. The chambers or *cellæ* where the harlots would entertain their customers, were small and bare, with a small stone bed in each. The name of the girl, and perhaps her price, would be affixed outside her cell. The price had always to be paid in advance. Often even the cells had erotic murals on the walls both as appetisers and, no doubt, for educational purposes, as they depicted various coital postures.

Harlots were often called *nonariæ* because *nonaria* meant the 'ninth hour', *i.e.*, four o'clock in the afternoon, which was the opening time for *fornices*. The girls either stood or sat outside, for which reason they were called *prostibulæ*. When engaged with a customer, the sign *occupata* would be hung outside a girl's cell. Messalina, first wife of Claudius who succeeded his nephew Caligula as emperor, was, as mentioned in a previous chapter, wont to visit a Roman brothel and there play the harlot.

The Roman love of baths is well known. Many of these were marble or alabaster-walled, and contained steamrooms as well as other rooms into the basins of which water from the Apennine mountains flowed. These baths often served as clandestine meeting-places for lovers. Prostitutes, too, are said to have had their own baths where they entertained customers; but, of course, no respectable women visited such baths. To facilitate trade, mixed bathing was introduced, the men bathing in the nude, but the women wearing brief costumes. Seneca, stern moralist that he was inclined to be, berated the licentious pleasures of Baiæ, a watering place which boasted of hot springs and drunken revelries on the beach and in the boats.

Christian Era riddled with Prostitutes

The splendidly Pagan attitude of the Greeks, with its extreme hedonism and love and worship of the body, was untainted by feelings of guilt. The Greeks were æsthetes *par excellence*. Not so the Romans who were grosser in their tastes as their debaucheries exemplify. Cruelty and sadism were prominent features of their sex lives, and these led to subconscious feelings of guilt.

With the dawn of Christianity, the guilt complex which, in the Romans of the pre-Christian era, had been but a glimmering, became, at first, more intensified, and, later, dominant. However, no amount of preaching and restrictive measures could purge the semi-barbaric Europeans of their Pagan practices. As we have noted in previous chapters, even the lay clergy and high dignitaries of the Church attempted to stem the tide of moral change and fought the Roman Church tooth and nail in the attempt to preserve the remarkable sexual freedom they had thus far enjoyed.

The Church's efforts to assert its moral restrictions took a few hundred years before its patrist guilt-culture was finally established, sounding the slow death-knell of the hitherto free and easy matrist societies. In the process, however, Europe passed through a long phase of psychopathic neuroses, and in mediæval times, aptly called 'the Dark Ages', there were outbursts of sado-masochistic practices such as flagellomania, hysteria, witchcraft, and nocturnal visitations and 'possessions' in the form of *incubi* and *succubi*, and 'choreomania' which will all be elaborated upon presently. Sexual repressions which the Church attempted to impose were undoubtedly the main factor in this sorry state of affairs.

In the present chapter, we are mainly concerned with prostitution and must, therefore, proceed to deal with its prevalence in the Middle Ages. The medical profession of the time wisely differed from the Church and prescribed rather than prohibited sexual indulgence. Even Thomas Aquinas spoke of it as a necessary moral purge: " A cesspool is necessary to a palace if the whole palace is not to smell ", a pronouncement that was echoed by Lecky, six hundred years later. Whoredom was not despised by the Church dignitaries, and in England the phrase ' Winchester Geese ' for prostitutes came into existence because the Bishop of Winchester treated it as a lucrative business. The Bishop of Sens drove the monks out of the Abbey of St. Peter, and converted it into a harem of concubines in the tenth century. Far into the Renaissance, bishops and even popes consorted with strumpets, most prominent among these being Popes Alexander VI and John XII, the latter converting St. John Lateran into a brothel.

In the early Middle Ages, prostitution had many enemies, and, from time to time, efforts were made to penalise it severely. In the sixth century in Eastern Europe, the Byzantine Emperor Justinian's consort, the Empress Theodora, whose own way to the throne had been paved with vice, had the brothels of Constantinople emptied of as many as five hundred prostitutes whom she had exiled to an ascetic existence on the remote shore of the Bosphoros which many of them never reached, as, in sheer desperation at the fate that awaited them, they drowned themselves during the voyage. Others took their lives later.

In Western Europe, a stern enemy of harlotry was Charlemagne who was determined to uproot prostitution which his laws considered as one of the three main sexual offences. His attempts were not conspicuously successful, so that one of his successors had to introduce the penalty of throwing a whore into cold water and presumably letting her drown. The law decreed that passers-by were not to help her but to mock and curse her. The punishments continued in various forms without wiping out the eternal strumpet. Flogging, the pillory, the stocks, shaving of the head—she survived them all. If a prostitute were caught *in flagranti,* she faced the death penalty or torture, yet her partner went scot-free.

With the Crusades, prostitutes reaped a rich harvest. Men torn from their wives and sweethearts had to have alternative sexual indulgence. So harlots thronged the ports and even went aboard the ships to give the men their bit of sexual solace. A fair living was thus provided thousands of prostitutes. But the end of the Crusades brought them a fresh problem. They deserted the ports and fled back to the towns and cities where they prostituted themselves within or outside the city gates. Rather than encourage indiscriminate soliciting, the authorities placed them in public houses where they were supervised by the police.

The Church adopted a wise attitude to the problem: It sponsored the activities of these women. In the papal town of Avignon, was opened a brothel euphemistically called an *Abbaye* or abbey. Even royalty gave its patronage to the brothel, for Queen Joanna of Naples preferred an establishment in the city to indiscriminate harlotry. The inmates of the new brothel had to conduct themselves as good Christians. They had to attend service and observe the hours of prayers. They were to entertain Christian customers only, and were forbidden to accept Jewish or heathen searchers after carnal pleasures. This venture was eminently successful, so much so that a similar institution was established in the holy city of Rome by Pope Julius II.

The Church in other Italian towns did not openly encourage prostitution, but turned a blind eye to its existence. The premises on which the trade was carried on often belonged to dignitaries of the Church or Mothers Superior of convents. One learns from Lewinsohn that in the houses owned by the Archbishop of Mainz, there were " as many prostitutes . . . as books in his library."

In days when beliefs in the supernatural were rife and communion with Satan was not ruled out of the realm of possibility, a brothel-keeper was well protected from accusations of witchcraft if a clergyman happened to be his landlord. How could the spirits, leave alone Lucifer, haunt the property of a man of God ? Hence the Inquisition did not pry into the goings-on in brothels, so long as married women, runaway nuns, and diseased girls, did not find shelter in them. The lone prostitute, however, was often accused of being a witch.

As early as the twelfth century, the Church encouraged attempts to redeem the prostitute from her life of sin. Pope Innocent III asked well-placed citizens to grant such women a refuge by taking them on as domestics after they had purged themselves of their immorality and become truly repentant. In some places, Magdalene Houses—so called after Mary Magdalene the reformed prostitute of Christ's time—were established. In 1226, an Archbishop established a ' rescue home ' for prostitutes in France, known as the *Maison des Filles-Dieu* or House of God's Daughters.

At the start of the fourteenth century, at St. Jerome's in Vienna, a penitents' house, popularly called the Soul House, was started by some rich citizens. So many gifts were received by the institution, which also owned rich vineyards, that when the inmates got married, as they often did, there was enough money to give each one a marriage settlement. Unfortunately, in the last quarter of the fifteenth century, Frederick III recklessly granted the penitents a retail licence for selling the produce of their rich vineyards. Intoxication of one kind led to another and many of the inmates once again answered the call of the flesh. One of those who so succumbed was Maria Kleeberger, a Superior, who formed a liaison with a priest named Laubinger, and reverted, on the sly, to her old profession. The scandal blew the institution sky-high in the chaotic times of the Reformation. The penitents were driven out and Franciscan monks now occupied the cells bringing back to Vienna the Catholicism of the old days, which, however, did not prevent the brothels from carrying on their trade. In England, the first Magdalene houses appeared as late as the eighteenth century.

'Bagnios' and 'Houses of Women': Mixed Bathing

A favourite place for prostitution in the Middle Ages, was the *bagnio* or bath, imported into Europe by the Crusaders as they returned home bringing with them the secrets of the Oriental *hamams* or warm baths. Mixed bathing was the order of the day. In twelfth century France, practically every village had its bath, and in Paris many of the streets had theirs. In Germany, the keeper of the bath would stroll through the streets in the morning blowing a horn to announce that the baths were ready. The lower order of society and even the middle classes, are described as having wended their way through the streets to the *bagnios*, either semi-clad, or even naked, sometimes whole families together. However, this does not seem to tally with the strictures on nudity enforced at the time. and one cannot but take these reports with a large pinch of salt.

These baths soon became hothouses of sexual immorality and prostitutes found this to to their advantage. We are told by Rattray Taylor, in **Sex in History,** that many bath-houses had but one dressing room where both the sexes undressed, and even " two-seater bath tubs were often used by persons of different sexes at the same time." It is no wonder that in France and Germany, the *bagnios* deteriorated into houses of illicit love.

Among the Germans and German-speaking Europeans, the bath was called *frauenhäuser* or a woman-house. These disguised brothels were often situated near churches. The tubs were shared by several persons of both sexes. Customers could withdraw to a dry room if they wished. Fifteenth century Paris boasted of no less than thirty such establishments.

In the streets, the main problem was to distinguish the harlot from the average respectable woman so as to leave the latter unmolested by obscene proposals from the 'wolves'. Just as the Romans of old had made the whore wear a short *tunica* or a male toga, as opposed to the longer gowns of the matron, the Parisian prostitute of the fifteenth century was not allowed to adorn her clothes with furs which were fashionable in high society, or to wear a full skirt or a golden girdle.

Renaissance revives
Joy of Living

The guilt-culture which the Church imposed on mediæval Europe was always at war with the paganism of old, and it is little wonder that the phallic and fertility cults of the pagans infiltrated Christianity, the former in the shape of St. Foutin—a parody of the name of Pothin, Bishop of Lyons—and the latter in the person of the Virgin Mary. Were these restrictions healthy ? The verdict must go against the Church, for the repressions it bred led to neuroses and curtailment of personal freedom by a few fanatical despots. The swing of the pendulum came with a vengeance with the budding of the Renaissance when men threw aside the shackles of intolerance and patristic dominance. There was a resurgence of matrism, and the Renaissance counterpart of the Greek hetæra, to whom the French gave the name of *courtesane*, a lady to whom men paid court, emerged.

The patrist conventions that regarded woman as a sinful vessel, nudity as shameful, and sex as a guilt-ridden urge to be avoided or repressed, went by the board with the dawn of the Renaissance that ushered in a very permissive period of matrism. Since sex lost its guilt, the energy that had gone into repressing it, flowed into creative channels, for, while intellectual labour may thrive on continence, art needs sexual freedom. Some of the finest nudes, and voluptuous paintings, as well as nude sculpture, were produced during this efflorescence.

The authoritarian Christian Church found its voice unheeded. Even some of the Popes of this era were atheists, oustanding among them being Leo X. But he, and such popes as Nicholas V and Julius II, were essentially humanists typical of the matrist trend of the times. They were connoisseurs and patrons of art, pleasure-loving and kindly.

The emancipation of women had begun to appear in Italy with poets such as Petrarch and Dante, who, out of their respective reverence and love for Laura and Beatrice, glorified woman and placed her on a pedestal. Rattray Taylor points out that Dante's abstraction of Beatrice till she becomes merged with Divine Knowledge, was a typically matrist symbol opposed to the patrist representation of a male deity symbolising authority. It is therefore not surprising to discover from P. G. Molmenti's **Venice** that the courtesan· with her social grace and usually good breeding, was readily accepted in artistic and political circles. The list of such women was a long one and included Bianca Saraton, Julia d'Aragona, and Margherita Emiliani. A friend of the painter Tintoretto was Veronica Franco who was also honoured by the court paid her by Henry VIII of England and other prominent men.

Even the Madonna was brought into line with the prevailing view of feminine beauty. Artists such as Andrea del Sarto and Solario sometimes portrayed the Virgin with a breast bared to give suck to her child. Mythological goddesses, such as the Florentine Boticelli's ' Venus Anadyomene ', were protrayed in the nude with chaste gestures of the hands attempting to conceal their nudity, and wearing slightly guilty expressions A pupil of the famous Bellini, one Giorgio Barbarelli, a Venetian, painted a nude 'Sleeping Venus' in a rustic setting—one of the most beautiful Venuses in existence now in Dresden. The famous Titiano or Titian, turned out many a 'Venus in Repose' with the skin a beautiful golden brown. The male form, too, was proudly disrobed in painting and sculpture. Perhaps the greatest representations of male nudity were by Michelangelo whose splendid 'Boy David' in Florence testifies to his genius in this direction, no doubt impelled by his strongly homoerotic urge.

The erotic temple sculpture of old India, depicting coital positions with unashamed precision, might have had their counterparts in Rome, but for an unfortunate incident. The great Raphael had a favourite pupil named Giulio Romano who had assisted him in his work on the halls and loggias of the Vatican. When Raphael died in 1520, young Romano, then but twenty-five, was inundated with commissions from patrons who were mostly church dignitaries. He conceived the idea of depicting human copulation, without the use of mythological figures, in sixteen postures. Four years after Raphael's death, Romano completed his sketches and commissioned Raimondi, Rome's most talented engraver, to make copper figures of his sketches meant purely for private circulation. However, due to some mishap, some of them came up for sale in the market. Even Renaissance Rome, with its exuberant love of nudity, was shocked. Pope Clement VII, a broadminded man descended of the Medici family, was perturbed, particularly by the inscription: 'In how many different ways, attitudes and positions loose men lie with women'.

Clement VII was about to order the arrest and trial of the artists, but was dissuaded by Pietro Aretino, famed poet and diplomat, who was one of his advisers. However, it later transpired that Aretino himself had composed sonnets to accompany the pictures. The Pope thereupon ordered all the plates to be destroyed. Romano, meanwhile, had fled to Mantua with the Mantuan envoy to the papal court, and was given refuge by a relative of the Pope. Only the poor engraver, Raimondi, found himself in prison from which he was rescued by the entreaties of influential friends.

A copy of the engravings is said to be in the Biblioteca Corsiniana in Rome, shut away from public gaze. Only Aretino's sonnets survive which are crude and vulgar. He settled in Venice, the centre of pornographic literature in the sixteenth century, and thus found in this free city an outlet for the sensuality of his themes. This sixteenth century Ovid who wrote of adulterous women, sensual nuns, and courtesans, won, in his lifetime, the soubriquet il divino or 'the divine', and even wrote three volumes full of piety called *Humanita di Cristo*. He was forgiven by Pope Julius II and by some mischance missed becoming a cardinal. He was not lacking in hypocrisy and is even said to have written to Michelangelo criticising his nudes for the Cistine Chapel.

All through the Middle Ages, the human anatomy had not been carefully studied. Dissection of corpses was not permitted even in 1515 by Pope Leo X, another Medici, and even Leonardo da Vinci, whose anatomical illustrations are well known, was not allowed to carry out autopsies in hospitals. However, Venice was then a free state and fortunately the University of Padua was under its sovereignity. Its real founder was always considered the Belgian Andrea Vesalius, who, at the age of twenty-nine, produced an atlas of anatomy depicting every part of the human body. Thus Padua was the cradle of modern anatomy and surgery.

The Renaissance, which saw the flowering of man's artistic genius in Europe, was also the period which marked the appearance of a new scourge: Venereal disease. It appeared first in Naples, in December 1494, among soldiers of the French Army who were garrisoned there, and was, therefore, called the *morbus gallicus* or the ' Gallic sickness '. However, syphilis had been unknown in France till then, and doctors concluded that it was Christopher Columbus's men who had brought it to Europe from the West Indies. Columbus was already on his second voyage to the islands, about twenty-one months after returning from the voyage of discovery.

A few years later, Rodrigo Diaz de l'Isla, a Spanish physician, confirmed that the disease had afflicted First Mate Pinzon on the first return voyage from Haiti or Hispaniola as the Spanish then called it. The passing of the buck to Polynesians is stoutly refuted by Lewinsohn who claims: " . . . but there were also other indications suggesting that the sickness had existed in Europe before that and had been carried to America by Columbus's crew. The origin of syphilis is one of the unsolved riddles of sex history . . . Only so much is certain, that whether or not syphilis had existed previously in Europe, it appeared in the Mediterannean countries towards the end of the fifteenth century with the virulence characteristic of new plagues. Shortly after, it crossed the Alps. It made no distinction between friend and foe. The prostitutes and wenches in the seaport taverns on whom the French soldiers had bestowed it passed it on to the German mercenaries. At first a typical soldiers' disease, it soon infected the civilian population, and assumed such alarming forms that the authorities were impelled to issue warnings . . . "

The French resented the disease being named after them, and, in turn, called it ' the Neapolitan illness ', *viz, mal de Naples,* or merely *vérole,* meaning ' pox '. Jacques de Béthencourt, a French doctor, thought of the most sensible name of all: *morbus venereus,* ' the sickness of Venus ', goddess of Love. Thus we talk of venereal desease, and often use the term in the plural for we know that there are several such diseases which are the outcome of sexual intercourse, the best known being syphilis and gonorrhœa.

Traffic in Human Flesh

Glimpses of the traffic in flesh in a few countries of the world must end this chapter.

The French have always displayed a sensible attitude towards matters sexual. It is, therefore, not surprising that during the French Revolution venal love had its heyday. On the first anniversary of the Revolution, a tariff was published giving the names, addresses, and even the prices of the girls of the Palais Royal, the adjacent districts, and other environs. The fares varied. You could buy love and a bowl of punch for six *livres* at 'La Bacchante', or the 'Victorine', but the four young women in Madame Dupéron's charge would cost nothing under twenty-five *livres*.

While the French Police were indulgent, the new members of the Constituent Assembly introduced restrictions for prostitutes in July 1791. If a prostitute did not conduct herself suitably in public, she would be arrested. In 1793, the Jacobins showed even greater zeal. The favourite haunt of the ladies of the night, the Palais Royal, was cordoned off and the political records of the women were examined. This measure was the forerunner of a drastic purge during Robespierre's reign of terror when many of the women disappeared from the streets.

Robespierre came and went; the *courtesane* continued on her merry way long after he had gone, and a tempestuous, lucrative time lay ahead. After the 1939-45 War, both France and Belgium outlawed brothels, but in Antwerp, as in Amsterdam today, prostitutes continued to exhibit themselves in the windows of their apartments, and in France, after 1946, street-walkers swarmed on the boulevards and avenues, and illicit houses of love sprang up.

In Germany, King Frederick William IV, who was considered a pious man, albeit he died of paralysis resulting from a syphilitic taint, attempted to stamp out prostitution, which resulted in Berlin at least abolishing brothels in 1844. By then their number had declined to about twenty-six, having been a hundred in 1780 in the time of Frederick the Great, with about seven or eight inmates in each to serve a population of but 150,000 people. As a result of the abolition, more street-walkers appeared and 'underground' brothels did a gala trade.

In Japan, in 1956, it was announced that the houses of ill fame would be shut down in two years' time, the period being allowed for the *geishas* to rehabilitate themselves in other callings. In the Soviet Union, and in China, reform houses for prostitutes have been established which would, undoubtedly, help to place the women in suitable jobs.

CHAPTER 11

ENGLISH HARLOTRY AND RANDOM SEXUAL MORES

*English Characteristics : Stability, Insularity, Independence, Pru-
dery, and Hypocrisy—English Sexual Phenomena—Vicarious Sexual
Thrills from Sensational Newspaper Reportage—Obsession with
Cruelty, Virginity, Homosexuality, and Defloration—Cuckolded
Husbands exhibit Wives' Shame—English Whoredom—' Bagnios '
synonymous with Brothels in Mediæval Age—Pedærastry in Norman
Times—Act of Parliament regulating ' Stews ' or Bath-Brothels—
English Renaissance-cum-Restoration moves with Steady Gait—The
Restoration : Peak of English Immorality—The Puritan Kill-Joys—
Sexual Libertinism side by side with Puritanism—Outrageous Sexual
Eccentricity of Lord Castlehaven—Sexual Exhibitionism—' Serag-
lios ' or Restoration Brothels—The Exploits of the Rakes and Bucks
of Clubland—Satanism and the Order of St. Francis of Medmenham
Abbey—Sado-Masochism of the Georgian Era—Flagellomania and
the Berkeley Horse—Brothels in Victorian Times—Male Brothels
for Women Customers—Places of Assignation : Taverns, Gin-Palaces,
Ranelagh and Vauxhall Gardens—English Worship of Virginity :
The Defloration Mania—The Gay Young Royal Blade : Edward VII
—World of Changing Values—A Popular and Much-Beloved Prince
of Wales—The Gay, Roaring, Fabulous 'Twenties.*

IN order to understand English morality, one must first fathom the
national character of the people. The geographic position of
England, an island with slippery cliffs and surrounded with raging
seas, has served to isolate it and to breed in its inhabitants a peculiar
insularity which is only just beginning to crumble in this Jet Age in
which mechanical speed defies frontiers and makes the world shrink
into a small globe. Except for the early invaders all of whom, except
the Normans, came to this island when it was yet barbaric, very few
citizens of other nations bothered to visit her shores till the eighteenth
century. This complete isolation brought about that suspicion and
mistrust that still exists to a certain extent among the English, and
which today we call xenophobia. While being cut off from other
people deprived them of the advantage of cultivating a cosmopolitan
outlook, at the same time it gave them an independence of spirit and

a self-reliance that has made them far more stable than most other European nations.

However, self-assurance, too, has its disadvantages. Says Dr. Ivan Bloch in his **Sexual Life in England,** " English self-assurance does not attract by gay candour, but repels by a certain moroseness, a sullen earnestness, which has been attributed, not without justice, to the fog which is a feature of the country's climate . . . All through their literature and public life the voice of this English national pride is continually in evidence. In Chauvinism John Bull leaves all other peoples far behind him . . . Exaggerated self-assurance is apt to develop very easily into coarseness and brutality. As a matter of fact brutality was one of the most conspicuous traits of the English national character and was manifested in a vast variety of ways. The independence, the straightness and energy of the Englishman is apt to become insensitive coarseness. The Englishman was downright, thorough and logical in his brutality as he was in everything else. Macaulay gives countless instances of this, especially in his brilliant description of the manners of the seventeenth century . . . "

In England, today, we shudder with horror at the cruelty of the Spaniards and their bull-baiting, yet this country's sports have not always been bloodless ones. Cock-fighting, donkey-baiting, chasing of greased pigs by dogs, and fox-hunting, which last still persists, with its peculiar ritual of ' blooding ', to say nothing of the fights which take place even today between factions supporting opposing teams in football matches, all testify to the aggressive streak and blood lust beneath the surface.

The independence of character of the English, bred yet another quality—eccentricity. This, by itself, is but a harmless, and one may venture to say, a sometimes lovable trait; however, when mixed, paradoxically, with puritanism, it tends to promote prudery and hypocrisy, the major defects in English society. Puritanism was born as a cover for concealing the basic brutal and eccentric qualities. " This is the only psychological explanation of English prudery ", comments Bloch, adding: " For prudery and hypocrisy love only the surface veneer under which the darkest depravity may often lurk . . . " Again: " It is obvious that a human being who is perpetually worrying about what is decent and what is indecent, must for ever be letting his thoughts dwell on indecency; whereas the naïve and innocent person keeps easily without any bother within the bounds of decency; it never occurs to such a person to denounce anything as obscene when it is only the twisted thought of the prude that makes it so."

English Sexual Phenomena

The sex urge being the most powerful in a man, it is in this domain that he generally betrays his true nature. Similarly, the peculiarities of a nation reveal themselves only too well in the sexual sphere. One has only to read the popular press of England to realise what a delight readers take in gulping down sensational cases of sex murder, divorce, cruelty to both humans and animals, blackmail, homosexual offences, and rape. English sexual life is permeated with several bugbears: Sadism which results in cruel sex murders; the defloration mania and the incessant obsession with virginity; flagellomania which had its most thriving period in the time of the Georgians; and finally the preoccupation with homosexuality among men and its punishment even when it occurs between consenting adults.

Though extra-marital relations thrive in English society, it must be admitted that, compared to other nations, family life in England is more permanent and stable. Though women here are probably among the most emancipated in the world, yet in the home, the woman, however well educated and modern, is willing, and often quite proud, to play the role of the wife who leans on her husband for support. He still remains the master of the house, be it castle or suburban cottage. This is a relic of the old Anglo-Saxon law which compelled the woman to submit to her 'lord and master'. Hence, as we noted in the chapter on marriage, the odd custom of selling a wife or daughter still prevailed in this country right up to the 'eighties of the last century when an Englishman could sell his wife or daughter at Smithfield Market. In the eighteenth century, the custom was all too common, and Archenholtz has commented on the frequency of bride-purchase in the latter half of the century. The name 'Horn Market' was applied to such sales which were allowed by the law. Sometimes advertisements for such transactions were inserted in the newspapers.

Today's Gretna Green marriages are an echo of the Fleet Marriages that existed in the eighteenth century. They were so called because outside Fleet Prison a man hung around tempting couples to form an alliance, the parson performing the marriage for but a few pence. Even clergymen went around to ale houses around Ludgate Circus, urging the customers to get married.

At first it may seem surprising that the newspapers of a country that is so concerned about propriety in sexual matters should probe into the details of a divorce case and highlight all the unsavoury details. However, if the matter is given some thought, it is easy to see that the repressed seek an outlet readily in vicarious experiences which they have not the courage to undergo themselves. Similarly, prior to 1857, when the Matrimonial Causes Act was passed, while a husband could yet claim from his wife's seducer damages in what was known as a 'Crim.-Con.' case (abbreviation for Criminal Conversation), magistrates, many no doubt from motives of vicarious sexual gratification, would ferret out from witnesses by means of probing questions, the most intimate and obscene details. Says Bloch, "With some justice Hector France described Crim.-Con. magistrates as the worst pornographers." Of course all the dirty linen was rewashed in the newspapers in which the cases were reported avidly.

Bloch quotes Archenholtz in two cases where the cuckolded husbands were only too eager to expose the adulteries of their wives. In one case, a nobleman, suspecting his wife of adulterous relations with an officer, pretended to go on a trip and returned home to discover the lovers *in flagranti*. He had them tied with cords to the bed-posts, and exhibited them to his circle of friends. In the other case, a ship's captain, having discovered his wife in a similar situation with a sailor, had her stripped, and along with her lover, tied to a mast which sailors carried through the streets of East London. Such was the sexual eccentricity of the cuckolded Englishmen of the eighteenth century.

The very first Crim.-Con. case was that of Lord Audley, Earl of Castlehaven, in the seventeenth century, and has been described elsewhere in this work. In the next century, came the divorce case of the Prince Regent, the future George IV, against his wife, Caroline, whom he had treated disdainfully from their very first meeting. The trial lasted for three months in 1820. Among the witnesses against her were hotel waiters and chambermaids, all of whom were cross-examined in respect to the minutest sexual details. Queen Caroline was acquitted, but died the following year, no doubt the humiliation of the proceedings having told on her health. The poet Shelley later wrote his ' Œdipus Tyrannus ', satirising the trial.

English Whoredom

As in Europe, in the Middle Ages, *bagnios* or public baths flourished in England where they were establishd officially as brothels. It was in the second half of the twelfth century, under Henry II, that regulations were introduced as to the manner in which these ' stews of Southwark ' should be conducted, eighteen of them being owned by the Bishop of Winchester. Even an English cardinal is reported as having purchased a brothel " as an investment for Church funds ", and G. Rattray Taylor, in his **Sex in History,** informs us that jurists argued whether the Church was entitled to ten per cent. of the prostitutes' earnings. The steam baths were mostly referred to as ' hothouses ' but at times the Oriental term, *hamam*, was used. These *bagnios* and hothouses soon became synonymous with brothels. The women would undress and exchange choice morsels of gossip in one room, while in an adjoining one they would dally with men as a woodcut of the period of James I indicates.

When the Normans invaded England, immorality ran rampant. Englishwomen are said to have matched Frenchwomen in their immodesty. The French *joie de vivre*, particularly in the sexual sphere, penetrated deep into the higher ranks of society and the clergy. Pæderasty is supposed to have been popularised on a large scale by these Norman invaders. During the Xmas festivities, the noblemen were hosts to both their male and female serfs. To preside over the festivities, which have been described as being both merry and indecent, a clergyman was appointed by the feudal lord, and this worthy of the Church was playfully dubbed ' the Abbot of Misrule'. Homosexuality flourished in the reign of James I, who was reputedly himself homoerotic.

The Plantagenet kings, such as the first two Henrys and *Cœur de Lion* or the ' lion-hearted' Richard I, gave full reign to their polyerotic inclinations and begot more bastards than legitimate children. In 1161, in the reign of Henry II, an Act of Parliament stipulated that no stew-holder of a public bath should hinder a woman from going and coming freely into the stew, and she was to be charged no more than fourteen pence for a room, nor kept in the stew against her wishes. The main restrictions were that a married woman was not to be accepted; no woman was to be allowed to take money from a customer unless she spent the whole night with him; a man had to come in voluntarily rather than be cajoled or tempted; and there had to be a weekly supervision of the stews by a bailiff, or constables.

These English *bagnios* boasted fancy names such as ' the Cardinal's Hat' or ' the Bell'. They continued into the thirteenth and fourteenth centuries, both Edward III and Henry IV confirming the Act of Parliament of 1161. In the second half of the fourteenth century, even a special way of dressing was prescribed for the prostitutes who were not to wear attire similar to that of noblewomen and others who did not follow their profession. In the last quarter of the fourteenth century, Bloch reports that the Mayor of London, William Walworth, owned all the *bagnios* which he rented out to procuresses. An attempt was made, at the beginning of the sixteenth century, by Henry VI, to shut down the stews, but public demand forced at least a dozen of them to be opened anew.

The Renaissance and the Reformation were ushered into England, as we saw in the previous chapter, more or less at the same time, unlike the happenings on the Continent where the Reformation followed the Renaissance, being a reaction to it. It was the private life of Henry VIII that precipitated the new movement. The English Renaissance did not scintillate with the same brilliance or excesses as on the Continent. Its gait was steadier and it was marked by moderation. The guilt complex of mediæval times in regard to sexual pleasures disappeared, and was replaced by robust, hearty revelries at Easter and Whitsuntide festivities and during Christmas. The Maypole, the ox, the holly and the ivy, came into their own. When the common folk returned from the countryside, from which they brought back the Maypole, and oxen with flower-decked horns amidst the waving of flags and handkerchiefs, more than half the number of girls in the throng are said to have returned ' defiled '.

In the Tudor Period, England's merry, roistering monarch, the much-married Henry VIII who ushered the Reformation into the country, exhibited an odd puritanical streak by shutting down the remaining *bagnios*.

The Restoration : Peak of
English Immorality

Following the Renaissance-cum-Restoration, in the seventeenth century, dawned an era of conflict between the Puritan and the Rake. For a time, patrism held ascendency. Puritanism turned a large section of the jolly, convivial, hearty, whoring English of Tudor times into morose, dour, wet-blankets. It is to Puritan times that one can trace back the birth of the phlegmatic, hypocritical, and insular traits that often mar, with their prudery and false reserve, the affability of the English temperament.

The Puritans, particularly the Calvinists, sought not merely to subdue the flesh as the mediæval Church had done, but stretched the guilt complex still further by extending it to cover all manner of transgressions, some of them utterly trivial. Attire, especially men's, was was made simpler and severer, churchgoing was enforced on Sundays and even Wednesdays, and looseness of the tongue was curbed, blasphemous and scatalogical language being outlawed. There was a penalty for the slightest offence. Parents, we are told by Burgo Partridge in his work, **A History of Orgies,** could be arrested for treason and blasphemy if the priest christened their child with a name other than the one they had chosen for it, and they dared to object. There was a clearly patrist pattern in the violence and cruelty by which the Puritans sought to enforce their odious laws and to blanket the national atmosphere with gloom.

At the commencement of the seventeenth century, an order was issued empowering the Aldermen of London to arrest prostitutes who were found in inns. A penalty of twenty pounds was introduced for any public bath that permitted a prostitute on its premises, and the baths which were meant only for women were enjoined to keep out licentious men. Thus baths were no longer synonymous with brothels.

Side by side with the restrictive practices imposed by the Puritans almost throughout the seventeenth century, existed a strong element that champed at the bit of restraint, particularly in the sexual sector. This was the hard core, with its joy of living and its sexually anarchistic tendencies, that was eventually responsible for the Restoration so called because royalty was once again restored to the throne of England.

Sexual libertinism kept its dubious flag flying right in the midst of puritanical gloom. A scandalous case mocked the tender susceptibilities of the Roundheads. In 1631, took place the trial of Mervyn, Lord Castlehaven, before his peers in Westminster Hall. The charges against the noble lord were that he had instigated and abetted the rape of his countess, committed sodomy with his men servants, and had encouraged the debauchery of his own daughter. The male servants had been forced to rape the Countess in the presence of her husband who then proceeded to indulge in homoerotic relations with his underlings. He had, moreover, compelled his daughter to marry one of his favourite servants after he and the rest of his domestics had watched the two in the act of coitus several times from the girl's twelfth year.

In the course of the notorious trial, the Countess, Lady Anne, revealed that on the very next night after their wedding, Lord Castlehaven had indulged in lascivious conversation with her and had then brought in a man servant naked to their bed, forcing the latter to have intercourse with her, while he himself held her down forcibly to prevent her resistance. The servant in question also testified to this, as well as to the fact that after he had raped Lady Castlehaven, the noble lord had committed sodomy on him. His lordship had also indulged in homosexual practices with other servants, and had kept a harlot in his house. He would both participate in, and take a scoptophile's delight in watching, the sexual act between others. Needless to say, Lord Castlehaven paid with his life for the outré existence he had led in defiance of the then existing puritanical creed.

With the Restoration, English sexual life attained the summit of immorality, the like of which had not been seen in previous Christian times in England, nor has been seen since. The Georgian rakes of the eighteenth century revived the gaiety of the European Renaissance. Excesses, coarse and brutal, marked their debauchery. The historian, Macaulay, declared: " Unbridled debauchery, the natural consequence of unnatural severity, was the prevailing fashion in these days, involving, of course, the moral degradation of women. It was good taste to idolise feminine beauty in a coarse and shameless manner . . . "

However, even in good King Charles's golden days, the puritanical values died hard, except among the aristocracy and in royal circles. Charles II himself, of course, set an example of good living with his spaniels, his ostentation, and his many mistresses. Sexually he was a veritable satyr, and at the same time, athletic, so that his excesses told little on him. It was during his reign that Sir Charles Sedley, typical of the Restoration rakes, is reported by Dr. Johnson, in his **Lives of the Poets,** to have exposed himself, along with Sir Thomas Ogle, " in indecent postures " on the balcony of the ' Cock ' in Bow Street, both being drunk. Sedley apparently did a strip-tease till he stood naked before a crowd at whom he hurled indecent abuse. He was fined for the offence.

Five years later, in 1688, we learn from the famed **Diary** of Pepys that Sedley and one Buckhurst, the first lover of Nell Gwyn, ran up and down the streets " with their arses bare ". However, King Charles himself being involved in the party earlier in the evening, pressure was brought to bear on the matter and the constable who had arrested the two exhibitionists was tried instead of the miscreants ! The Restoration plays of Sheridan, Congreve, and their ilk, amply testify to the licentious mores of the time. Never before, or since, has English sexual eccentricity reached such fabulous proportions.

The *bagnios* which had become, literally, baths, once again reverted to the old pattern towards the end of the seventeenth and the start of the eighteenth century, the age of the Gallants, and later, at the tail end of the period, the Regency Bucks. A foreign traveller, Archenholtz, reported that girls did not live in the *bagnios* but were fetched from outside in sedan chairs, no payment being necessary if a particular girl were rejected. "The English retain their solemnity even as regards their pleasures", adds Archenholtz, "and consequently the business of such a house is conducted with a seriousness and propriety which is hard to credit . . . Old people and degenerates can here receive flagellation, for which all establishments are prepared . . . "

Covent Garden was the district where brothels abounded. Fashionable houses were run by Molly King, Mother 'Cole', Mrs. Gould, and Mrs. Stanhope. Mother Cole's were visited by royalty and princes of the realm, Mrs. Gould's contained aristocratic and well-bred women to please the customers who were mostly wealthy merchants and professional men. The old name of *bagnio* was replaced by the more modish one of *seraglio*. Thus the brothel proper, which no longer masqueraded as a public bath, was introduced into England by one Mrs. Goadby, after the pattern of the Continental, particularly the Parisian, *sérails*. Mrs. Goadby's first house was opened in the mid-eighteenth century in an elegant house in Berwick Street in Soho. The women she installed in it were well bred, and she even employed the services of a surgeon to look after their health.

Charlotte Hayes, herself a demi-rep or woman of the twilight world, opened another house in King's Place, Pall Mall, which became known as a 'Cloister'. This establishment catered especially to debauchees whose organism required extra stimulus. The prices of the 'nuns' differed according to their age and allurements. Among other owners of brothels in Pall Mall were Mrs. Nelson who often had school girls enticed to her lair, and a Miss Harriot, a negress.

A novel *seraglio* belonged to Miss Fawkland, the mistress of a Major. It was divided into three 'temples', the one dedicated to Aurora (symbolic of Dawn like the tender ages of the girls) providing a dozen girls whose ages ranged from eleven to sixteen. Impotent customers could play about with these girls thus ensuring the preservation of their virginity. As they grew up, they were transferred to the temple of Flora where they proved attractive 'goods' owing to their previous training. The inmates of these two temples were never admitted to the third—the temple of Mysteries—where took place sexual rites that were shocking in their excesses.

Married women turned prostitutes for the sheer enjoyment of sexual lust in the brothel of Mrs. Redson of Piccadilly. In Curzon Street, Mayfair, a male brothel was run by Mrs. Banks to which females could resort in search of sexual thrills. The Restorationists certainly knew where to take their varied pleasures. Even in the twentieth century it would be hard to find an establishment that was run for women visitors.

The Exploits of the Rakes
and Bucks of Clubland

The early Georgian period marked the beginnings of London's clubland. Men with similar tastes and interests banded themselves in the same clubs. The rakes, gallants, and bucks, as the young men were variously called, indulged in a great deal of rakish behaviour. The Mohocks or Mohawks were young clubmen who terrorised the streets by gouging out eyes or pulping noses. However, this element was crushed by the fourth or fifth decade.

The Bold Bucks, filled with drink, behaved like the animals from which they took their name. Lust was their guiding principle and they molested women on the open streets. Even their female relatives steered clear of them. In keeping with the licentious times, the Hell Fire Club sprang up, headed by the Duke of Wharton. The members used the mumbo-jumbo of mystic rites at their gatherings in taverns, and celebrated black masses. In their assembly hall was an altar dedicated to the devil, and every meeting began with an invocation to Satan. Hence this peculiar cult was given the name of ' Satanism '. A Bill for its suppression was brought up in the House of Lords.

An institution more or less burlesquing the worship of St. Francis was started under the name of the Order of St. Francis of Medmenham Abbey. Its founder had observed communities of monks and nuns in Italy, and being revolted by their extreme asceticism, had decided to found the order in mockery of the religious name given it. Instead of asceticism, hedonism was given full rein. A house called Medmenham Abbey was built on an island in the Thames near Hampton, and each member took along a woman of his choice. Licentious conversation prevailed at the table during meals. Bloch gives us an illuminating description of this mock Order:

" Reception into the Order took place in a special chapel, with peals of bells and music, before twelve knights . . . So long as the ladies stayed in Medmenham Abbey they regarded themselves as the legitimate wives of the monks, and each monk took care not to disturb the honeymoon of the others. In order that a woman should not be discovered there by her husband, father or other acquaintance, these unique priestesses of Venus arrived masked, passed all the monks in review, and only unmasked when they were sure there was no danger. Otherwise they could at once withdraw unhindered. At these gatherings of the monks and nuns of Medmenham Abbey, all 'forms of physical and platonic love' were tried out, and the conversation was often so obscene and licentious that the ladies used their fans to hide their blushes, and very often made the pretence of shyness an excuse to ' retire for a time with their lovers '. Particularly noteworthy was the fact that this pious cloister availed itself of the services of midwives and doctors to a great extent. In certain cases, the ladies, when they thought it necessary, could retire for a time from the world, and in Medmenham Abbey contribute to the increase of the population. The children resulting from these unions were 'sons and daughters of the Holy Francis' and were brought up at Medmenham Abbey."

For the brothelgoer, things were made easy by the publication of Harris's List of Covent Garden Ladies, a kind of Who's Who and What's Where of whoreland. These demi-reps found their way into society by pinching or cadging invitations to fashionable parties. Groups of bucks would descend on a *seraglio* such as Mrs. Stanhope's. The proceedings, both at the clubs and in the brothels, were livened by drink, drink, and more drink. Sometimes the bawdy houses even served as the venue for private parties.

Casanova's 'Memoirs' reveal that he was not greatly enamoured of the London *demi-monde*. Spending an evening with a male friend and two female companions, a private orgy was suggested. His three fellow pleasure-pursuers exposed their superb bodies while blindfolded musicians played on, yet he was left unstirred. "It was one of those moments when I knew many truths," he declares. "On that occasion I saw that the pleasures of love are the result, and not the cause of gaiety . . . "

An eighteenth century strip-tease act of a so-called 'Posture Girl' in a Great Russell Street brothel is quoted by one 'Urbanus' in **The Midnight Spy**: "Behold an object which arouses at once our disgust and our pity. A beautiful woman lies stretched on the floor, and offers to view just those parts of her body that, were she not without shame, she would most zealously seek to conceal. As she is given to drink, she usually arrives half-drunk, and after two or three glasses of Medeira exposes herself in this unseemly manner. Look, she is on all fours now, like an animal. She is ridiculed and men gloat over such prostitution of incomparable beauty."

Sado-Masochism of the Georgian Era

English sexual life in Georgian and Regency times pulsated with a sado-masochistic undercurrent. Flagellomania and defloration mania set in. Clubs and brothels specialised in gratifying such cravings. Mrs. Theresa Berkeley of 28, Charlotte Street, Portland Place, kept an armoury of instruments of flagellation including cat-o'-nine tails, some of them studded with sharp needle-points, whips, leather straps, and curry-combs. These were kept in water to preserve their suppleness. A customer, if he so wished, could be scourged with green nettles (which Mrs. Berkeley preserved in the summer in Chinese vases), whipped, or curry-combed mercilessly until he bled.

In 1828, this notorious woman invented the Berkeley Horse, a copper-plate of which was published in her 'Memoirs'. The contrivance was a sort of extensible ladder the length of which could be adjusted. It had apertures for the head and the genital organs. The victim would be strapped to the *chevalet* under which Mrs. Berkeley herself would sit on a chair flogging his bare posterior, while a young woman, suitably underclad, would act as 'frixtrix', as Bloch puts it. A masochistic customer who had tried other floggers and been insufficiently subdued, once wrote to Mrs. Berkeley offering her a sliding scale of fees commensurate with the severity of the pain inflicted on him: She would receive a pound sterling for the first sign of blood; another pound if the blood trickled down to his heels; yet another if there were a pool of his blood on the floor, and a fiver if the ecstasy of the torture could render him unconscious.

Female flagellants had their exclusive clubs in the eighteenth century. The 'Bon Ton' Magazine of December, 1792, gave a vivid picture of such a club: The members were mostly married women who, having grown indifferent to the pleasure of conjugal love, would scourge one another with stout rods. Lots were drawn to determine the order of procedure and a speech would be made, no doubt to stimulate the libido of the members, on the effects of corporal punishment of various parts of the body. During the flogging, the victims would bare the most delicate parts of their bodies such as the bosom or the buttocks. The most notorious female flagellant of all was Elizabeth Brownrigg, the wife of a Fleet Street plumber. She was a midwife in St. Dunstan's parish and inflicted atrocious daily floggings with sticks and brooms, on three girls she took in as apprentices. One of them was often beaten, disrobed, and kept in a cellar on bread and water. On one such occasion, after having been beaten no less than five times, the girl succumbed to her injuries after a few days in hospital. Brownrigg was hanged at Tyburn in September 1767.

Brothels in Victorian Times

From the end of the eighteenth century, and throughout the Victorian era, when prudery and hypocrisy concealed shameful vices, flagellatory brothels were the vogue. Many of the females who worked as assistants to administer the floggings, were obviously female sadists or, as Dr. Magnus Hirschfield would prefer to call them, 'metatropists', for sadism, being basically a masculine urge, when found in the female is a gross abnormality, just as masochism, being basically a feminine urge, is metatropistic in a man.

One Mrs. Collet who started a brothel in Covent Garden, then moved on to Portland Place, and finally to Bedford Street off Russell Square, was particularly renowned as a flagellant, and is even said to have been visited by George IV for that purpose. Her niece, Mrs. Mitchell, was brought up in the same tradition, and followed the same calling at 22, Waterloo Road, and later at Kennington. Another such brothel-keeper was Mrs. James, who once belonged to the domestic staff of Lord Clanricarde, and who kept a house in 7, Carlisle Street,

Soho, ending up a wealthy woman with a luxurious house in Notting Hill Gate. However, compared to Mrs. Berkeley, these were smaller fry.

In the second half of the nineteenth century, when Queen Victoria's reign was well under way, flagellation brothels abounded. One Mrs. Sarah Potter, alias Steward, ran an ostensibly respectable establishment. She provided free clothes, board and lodging for the girls she took in, and then made them submit to the perverted tastes of her clients. Veritable orgies of flagellation took place, the girls being flogged while bound to a ladder, or laid in bed, or whipped round the room.

Male flagellants were mostly metatropists, and were called flogging ' cullies ' because they excelled in the passive, masochistic role. Impotent or semi-impotent men belong to the ranks of these. As long ago as the sixteenth century, the poet, Christopher Marlowe, had composed the following satirical verse about one such man:

> " When Francis comes to solace with his whore,
> He sends for rods and strips himself stark naked,
> For his lust sleeps and will not rise before
> By whipping of the wench it be awaked . . . "

Two of the most notorious owners of *seraglios* in Victorian times were Marie Aubrey and Mary Wilson, the latter being known also for her efforts to revive English erotic literature. Her temples of Venus were shifted from locality to locality such as Old Bond Street and St. Pancras.   Her houses provided, among other refinements, the popular one of flagellation. In 1842, she published the ' Voluptarian Cabinet ' in the second part of which she outlined her plan for a male brothel that women could visit. It was called ' the Eleusinian Institute ', and her description of it runs as follows:

" Any lady of rank and means may subscribe to this institute, to which she shall always have the entry incognito; the married to commit what the world calls adultery, the unmarried to obey the commands of all-powerful nature, and to offer a sacrifice to the oldest of the gods, Priapus . . . I have erected a very elegant temple, in the centre of which are large salons surrounded by charming and comfortable boudoirs. In these salons, arranged according to their class, can be seen the most attractive men of all types that I can obtain, expert in all forms of pleasure to suit all tastes, and all in a state of great exaltation produced by good living and inertia. The ladies never enter the salons, but are shown the occupants through darkened windows in the boudoirs. In one room can be seen beautiful, elegantly dressed young men playing cards or music, in others, athletically built males, completely naked, wrestling or bathing . . . As soon as their minds are made up, they ring for the chambermaid, call her to the window and show her the object of their desire, and he is forthwith brought to the boudoir."

Marie Aubrey was a Frenchwoman who ran a brothel in Seymour Place from 1825-1837. All the dozen or so rooms in the establishment were exquisitely furnished and contained silver table ware. Her 'bully', one John Williams, helped her to run the brothel, and a doctor in the neighbourhood aided in procuring girls for the *seraglio*.

In 1840, the number of brothels in London were estimated at 1,500. Probably double the number existed. Very often the brothels were near churches. Leicester Square was well favoured with such houses, and of course the dock areas.

Places of Assignation

The Restoration, with its laxity of morals, made the taverns popular places of assignation in the seventeenth and eighteenth centuries. One writer commented that there were so many such taverns and inns that London had no need of brothels. Well-known taverns in the eighteenth century were the 'School of Venus', the 'Golden Lion' in the Strand, and the 'Weatherby', the last of which was frequented by women of all classes from 'kept' women to harlots.

In the nineteenth century, the long rooms and saloons of the taverns became crowded with prostitutes. They were not to be found merely in the West End, but were spread out all over London, especially near the Thames. Often sailors who frequented the long rooms of these riverside taverns which could hold a few hundred persons, were taken to brothels and there robbed, or sometimes, even murdered. The tavern owners made it a point to attract prostitutes, with free food and wine, to their premises, so as to draw male customers.

Gin palaces, of which five thousand are said to have existed in 1838, were also popular picking-up places for whores, as well as oyster houses and dining rooms near Covent Garden and Drury Lane which advertised 'beds' in their windows. Often boarding houses were a blind for brothels. Massage institutions also existed. These offered not only pleasures in the arms of harlots, but also purveyed subtle sexual perversions or 'refinements' according to individual taste. Manicurists and governesses were often the poses assumed by harlots just as today they call themselves 'models'.

The Coffee-Houses of London which flourished at the turn of the seventeenth century were not actually places of assignation and so we need only quote briefly from the second volume of Macaulay's **History of England**: "There were Puritan coffee-houses where no oath was heard, and where straight-haired men in their nasal voices discussed predestination and damnation; Jews' coffee-houses, where black-eyed money-changers from Venice and Amsterdam met; papist coffee-houses where, according to the notions of Protesants, Jesuits made plans for another great fire and cast silver bullets to shoot the king with."

Gardens, parks, and places of amusement generally serve as the haunts of prostitutes. Such a purpose was fulfilled by the numerous tea-gardens in London and elsewhere. In ' Bagnigge Wells ', more than a thousand people crowded on Sunday mornings. The most notorious tea-gardens were between Southwark and Lambeth on the Surrey side of the Thames, in the eighteenth century, of which the ' Dog and Duck ' acquired such an evil reputation for immorality that it was closed down at the start of the second decade of the nineteenth century. It had a pleasure boat which cruised round on a canal that ran through the garden. Yet another fashionable tea-garden in St. George's Fields was the Apollo Garden which boasted of an excellent orchestra but was overrun by prostitutes.

In the first quarter of the eighteenth century, Belsize House, near Hampstead, with its lovely gardens, springs, a racecourse, and dance halls, was the stamping ground of prostitutes. But their licentious behaviour caused its closing down in 1730. Between Chelsea and Pimlico, where Victoria Station now stands, was ' Jenny's Whim ' much frequented by the working classes on a spree. May Fair, between Piccadilly and South Audley Street, was the playground of the wealthy and has remained so to this day, Curzon Street having been the most popular haunt of the modern street-walker till driven from the streets by recent legislation following the Wolfenden Committee Report on Prostitution.

In the eighteenth century, prostitutes " paraded sitting in high phætons through the streets, in wonderful Amazon costume, and accompanied by other girls, similarly dressed, riding alongside the phætons ", according to the fifth volume of Archenholtz who describes the temple of Flora in the Garden of Venus. Two gardens that achieved distinction for their beauty in the eighteenth century and continued to exist into the early nineteenth century, were Ranelagh and Vauxhall. The latter was in the Borough of Lambeth on the south or Surrey side of the Thames. Though famed for their beauty and the recreation they afforded, the Vauxhall Gardens fell into disrepute as early as the mid-seventeenth century, for Pepys comments in his diary of 30th May, 1668: " But oh Lord ! what a loose company it was there to-night, one need only go there once to perceive the kind of doings there are." The prostitutes often wore masks as they half concealed and half flaunted their gaudy charms. Pepys again wrote, on 27th July, 1668: " . . . observed how coarse some young gallants from the town were. They go into the arbours where there is no man and ravish the women there, and the audacity of vice in our time enraged me . . . "

For almost a generation, from 1712, Vauxhall lost its popularity. But is was reopened in 1732. In 1792, the entrance fee was raised from one to two shillings, and went up to four shillings, but was reduced to one shilling from 1850 onwards. Nine years later, the 25th July, 1859, saw the closing down of the Vauxhall Gardens for ever. Bloch declares: " The arbours and dark bushes in Vauxhall particularly served the purpose of prostitution and were always mentioned as a great attraction."

In the middle of the last century, the Argyll Rooms in Great Windmill Street served as glittering dance places, but a decade later were deserted for the National Assembly Rooms in Holborn, which served as " a dancing centre for prostitution." The Cremore Gardens on the banks of the Thames at Chelsea also provided a magic fairyland for dancers among whom were many prostitutes.

" Prostitution on a large scale is a sign either of an age of extreme licence, or an age of extreme restriction . . . " says Partridge in **A History of Orgies.** In the case of the Victorians, it was obviously the latter. The Victorian home was sacrosanct and family life was the ideal. But Victorians were no romanticists and hence very practical. They took their sexual pleasures outside the home . . . Concealment of feminine allure which prudery deemed necessary in the Victorian mode of attire must have provoked their libido to bursting point.

According to the **Lancet,** the journal of the British Medical Profession, in 1857 in the county of London there were no fewer than 80,000 prostitutes out of a population of 2,235,344. It also claimed that one in sixty houses was a brothel, and that one in every sixteen women was a harlot. These figures are astounding and stretch one's credulity. One may venture to suggest that the medical profession was representing the Victorian witch-hunt against prostitutes who were used as scapegoats for the covert sins of a patriarchal and hypocritical society.

Factory girls and domestic servants, both of whom were underpaid, swelled the ranks of prostitutes. Regent Street, the Burlington Arcade, and the Haymarket, were the favourite venue of many of these women. The hub of the world, with Piccadilly rightly presided over by Eros the Greek god of Love, became also the hub of prostitution and has remained so till our own time, except that the women no longer lurk around the corners or clutter the streets in and around Piccadilly as they did only a few years ago.

The mid-Victorian era boasted of a luxury brothel just off Leicester Square, over which presided Kate Hamilton, the corpulent owner. A subterranean passage led to the domain over which she reigned literally like a monarch, seated on a velvet throne with beautiful young ladies-in-waiting to obey her slightest command. The customers were scrutinised very carefully through a peephole in the door, before being admitted. Even the Shah of Persia and two Siamese princes were reputed to have patronisd Kate Hamilton's whore-house.

English Worship of Virginity :
The Defloration Mania

The demand for virgins, or what is known as the defloration mania, has a firm hold on the mind of the English male. In the eighteenth and nineteenth centuries, it became widespread. Psychologically, the mainspring of the desire is the wish to possess that to which nobody has had access before. It is indeed the urge of the explorer and the conqueror.

Child prostitution which was rife in England, was, as one can plainly see, the direct result of Englishmen's defloration mania. Archenholtz commented on the immaturity of many London prostitutes in the eighteenth century. In the early part of the nineteenth century, child brothels sprang up like mushrooms, many near Bedford Square. One such brothel was run by a married couple for the span of a quarter of a century. Young girls were sent out of these brothels to entice boys of their own age as well as older men. One William Sheen is said to have set up brothels with almost thirty children in them, where gross acts were committed between them and adults.

The **Pall Mall Gazette** exposed child prostitution and the sale of children for immoral purposes, in 1885. The attack was headed by the editor, Wickham Steed, himself. A secret commission formed under the auspices of the paper, made its own investigations independently, though the committee worked in collaboration with the Home Office. The revelations regarding the rape of virgins were astounding. The girls were forced to submit against their wishes and the miscreants who had led them astray were seldom punished. Certificates of virginity were procured and traces of seduction were cleverly concealed so that the same child could be offered as a virgin to another customer. Bloch reproduces Wickham Steed's revelation of what a brothel-keeper confessed to him:

" ' There is always a demand for virgins as you call them, fresh girls as we call them in the trade, and a pander who understands this business has his eyes open in every direction. His stock of girls is always being exhausted, so that he has to be continually filling it up and looking out for suitable numbers in order to keep up the reputation of his house. The hunt for fresh girls takes a good deal of time . . . ' "

The brothel-keeper went on to explain the manner of enticing young girls. He himself had occasionally posed as a minister and proposed marriage to a girl so as to procure her for a client. He would then ' wine and dine ' her, take her to a show, and make her miss her last train, following which the victim would be taken home to the waiting customer for defloration. He also explained that prostitutes would often sell their daughters for anything between twenty to forty pounds when the girls had reached their twelfth or thirteenth year.

" ' We deal in virginity but not in virgins ', archly explained one young procuress to Stead as quoted by Bloch. " ' My partner procures the girls who are seduced and taken back to their relatives. The business is then at an end as far as we are concerned. We deal only in first seduction; a girl goes through our hands once. Our

customers desire virgins, not damaged goods, and usually they only
see these once.' "

Nursemaids, governesses, domestic helps, and working women
in general, were pounced upon in parks and places of recreation by
the hounds sent out by the brothel-keepers on the virginal scent.
Hyde Park, Regent's Park, and Green Park, were infested with these
hunters who cajoled the girls over a period of weeks, into making
' easy ' money.   When a girl was offered to a customer against her
wishes, she was given narcotics and kept in a room from which her
cries would not reach the streets.   Some of these poor victims were
too scared to reveal how they had been tricked into losing their
chastity.   Some of the brothel-keepers themselves took a keen delight
in listening to a girl's cries while she was being deflowered, and they
averred that the customers often got an extra thrill from hearing
them.   Girls who would not surrender easily were often tied down
to the beds.   Many of the establishments kept their own doctors who
provided certificates of virginity.   After such medical examination,
the girls had sometimes to sign a document agreeing to being seduced.

The **Pall Mall Gazette** also exposed the practice of infibulation,
or the restoration of virginity by artificial means such as stitching
in the appropriate parts.   This was a revival in the last part of the
Victorian era of the custom which had prevailed in the Middle Ages
and right up to the eighteenth century.   Victorian England was
shocked at having the beam plucked so rudely from its eye, and for
a time there was a campaign afoot to prosecute the staff of the paper
that had actually done such a service to the country.   Here was
Victorian hypocrisy revealing its shabbiest side.   The Government
promised to investigate the matter with the co-operation of the Police.

Eventually, the public went over to the side of the **Pall Mall
Gazette** and a crusade was started for putting an end to the traffic
in girl prostitutes.   In the August of 1885, 250,000 people are reported
to have collected in Hyde Park with Wickham Stead, the editor,
riding in triumphal procession on a waggon.   Bouquets of white
roses, symbolising purity, were carried by many of the marchers.
However, the trade was not checked effectively, which Partridge explains by claiming: " Lip-service was the motto of the Victorians
and would remain so."

The strain that Victorian prudery imposed on its young did not
make them abstain from sexual indulgences even outside of marriage.
" All that the Victorians really practised was hypocrisy, and the kind
of controlled schizophrenia we have already seen ", observes
Partridge.   " Even the strain of this was too great.   In fact, in particular the strain of this.   The reaction was sudden and violent."

Immorality   became fashionable and daring among the minority
of rebels belonging mostly to the smart society set.   Once again the
courtesan came into her own.   Agnes Willoughby, Laura Bell, Kate
Cook, and above all, Cora Pearl, were accepted in Victorian society
though known to be 'scarlet women '.   Cora Pearl threw many un-

conventional and rowdy parties for which she always thought out something unusual.   Once she was 'served up naked' during a banquet, another time she had a champagne bath in a silver tub before her guests, and on yet another occasion she danced the can-can on a carpeted floor strewn with roses.   When on the point of writing her memoirs, she blackmailed former lovers who paid up rather than be compromised in the pages of her book.   She died in a garret in Paris in the 'eighties of the last century.

The Gay Young
Royal Blade

Edward, Prince of Wales, son of Queen Victoria and Prince Albert, was a gay young blade who, during his mother's long reign, was able to lead a carefree hedonistic existence.   Among his friends were Lily Langtry, the famous actress, and Mistinguette, of the *Folies Bergère*. The Edwardian Period which covered his short reign as Edward VII for about a decade, was a far more relaxed and naughtier society than the Victorian era.   It was also the last colourful and elegant period of English history.   Costumes were brilliant, balls were gay, wealth was lavishly spent.   All over Europe, the swansong of old-fashioned gallantry, blazing spectacle, pomp and pageantry, was being sung. The first World War of 1914-18 was to bring a tremendous upheaval in the old values.   The Blue Danube that flowed to the strains of the lilting music of the Strausses, and saw the gaiety of the Old World of charm and grace, would never again witness such colour, romance, and pageantry.

The end of the 1914-18 War, brought a feverish, short-lived gaiety, more boisterous, far less elegant, and for the upper crust a glorious freedom fling which was a kind of cry of despair from souls living in a fast-changing world in which old social values were thrown overboard and a more democratic spirit swept in.   This was the era of the gay young things of the Roaring 'Twenties, when women were emancipated, feminine legs and even knees were bared, the Charleston was danced till dawn, and women bobbed and shingled their hair and smoked through long cigarette-holders; when Judge Lindsey's companionate marriage proposal went off with a bang in the U.S.A., resounding the world over; bootleggers in America thrived on Prohibition, and Al Capone strutted around as King of her underworld, while in England a new Prince of Wales, almost as young as the twentieth century, a worthy grandson of the gay Edward VII, himself to become Edward VIII for a brief, sad spell in the future, shocked royal circles and won the approbation and love of the Common Man all over the world, with his democratic spirit which made him equally at home in court circles or night-clubs, where he consorted with 'hoofers' such as Fred and his sister Adele Astaire, the famous dancing team.   But on the throne sat a stern, humourless though benign monarch, with his dignified, regal consort: George V and Queen Mary.

So much has been written of the Jazz Age of the 'Twenties by men and women who savoured fully of the life of that decade that the present writer, living but his early childhood then, does not feel qualified to expand too much on the revolution in manners and morals that the period ushered in. Sexual mores became slacker as a revolt against the guilt complex and restraints of former times. 'Petting' and 'necking' were common pastimes among the flaming youth, particularly in the America of F. Scott Fitzgerald, graduate of Princeton, a typical product of the age, who, in his novels, depicted a fervid picture of the neurosis of his time. The clinging of young bodies as they danced the fox-trot, invented by Vernon and Irene Castle before the former's tragic death in the war years, was described as " a syncopated embrace ". Frederick Lewis Allen in **Only Yesterday,** his classic account of the Fabulous 'Twenties, describes all this amusingly:

" No longer did even an inch of space separate them; they danced as if glued together, body to body, cheek to cheek. Cried the Catholic Telegraph of Cincinnati in righteous indignation: ' The music is sensuous, the embracing of partners—the female only half-dressed—is absolutely indecent; and the motions—they are such as may not be described, with any respect for propriety, in a family newspaper ... ' "

Charming sheikhs à la Valentino, beautiful ' jazz-babies ', champagne baths, midnight revels, glimpses of speakeasies, pleasure-mad' daughters, sensation-craving mothers, flaming youth, hot love-making : these choice epithets used in ' blurbs ' of film posters of the time, promising a vicarious thrill to picturegoers, express adequately the feverish, strident spirit of a decade that sent old morals toppling in favour of brand new ones.

In England, the atmosphere of the Gay 'Twenties was much the same as across ' the Big Pond ', if one counts out the ' speakeasies ' of the American Prohibition era. Prostitutes walked about and mingled more freely with the throng. They were occasionally glorified on stage and screen. Outstanding among such creations was Somerset Maugham's Sadie Thompson, the leading character in his play, ' Rain '.

CHAPTER 12

SEXUAL ORGIES IN CLASSICAL TIMES

*Conformist Group Orgies—Orgiastic Revels—The Greek ' Aphro-
disia '—Corinthian Harlotry—Dionysian Orgies and ' Bacchæ '—
' Phalli ' carried around in Processions—The Women's Festival of
Thesmophoria—The Boisterous ' Mænads '—The ' Olympiad '—The
Debaucheries of Corinth—Roman Revels—The ' Bacchanalia ' of the
Romans—Fornication, Hysteria, Sodomy, and Violence, linked with
' Bacchanalia '—Phallic Cults and the ' Saturnalia '—The Cult of
Priapus—The Worship of Cybele—Eunuchs as Priests of Cybele—
Cults of Isis and the ' Bona Dea '—Bawdy Priestesses of Isis—
Orgiastic Worship of the Good Goddess—The Feast of the ' Luper-
calia '—Whipping of Barren Women—Cæsar orders Mark Antony
to flog Calpurnia during the Lupercalian Games—" A Hairy Goat
shall leap the Roman Wife ".*

ORGANISED societies, whether primitive or savage, impose sexual
restraints on their members in the form of taboos which create
in hypersexed individuals certain tensions that often reach
breaking point. The human creature, though evolved higher than
baser forms of animal life, yet has propensities of a distinctly animal
nature that cry out for release like spirited steeds champing at the bit.
Relief from such accumulated tension is often obtained, in modern
society, by fornication and extra-marital relations. But in primitive
societies even today, and among civilised races in ancient times, a
form of organised licence served the purpose of releasing such tensions
by removal, for a set period, of the normal restraints.

This organised release of paroxysmal desire is called an ' orgy '.
Apart from serving as a safety-valve for pent-up emotions, it has the
added advantage of preventing a guilt complex, such as may afflict an
individual breaking social taboos, by the licence being indulged in
en masse, and the guilt thus being shared so that the individual blame
for it is reduced to nil. Such group debaucheries are primarily conformist, and it needs a De Sade, a Sacher Masoch, or a Jack the Ripper,
to outrage convention and revel in an individual and rebellious orgy
of torture, cruelty, suffering, or murder. However, such a lonely

195

rebellious orgiast is bound to suffer from acute feelings of guilt which may prey on his mind and make him a schizophrenic or split personality. The advantage of conformist group debaucheries is that once sated, the participants normally yearn for the temperances of daily life. Just as abstinence provokes lechery, satiety evokes temperance.

Orgiastic Revels

The Greeks of antiquity based their lives on the pursuit of *hedone* or pleasure. Their preoccupation was not with money and status, as in civilised societies in modern times, but rather in living a full life for which a healthy body was considered to be a prime necessity. Thus arose a worship of beauty and of the body beautiful, and a complete lack of the shame-cult in regard to nudity. A frank and honest sensuality was part of their culture—a long way from the sin-consciousness and consequent guilt complex of Christianity. It is significant that Greek, Hindu, and Roman mythological legends depict gods and goddesses who revel in the fleshly joys and frailties of mortals.

The orgiastic festivals of the Greeks were of a conformist group nature. Corinth, a wealthy maritime city, stood on an isthmus and was the Mecca of pleasure-seekers. " . . . What human fancy elsewhere was content merely to imagine in the way of licentiousness, found in Corinth its home and visible exemplification," says Hans Licht in his **Sexual Life in Ancient Greece,** " and many a man who could not find his way out again from the whirlpool of the naturally very expensive pleasures of a great city, thereby lost reputation, health, and fortune so that a verse became proverbial: ' The journey to Corinth does not profit every man.' The priestesses of venal love crowded about the city in incalculable numbers. In the district of the two harbours were swarms of brothels of every degree, and prostitutes without number lounged about the streets . . . "

The ' Aphrodisia '

The focus of attraction in Corinth was the temple of Aphrodite Porne, the Goddess of Love in her aspect of a prostitute. Here, according to the historian Strabo, were kept no less than a thousand *hieroduli* or temple girls, who, in actuality, were *hetæræ* or harlots who served the lusts of men. The temple rose from the ground of the Acrocorinthus citadel, and seafarers, whether approaching from East or West, could sight it while yet afar at sea.

About half a millennium before Christ, Xenophon of Corinth, as observed in a previous chapter, celebrated his victory at the Olympic games by dedicating a hundred girls to the temple of Aphrodite. The renowned Greek poet, Pindar, composed an Ode of Victory for the occasion, and a hymn which was sung in the temple.

Aphrodite, known to the Romans as Venus, was no faithful spouse. She once committed adultery with the sun-god Ares, and so beautiful was the sight of the two mating, that her husband, the lame Hephæstus, is recorded in Greek mythology as calling all the gods to witness the act. She also had love affairs indiscriminately with a succession of mere mortals such as Adonis, Anchises, and Pygmalion. No wonder that harlots participated prominently in the *Aphrodisia* or festivities dedicated to the Goddess of Love, which mostly took place in the Spring, and which, though not recognised by the State, or perhaps because of this very fact, were immensely popular and were celebrated throughout the land.

The birth of Aphrodite in Greek mythology is described in Æschylus's **Danaïdes.** Uranus, as the Greeks called the sky, " . . . desires to penetrate the earth, and love seizes the earth and (it) longs for union with it; the rain falling from the fair-flowing sky fructifies the earth which bears for mortals fodder for flocks and the sustenance of Demeter." From the union of Uranus and Gæa, the earth, are born the Titans, the Greek Cyclopes (not those in Homer) and the hundred-armed Hekatoncheires. Uranus, fearing the Cyclopes and the Hekatoncheires, buries them deep in the earth. But Gæa calls on her remaining sons, the Titans, to avenge their father's foul deed. Only Cronos is willing to help his mother: When Uranus bends down to embrace Gæa, Cronos cuts the former's generative organ with a sickle. The *membrum virile* falls into the sea, and from its white foam, which is the sperm of Uranus, springs Aphrodite on the beach at Paphos in Cyprus.

Long sexual abstinence, as in the case of sailors away at sea without touching port for a long while, is an aperitif to cupidity. It is therefore understandable that the term ' Aphrodisia ', according to Plutarch, came later to be applied to the revelries of concupiscent sailors letting off steam. Sensuality and boisterousness reigned supreme at the *Aphrodisia*. Corinthian harlotry turned what was supposed to be a religious festival into a veritable orgy of lasciviousness. All through the night, the prostitutes would roam the streets selling their favours cheap, such nightly festivity being known as *pannychis*, a name that stuck to the harlots themselves.

The *Aphrodisia* of Ægina concluded the festival of the god Poseidon. A prominent part was played in the *Poseidonia* (and in the *Eleusinia*) by Phryne of Thespiæ, a harlot famed for her luscious beauty and her wiles as we have noted previously. Athenæus tells us that more beautiful even than " the apples of her breasts " which, as we know, her defender, the orator Hypereides, exposed to save her from a death sentence, were her private parts which she concealed with a *chiton*. These she exposed only during the *Aphrodisia*, when she would " put off her himation, let down her hair, and go into the sea . . . "

In Thessaly was celebrated the festival of Aphrodite Anosia at which men could not be present. Presumably it was a Lesbian orgy with sado-masochistic undertones, as one learns that erotic floggings were a prominent feature of the festivities.

The revels at the Cyprian Aphrodite festivals highlight the element of sexual abandon when marital fidelity counted for nought. The festival at Palaipaphos, near Paphos, which took place every year, was dominated by erotic ceremonies when even married women would give themselves to strangers in the precincts of temples. All this is understandable when one considers that the Goddess of Love was originally looked upon as the goddess of fertility too.

The love feasts in Cyprus commemorated Aphrodite's birth on the shore of Paphos. An image of her was always washed in the sea by the women and decked with flowers, after which the fair adorers themselves would take a bath and get ready for the festival, or rather the orgies, of love.

Aphrodite was also the goddess of beauty and a temple was built glorifying even the loveliness of her posterior. In this aspect she was known as ' Aphrodite Kallipygos ', *i.e.*, the goddess " with beautiful buttocks ". In the east wing of the famous Neapolitan *Museo Nazionale*, is still to be seen in the room called ' Veneri ', a statue of Venus on a revolving pedestal showing her naked posterior while she glances over her shoulder at her bared anatomy.

Dionysian Orgies
and ' Bacchæ '

The worship of Dionysos or Dionysius, though of a religious nature, was, basically, cathartic, *i.e.*, the revelries were meant to purge and cleanse the system of accumulated erotic tensions. As W. K. C. Guthrie explains in his work, **The Greeks and their Gods,** when a man deviated from normal behaviour, as in the case of the insane and the epileptic, which today we should attribute to subconscious motivation, the Greeks considered that he was " Possessed by God ", a state to which they applied the term *theolepsy*.

The origin of the custom of inducing a theoleptic state with the aid of dancing, music, and wine, was to be found in Thrace whose people climbed mountain tops to the tune of flutes and kettledrums, madly dancing the while, and copulating freely atop the mountains, as the culmination of the sexual act liberates the individual from his or her personality and fuses it with the infinite.

When the Greeks gave festive form to this cult, they chose, appropriately, Dionysos, the god of grape and wine, son of Rhea, the mother of the gods, and father of Priapus who symbolises sexual desire, as the presiding deity. In the beginning the celebration was esoteric and practised by limited groups called *thiasoi*, which consisted only of women who indulged in tribadistic intercourse, *i.e.*, pseudo-copulation among themselves. Later, both sexes were admitted to Dionysian worship, which, apart from communion with the divine, also served the purpose of providing a safety-valve for sexual tensions, as well as for thanatic or destructive instincts.

The aggressive and sadistic desires were got rid of by the sacrifice of an animal at the end of the ceremony when a kid symbolising the god Dionysos himself, was torn and devoured, or even a human, perhaps the sacrificial priest himself. The similarity between this custom and that of the totem-feast of primitives who consume their totem-ancestor, is striking. Sadism also found an outlet in the flogging and scourging of women as at Alea in Arcadia.

The followers of Dionysos were called *bacchæ* or *bacchantes* after Dionysos's other name, Bacchus or Bakkhos, derived from a Greek word meaning ' communion with the divine'. Plutarch's description of a Dionysian celebration is as follows: " The festival of Dionysius was in old times celebrated in a popular and cheerful manner; a wine-jar was carried around and a vine-branch; then someone brought a goat, another a basketful of figs; and over all the phallus . . . "

In the country, an enormous phallus or several such phalli, were borne in procession through the streets amidst dancing, jesting, and the indecent behaviour of some. On the second day of the festivities, naked boys carried around wine skins or sacks which were slippery and on which they hopped about attempting to avoid slipping, no doubt causing great merriment with their merry antics.

Following the country *Dionysia*, came the *Lenæa*, which took place in Athens in the district of Lenæum to the south of the Acropolis. The meat for this festival was provided by the State. Wanton dances were included in the processions, the participants being dressed up as bacchantes, satyrs, and nymphs, as many famous paintings of the bacchanalia show, prominent among them being one by Rubens which can be seen in the National Gallery, London. Many revellers drove in carriages from which they played practical jokes. The *Anthesteria* followed in the next month known as Anthesterion. On the first day, the casks of liquor were pierced, the next day, the new wine was imbibed, and the third day pots of boiled vegetables were placed for dead souls.

The city *Dionysia* lasted several days in the month of Elaphebolian, equivalent to our March-April. The usual processions wended through the streets, boys singing in chorus and executing dances. Drinking went on among the spectators who watched the processions, and, of course, phalli were carried around to the accompaniment of dance and song. From Licht, we learn that in quite a few parts of Greece, particularly in Parnassus and Cithæron, and on the islands, Dionysian orgies confined to women, took place. These females were garbed in the costumes of bacchantes, or in goat-skins, and carried tambourines on which they played. Spurred on by the heady wine, no doubt many tribadistic orgies occurred

The 'Thesmophoria' and
Sundry Festivals

Many other Greek festivals were popular. The Attic *Thesmophoria* was a national feast lampooned by Aristophanes in his *Thesmophoriazusæ*. The women participants practised sexual abstinence for a little over a week preceding the occasion. They are said to have eaten garlic to keep their men folk away from becoming too ardent during this time. The five-day festival was in honour of the goddesses Persephone and Demeter, and the celebrants were confined to the fair sex. The name of the festival derived from the month of Thesmophorius as the Cretans and Sicilians called the month of sowing. The festival may have been confined to women because the goddess Demeter was the goddess of sowing and this activity corresponded to child-bearing. On the other hand, the women's abstinence before the festival makes one wonder whether a tribadistic element was perhaps connected with it.

The *Hyacinthia* was in honour of Apollo's favourite boy, Hyacinthus, who was killed with a discus aimed at his head by the jealous Zephyrus or god of the wind. As Greek gods enjoyed all the fleshly joys of mortals, the legends of Hyacinthus and Ganymede are obviously meant to indicate that even the gods were homoerotic. This feast was marked by boys playing on the cithers and singing or riding on horseback. Women in basket carriages, or in wooden chariots, led the processions. Another boys' festival was the *Gymnopædia* which consisted of dancing by naked boys after whom it was thus named; it was held in Sparta and celebrated in the market-place.

In the Autumn, in the Greek month of Bœdromion (September), were celebrated the *Eleusinian Mysteries*, the festivities lasting over a week. The ritual baths in the sea and the purification ceremonies were not very decorous. As the secret cult symbolised the death and reburgeoning of the grain, on the sixth day a procession wended its way from Athens to Eleusis but nine miles distant, with the processionists wearing crowns of myrtle and ivy on their heads, and with ears of corn and farming implements in their hands. Iacchus, the Eleusinian name for Dionysos, was supposed to lead the procession of *mystæ* or initiated, of whom there were thousands, to the Bay of Eleusis where the air reverberated with singing and mirth-making.

In the month of Pyanepsion, in Winter, around November-December, came the *Pyanepsia*, during which boys carried an *eiresione* or olive-branch shaped like a crown, from home to home while singing songs rather like Christian carol singers. In the same month, the *Oscophoria* took place in Athens with a transvestite element, two boys dressed as women, carrying *oschoi* or vine-branches bearing grapes in front of a procession. The boys had to have both parents alive. The branches were carried in relays by handsome *ephebi* or youth who ran from the temple of Dionysos to another in Phalerum, in competition, the first one receiving a concoction of wine, cheese, meal, honey, and oil, the year's produce; after that, in company with other ephebi, he danced merrily.

Another boys' festival was the *Theseia*, a parade of youthful Athenians who displayed their gymnastic skill. The *Adonia* in the month of Munchion, our April-May, celebrated the return of the slain Adonis to his beloved Aphrodite to dwell with her for a short spell. In this festival, statues of the two lovers were taken around in procession. In May-June, in the month of Thargelion, the *Daphnephoria* or festival of laurel-bearers was celebrated once in every nine years. It was so called because a *daphnephorus* or laurel-bearer, a young boy with both parents still alive, carried in a procession, a *kopo* or olive branch wrapped in wool, with little bronze globes attached to it to symbolise the planets, and with flowers decking it. The laurel-branch was thus ceremonially taken to the temple of Apollo Ismenius.

The *Thargelia* was held in honour of Apollo and Artemis, at Colophon. It seems to have been a sadistic celebration, for the most hated individual in the district was selected as a scapegoat or *pharmakos*. It was held only in times of disaster when some great calamity, such as a plague, or famine, visited the community. The scapegoat was paraded through the streets and after having presumably taken the contamination upon himself, was banished, being provided with bread, figs, and cheese. Outside the city, his genital organs were submitted to a scourging with whips, while a flute sounded a special tune.

Erotic dances played a considerable part in the festivities. The retinue of Dionysos being ithyphallic, the humans, dressed as satyrs or nymphs, simulated indecent gestures and postures. Such orgiastic dances were frequent in festivals in honour of Artemis. The *mænads* were extremely boisterous, and one of them, Licht informs us, is depicted on a vase in the nude, dancing while swinging a phallus. Male and female cup-bearers were always present at banquets and often danced before the assembled guests.

Dances of an orgiastic nature were often performed in the cult of Artemis, the virgin goddess. In the festival of *Tithenidia* at Sparta, virgins performed dances that were positively indecent, and at Caryæ too, the Laconian virgins displayed a sensual element in their terpsichorean revels. Such dances were executed in the temple of Artemis Limnatis which stood in the shade of Mount Taygetos, as well as in South Italian colonies, and in Sicily.

The ' Olympiad '

Greece of antiquity was not strictly a nation but rather a collection of tribes living in different states. Once in every four years, however, there was a sort of unity throughout the country during the *Ekecheiria* or truce of God that existed for five days, at the time of the festival of Olympia. The celebrations took place every fifth year in the district of Elis, as it was Iphitus, king of Elis, who had revived them some eight centuries before Christ on the pattern of the contests supposed to have originated with Heracles or Pelops and then to have ceased for a time. While the Olympiad lasted, all weapons were laid aside.

The gymnastic contests were called *agones* and consisted of throwing the discus, wrestling, and running, while the contests with *hippos* or horses, or mules, were with teams of horses. Whoever won the first prize in running had that particular Olympiad named after him. The victor's prize that in ancient times was wont to be a valuable object had become a standardised and hallowed one: a crown made of olive-branches, the branch being cut by a boy whose parents were both alive.

The Hellanodikæ presented the prizes in the temple of Zeus where the crowns were laid out on a gold and ivory table. The herald announced the name of each victor round whose head a *tænia* or woollen bandage was bound before he was crowned with the laurel wreath. All the champions then repaired to offer temple sacrifice amidst hymns of victory. Semetimes a poet composed a special ode for the occasion.

A banquet was given by the exalted of Elis to the champions in the dining hall of the Prytaneum amidst general rejoicing both inside and outside, the hall resounding with songs of victory. An Olympian victor was feted even more than a general, and the Altis or sacred grove of Zeus would soon contain his statue erected there by his admirers. Dressed in the purple of victory, the victor's home town would welcome him right royally as he was driven through the streets in a carriage drawn by four white horses. A votive offering of the crown of olive-branches was laid down in the chief temple. The different states had their own special ways of conferring honours on the victor. Thus in Sparta, the Olympian victor could fight beside the king in battle.

The contestants at the Olympic Games, as mentioned previously, appeared stark naked at least after 720 B.C., before which time a brief apron covered their genitals. This description of the Olympiad has been in the nature of a digression, which was thought worthwhile in view of the importance of the games; but we are concerned mainly with orgies of an erotic nature—which the Olympic Games certainly were not, except that on the way to them most roads led through Corinth and here many of the spectators, having left their women folk behind, as was the custom except for small girls, regaled themselves with the proverbial wine, women, and song—and to such erotic orgies we must now return.

Roman Revels

The philosophy governing the lives of the Greeks and the Romans differed considerably. The former were æsthetes who struck a happy medium in the art of living, whether it was apparel, food, or sexuality. Greek festivities provided a safety-valve for getting rid of accumulated sexual tensions, and even these orgiastic festivities were romanticised into the theoleptic cult, seeking fusion with the divine; once over, the Greeks returned to normal living with greater zest for moderation. Perversions—and homosexuality was not considered to be one, being, as we know, idealised—such as acute forms of sadism were absent from Greek life.

The Romans, on the other hand, though superficially refined, indulged in gross debaucheries for their own sake. Their cruelty was proverbial; their games in the arena where men were thrown to wild beasts, or gladiators pitted their strength against one another or even against beasts, testify to their inhumanity, as do the lives of the members of the Julio-Claudian House which we have already surveyed. After the gladitorial shows, men who had witnessed human mutilations and feasted their eyes on the free flow of blood, were sexually aroused to fever pitch and fell easy prey to the wiles of prostitutes who gathered in vast numbers in brothels near the Circus Maximus.

The Romans were sybarites who indulged in luxurious living which caused in many of them a singular effeminacy as in the case of the Greek colony of Sybaris; their pursuit of pleasure was gluttonous and tinged with a singular morbidity. Greek hedonism was not sybaritic, the Spartans in particular being noted for their strict discipline. The sports of the Greeks were manly and not cruel; their admiration of the human body and their sane attitude to nudity were wholly untouched by guilt feelings. The very symbol of the Roman state betrayed its feverish eroticism: the *fasces* which consisted of a bundle of rods with an axe (reminiscent of flagellation and execution) and was borne by a *lictor* or officer who carried out sentences, or before a Roman dictator when the number was doubled. The *fasces* were also borne before a high magistrate.

The Romans adopted many Greek deities on whom they generally conferred Roman names. Thus Aphrodite became Venus, and Eros was called Cupid. They also imitated Greek orgiastic festivals, but with them these became debased and not a mere outlet for sexual inhibitions, being rather an excuse for debaucheries *ad infinitum*.

The 'Bacchanalia' of the Romans

The notorious *Bacchanalia*, in honour of Bacchus, the Greek god of wine, was a very debased Roman form of the Greek *Dionysia*. This cult sprang up in Italy at the end of the second Punic War and spread like a wild fire all over the country. Though officially frowned upon, the Bacchanalian orgies found great favour among the populace. Starting as a vineyard cult, with but a slight undercurrent of sexuality, this last quality came to dominate the proceedings and a secret society developed around the cult which Livy described in these words:

"... As to the *Bacchanalia*, I am assured that you have learned that they have long been celebrated all over Italy and even now within the City in many places, and that you learned this not only from rumours, but also from their din and cries at night ... but I feel sure you do not know what this thing is: some believe that it is a form of worship of the gods, others that it is an allowable pastime and play ... that it concerns only a few. As regards their number ... there are many thousands of them ... a great part of them are women, and they are the source of this mischief; then there are men very like the women, debauched and debauchers, fanatical, with senses dulled by wakefulness, wine, noise, and shouts at night ... "

Fornication, hysteria, sodomy, violence, and boisterousness, came to be inextricably linked with the *Bacchanalia* and Livy further describes the nature of the rites: "There were initiatory rites which at first were imparted to a few, then began to be gradually known among men and women. To the religious element in them were added the delights of wine and feasts ... When wine had inflamed their minds, and night and the mingling of males with females, youth with age, had destroyed every sense of modesty, all varieties of corruption first began to be practised, since each one had at hand the pleasure answering to that which his nature was more inclined ... "

Burgo Partridge cites, in **A History of Orgies,** an interesting case of one Æbutius who fell in love with Hispala, a freedwoman who had once been a prostitute. His mother and his step-father insisted on introducing him to the Bacchic rites in order to destroy him. Thereupon Hispala who had been present at a Bacchanalian orgy with a former mistress, described its horrors to him. She explained that for two years only young people up to the age of twenty had been initiated. A young man would be introduced "like a beast for slaughter" to the priests who "took him to a place which resounded with cries and hymns, and the beating of drums and cymbals ... so that no one could hear the victim's cries for help while he was being violated."

Hispala's lover, Æbutius, reported the matter to the consul Postumius who elicited further information from Hispala. She revealed that at first the Bacchanalian shrine had been reserved for women, married women being priestesses in turn, but a Campanian woman altered the ritual by introducing her two sons. "After the rites had become open to everybody, so that men attended as well as women, and their licentiousness increased with the darkness of night, there was no shameful or criminal deed from which they shrank. The men were guilty of more immoral acts among themselves than the women.

Those who struggled against dishonour or were slow to inflict it on another, were slaughtered in sacrifice like brute beasts. The holiest article of their faith was to think nothing a crime. The men prophesied like madmen with their bodies distorted by frenzy. The women dressed as Bacchantes with their hair unbound, ran down to the Tiber carrying burning torches which they plunged into the water and brought out still burning because they had been smeared with sulphur and lime. They said ' the gods had taken them ' when certain men were bound to a windlass and snatched away out of sight into secret caverns. These were the men who had refused either to take the oath, or to join in the crimes, or to be violated. The society had a huge membership . . . and among them were men and women of noble birth."

On the strength of Hispala's description, the consul Postumius persuaded the Senate to conduct an investigation. As a result, many Bacchantes were prosecuted, almost seven thousand we are told, and many were put to death, while many fled. In 186 B.C., a senatorial decree prohibited the *Bacchanalia* throughout the country, the decree being on a bronze tablet which is still extant.

In Etruria, Bacchic dances and orgies found great favour. The Etruscans were sybarites and were matriarchal in days of antiquity. They were attended on by nude slave girls and even the freedwomen often appeared in the nude. Promiscuity prevailed among them and adultery was commonplace. The paternity of a child was seldom known definitely and the children were all brought up together irrespective of who had fathered them. Copulation could take place in the open without being considered untoward or indecent. Slaves would take in harlots and boys to their masters, or their wives. Often the men were both active and passive pæderasts so that for the latter purpose they used lusty young men.

The Bacchic dances in Etruria, as revealed by murals at Tarquina, were performed by naked persons or with a cloth covering the loins of the dancers. Wine played a prominent part in the revels as the Etruscans were great bibbers.

Phallic Cults and the ' Saturnalia '

Liber and Priapus were fertility gods of the Romans. The two are sometimes considered to have been identical, probably because their worship was similar. The worship of Liber was described thus by St. Augustine in *De civitate Dei*:

" Varo says . . . that the rites of Liber were celebrated at the crossroads in Italy so immodestly and licentiously that the male genitals were worshipped in honour of the god—and this not with any modest secrecy but with open and exulting depravity. That

shameful part of the body was, during the festival of Liber, placed
with great pomp on wagons and carried about to the crossroads in the
country, and at last into the city. In the town of Lanuvium, a whole
month was dedicated to Liber. During it, all the citizens used the
most disgraceful words until the Phallus had been carried across the
market-place and put to rest again. It was necessary that the most
honourable of the matrons should publicly place a wreath on that
disgraceful effigy. The god Liber had to be propitiated to ensure
the future of the crops, and the evil eye had to be repelled from the
fields by compelling a married woman to do in public that which not
even a harlot might do under the eyes of married women in the
theatre."

From St. Augustine, such scathing criticism is not after all surprising. But Otto Kiefer seeks to refute it in his **Sexual Life in
Ancient Rome** by declaring that the custom " was not a proof of
debauchery, but an old custom of religious significance to avert destructive magical 'influences'", on the grounds that an honourable
woman performed the ceremony. However, even if an honourable
woman gave the custom an air of of respectability, it does not pre-
clude others from treating it as an excuse for debauchery. As to
religious implications, sex is very often the basis of mystical practices.

The phallus, or *fascinum*, we are told, was hung round the necks
of children, placed above doors of shops, and even graced the triumphant chariot of a victorious general, " as an amulet and a charm against
magic . . . " Here again even if the phallus was considered capable
of averting the evil eye and bad fortune, the fact that such power
was attributed to it goes but to prove that it held a compelling erotic
sway over the hearts and minds of people to the extent where its
physical potency led to its being given a metaphysical potency as well.

The cult of Priapus differed from that of Liber only in being
more obviously phallic. Known as the garden god, he was actually
a 'scare-god', *i.e.*, a scarecrow, in whom the genital organ was over-
proportioned. Often he was depicted as a huge phallus with a human
face and eyes. His worshippers conferred on him their own sexual
propensities, and he was credited with being able to solve their erotic
problems, and, being a fertility god, to restore fecundity to the barren
who prayed to him.

The phallus is sometimes jestingly referred to as a weapon of
punishment, and much more so that of the god Priapus in whose
honour were compiled obscene verses titled *priapeia*, through which
ran a distinct vein of sadism. Thus the simple garden god who was
but a scarecrow was converted, by the coarse thinking of his worhip-
pers, into a symbol of their own sexuality, so that the cult, in course
of time, increased in crudity. From the pen of the Patrician poet-
dramatist, Petronius, a favourite of Nero, came the *Satyricon* in which
he cleverly parodied the cult in a scene in which Pannychis, a girl of
seven, is deflorated by Giton, a boy of the same age.

We saw that in the worship of Liber obscene jesting played an important part as well as the garlanding of the phallus by a respectable matron. This was probably a deliberate belittling of her social status, for such denigration was exaggerated in the Roman *Saturnalia*. On the first day, master and servant reversed their normal roles amidst feasting and revelry. A remote link with this custom is that which prevails in the British Army on Christmas Day when the officers serve the men their food and are often made fun of. To preside over the *Saturnalia*, for a month, a king or lord was elected who had the privilege of doing whatever he wished for the period of his 'reign', after which he was put to death. During the Saturnalian revels, men and women undoubtedly mated promiscuously, whether married or single.

The Worship of Cybele

Kiefer reminds us that Bachofen says somewhere: "'It is by its religions that the East seeks to impose a second yoke on the West.'" With this one cannot but agree implicitly. All of today's existing religions have started in the East, right up to Christianity which was founded by a mid-Eastern Jew. Only offshoots of old religions have originated in the West. It has always been the present writer's contention that the essence of Christianity has never been grasped in the West for the Occidental mind is not subtle enough to penetrate the mysticism of the Oriental mind and its philosophies.

The worship of the goddess Cybele was definitely imported by Rome from Asia Minor after the wars with Hannibal, some two centuries before Christ. According to Livy, the *Decemviri*, or twelve men who acted as council or ruling power in Rome, had discovered the following prophesy in the Sibylline books which were a collection of oracles belonging to the Roman State: "Whenever a foreign foe brings war to Italy, he can be conquered and driven out if the Idæan mother is brought from Pessinus to Rome. Accordingly, the *Magnus Mater* or Mighty Mother was brought to the Eternal City and placed in the temple of Victory on the Palatine, the greatest miracle occurring when the ship bearing the statue got stuck on a shoal in the Tiber but started to float again when, as mentioned in a previous chapter Claudia Quinta, whose chastity was suspect, called upon the goddess to help her prove her innocence by letting the vessel float anew.

It was decreed that the cult of Cybele was to be celebrated only by Phrygian priests and priestesses called the *galli* who had accompanied the images. No Roman was to walk in the procession or worship with the frenzy of the Phrygians. As the procession wended its way to the tune of flutes and the beating of drums, the priest and priestess of the cult asked for alms for Cybele.

The priests of the Cybele cult were eunuchs. This was probably due to the idea of mortification of the flesh which is to be found in most religions including earlier Christianity. Fasting, celibacy, self-flagellation, and other rigours of the flesh, all belong to this category. The priests not only indulged in frenzied self-castration, but also dedicated their lopped-off genitals to Cybele. A ram's or bull's blood served the purpose of baptism of blood which was part of the ritual. The eunuch priests were following an example of Attis of legendary fame who is said to have castrated himself for love of the goddess as the following lines from Catallus indicate:

" *Over the billows Attis fled swift on a hurrying keel,*
till with eager step he hastened into the Phrygian grove,
to find the hidden sanctuary deep in the holy forest :
There the madness whipped his mind, there his spirit raved,
there with the flintblade's heavy blow he cut away his manhood.
Now when he saw his body stripped of all that made it man,
and the blood-gouts dripping freshly on the soil beneath,
he grasped (his hands were woman's hands) the rapid kettledrum,
the kettledrum and the trumpet, the sacred rites of Cybele,
shaking and sounding the hollow hide of a bull in his tender hands,
and thus he sang, trembling and pale, before his wild company :
' Up and away to the tall groves of holy Cybele . . .
you men-women, exiled folk, strange in a strange land,
following my leadership, companions of my worship.
With me you bore the rush of the brine and the wild ocean savagery,
with me unmanned your bodies in your hatred
*   of love and Venus . . . '*
Thus he cried to his company, proud of his bastard womanhood . . .
swiftly the unmanned priests followed their leader's precipitate pace."

The priests of Cybele are said to have been homosexual and to have indulged in sexual relations with peasant youths. Being eunuchs, anal intercourse in which they were the passive partners, was obviously one of the ways of sexual appeasement left to them.

Cults of Isis and the ' Bona Dea '

Isis, like her male counterpart, Osiris, was an Egyptian " goddess of crops and cultivation ". Later, she became a patroness of sea-voyagers and a law-giver, as well as a match-making deity who brought men and women together in the interests of procreation. With the introduction of her cult the Romans brought home yet another Eastern religion. However, it was not officially recognised except by Caligula. His predecessor, Tiberius, had even destroyed one of the shrines of Isis and cast her image into the waters of the Tiber because the priests of the cult had attempted a sexual offence on a noblewoman.

Many scholars opine that worship of Isis was a sexual cult. The Roman historian, Juvenal, certainly called the priestesses ' bawds '.

In the days of the later Roman Empire, the worship had a tremendous hold on the populace, probably because it facilitated adulterous liaisons and fornications. Little, however, is known of the cult with any historical accuracy. The theory that it was a sexual cult is contradicted by the verses of Tibullus and Propertius who complain, respectively, of " ritual nights spent on a lonely bed ", and " . . . What benefit to you, if girls sleep lonely ? " when their wives force them to sleep by themselves. Apparently a degree of asceticism was demanded of the devotees. But one is tempted to ask whether this was for the sake of asceticism itself, or merely a temporary measure to increase cupidity, at some temple ceremonial, for tribadistic practices, as only women practised the cult in secret ?

The *Bona Dea* or the Good Goddess and her cult seem to have been introduced to Rome in about 272 B.C. According to Plutarch, the Phrygians claimed that she was the mother of their King Midas of the golden touch; the Romans associated her with a dryad or nymph of Faunus; the Greeks declared her to be one of the mothers of Bacchos or Bacchus their god of grape and wine.

This cult again was confined to women, and has been suspected of having been tribadistic. At the time of the *Bona Dea* festival, the women would segregate themselves in tents with vine twigs for roofs, or in the home of a consul or prætor who, along with all other males, would leave the house with his wife in charge of the ceremonies.

In contradiction to Plutarch's description is that of Juvenal whom Keifer quotes as declaring:

> " *The rites of the Good Goddess! Shrieking flutes*
> *excite the women's loins; wine and the trumpet*
> *madden him, whirling and shrieking, rapt*
> *by Priapus. Then, then, their hearts are blazing*
> *with lust, their voices stammer with it, their wine*
> *gushes in torrents down their soaking thighs . . .*
> *This is no mimicry, the thing is done*
> *in earnest : even Priam's aged loins*
> *and Nestor cold with age would burn to see it.*
> *Their itching cannot bear delay : this is sheer Woman,*
> *shrieking and crying everywhere in the hall,*
> *' It is time, let in the men !' The lover sleeps—*
> *then let him snatch a greatcoat, hurry here.*
> *No? Then they rush upon the slaves. Not even*
> *slaves? Then a scavenger comes off the streets . . . "*

Eventually, we are told, if no men can be found, the women use an ass as a substitute. Whether this is a poetic prank on Juvenal's part is hard to say. Plutarch, a contempory, certainly does not share the view, and even tells us that the Consul's mother or wife performed, every year, a sacrifice to *Bona Dea* in the presence of the Vestal Virgins.

This section on Roman orgies could well end with their festival
of the *Lupercalia* celebrated in the middle of the month equivalent to
our February. In the course of the festivities, especially the games in
the arena, the young male participants, scantily clad in girdles round
their waists and genitals, lashed freely with their whips the women
who crossed their path, for superstition ordained that a barren woman,
thus flogged, would become fertile.

On their part, the women, also in flimsy apparel, no doubt having
faith in the superstition, rather than with any masochistic intent,
courted the stinging kisses of the whips, particularly on their bellies,
believing that these scourgings from the *luperci*, as those wielding the
whip were called, would open their wombs. Thus in Act 1, Scene 2, of
Shakespeare's **Julius Cæsar,** we are presented with the following
spectacle:

Cæsar: Calpurnia.
Calpurnia: Here, my lord.
Cæsar: Stand you directly in Antonio's way,
           When he doth run his course.—Antonius.
Antonius: Cæsar, my lord.
Cæsar: Forget not, in your speed, Antonius,
           To touch Calpurnia; for our elders say
           The barren, touched in this holy chase,
           Shake off their sterile curse.

This Roman superstition was connected with the goddess Juno
who decreed, "A hairy goat shall leap the Roman wife", in the days
of Romulus, when barrenness afflicted the Roman women and they
and their husbands prayed to Juno seeking her help. Accordingly, the
thongs used for flogging barren women with, were made from the
hide of goats.

CHAPTER 13

MEDIÆVAL, RENAISSANCE, AND VICTORIAN ORGIES

Mediæval and Renaissance Morality—Immorality of the Clergy— Mediæval Flagellomania—Subduing the Wicked Flesh—The Witch Hunt : ' Incubi ' and ' Succubi '—The Witches' Hammer—The ' Holy' Inquisition—Torture in the Name of Christianity—Farcical and Unjust Trials by Ecclesiastical Courts—The Inquisition's Orgies of Torture and Brutality—' The Iron Mother '—The ' Auto-da-fé ' —The Burning of Heretics—The Feast of Fools, May Games, and ' Choreomania '—Kissing the Devil's Rump—Masques and Carnivals —A Victorian Orgy : Jack the Ripper—Killer selects Prostitutes for his Butchery—Martha Turner's Death from Thirty-nine Wounds— Mary Nicholls's Throat slit from Ear to Ear—Annie Chapman's Throat severed from Trunk—' Leather Apron ' Ripper—George Bernard Shaw enters the Fray—Elizabeth Stride's Murder disturbed —Killer removes Catherine Eddowes's Kidney and Entrails—Jack the Ripper chooses his own Nickname—Letters and Verses from the Ripper—Queen Victoria takes an Interest in the Ripper Case—Mary Kelly hacked by Ripper's Butchery—Jack or ' Jill ' the Ripper ?— Individual Orgy on Grand Guignol Scale.

IN the paganism of the Greeks there was no trace of a guilt complex. Among the Romans, too, it was missing at least as far as their debaucheries went; but in them, due to the vein of sadism that ran through their licentious practices, the concept of sin emerged. This concept gathered strength by slow degrees in the early years of Christianity when even the lay clergy paid but little attention to the sexual prohibitions that the Church tried to impose on her followers, despite the fact that the prohibitions were not particularly stringent.

Mediæval and Renaissance Morality

The defiance of its taboos, especially by the priestly orders, led the Church, in time, to impose on a heretofore matristic society patristic restrictions of great severity. Thus was born a new guilt-ridden culture. Sexuality lost its former robustness and became a craven

211

thing ashamed of its own shadow and displaying psychoneurotic symptoms. These times, spreading over centuries, deservedly earned the name of the 'Dark Ages'.

We have noted, in previous chapters, the licentiousness of the early mediæval centuries. Lechery ran riot and the court cases of the time reveal incest, adultery, and homosexuality, among the besetting sins of the age. Prostitution was openly tolerated and even Thomas Aquinas concedes, as late as the thirteenth century, that it helped to check general immorality by protecting, to a certain extent, family morality. Ecclesiastical celibacy was not strictly enjoined till about the eleventh century, and the campaign on its behalf was not even started till the fourth century. One of its strongest supporters, St. Paul, preferred to choose married men with families as bishops in the very early years of Christianity.

The lax moral outlook was reflected in dress, men wearing coats that left their buttocks practically uncovered, their genitals being outlined in a *braguette*, a kind of tight bag or pouch. Nudity was not frowned upon at this stage. The Queen of Ulster and the ladies of her court appeared before Cuchulainn with their breasts bare, and even raised their skirts to expose their genitals as a mark of respect. Ordinarily, the women wore their dresses tight over their hips, and laced their breasts high so that their form was prominently outlined.

Pious Christian historians, mostly of later periods, particularly the prudes of Victorian times, have depicted mediæval knights as Galahads of purity and good intent, a highly glossed over picture, for, in actuality, they were as lecherous as the rest of the men of the times. Burgo Partridge, in **A History of Orgies,** quotes Traill and Mann as saying: " ' to judge from contemporary poems and romances, the first thought of every knight on finding a lady unprotected, was to do her violence ' ". He goes on to add: " and Gawain, the alleged paragon of knightly chivalry, raped Gran de Lis, despite her screams and struggles, when she refused an invitation to sleep with him. Celtic society remained, in spite of the prohibitions of the Church, essentially tolerant in its moral outlook and general character, and, as during the pre-Christian period, much of the running was made by women. Amazingly few of the clergy seemed able or willing to swallow their own medicine, and, like the sheep they sought to lead, they remained unpricked by guilt."

We have already dealt in earlier chapters with the debaucheries of Mediæval and Renaissance priests, bishops, and popes, such as the Bishop of Liege who fathered sixty-five bastards in the reign of Henry III; John XXIII who was deposed because he admitted to having committed adultery, incest, and even murder; the Bishop of Sens, who, in the tenth century, drove the monks away from St. Peter's Abbey and used it as a harem for his many concubines, and last but not least, Alexander VI whose papal orgies with prostitutes, and incest with his own daughter, Lucrezia, have been narrated elsewhere. We must here deal with other phenomena of the Dark Ages and the Renaissance which were orgies not so much of sexual fulfilment as of sexual denial manifesting perverse aberrations of the sex urge such as acute sadism, masochism, and brutality.

Mediæval Flagellomania

Subduing the lustful flesh is a part of the Christian creed. In mediæval times, the flesh was humbled by means of torture, the self-inflicted variety being mostly flagellation. Monks under vows of celibacy, quelled the voice of carnal lust by whipping themselves merci-lessly. It was, of course, a subtle form of masochism, for religious ecstasy can turn into psychopathic frenzy.

Peter the Hermit who lived in the days of the Crusades, resorted to self-flagellation when any attractive female aroused his libido. While reciting no less than thirty psalms, St. Rudolphe flogged himself. St Dominic was known to scourge his nude body with birch-rods while reciting the psalter in its entirety as many as three times. St. Lewis Gonzaga scourged himself till he was covered with weals and the blood flowed, and not only did St. Francis de Sales practise self-flagellation as late as the latter half of the sixteenth century, but also recommended this 'salutary' custom for others who wished to subdue the wicked flesh. Female penitents were not wanting in such ardour, and Catherine of Cordova is said to have employed a scourge with hooks to humble her flesh.

Orders of Flagellants arose, and Mediæval Europe saw the spec-tacle of these flesh-quellers parading in procession through the streets whipping one another's bared backs. In the heart of the town they would prostrate themselves and wield their whips mercilessly on one another. Mass flagellation became a cult. When the Great Plague of 1259 swept the district of Perugia in Italy, the Hermit of Umbria, one Fasani, went around preaching atonement through self-torture. Northern Italy became the scene of innumerable flagellants roaming around, naked to the waist, and scourging themselves with vicious whips, twigs, and sticks. Mass hysteria swept the land and more and more fresh 'blood' was recruited to ooze out in copious streams of mutual and self-flagellation.

Flagellomania came in recurrent waves to Europe, increasing in intensity after any natural catastrophe. Thus in the fourteenth century, when the Black Death, tornado-like, swept through Europe, flagellants went about throwing themselves prone in a circle on the ground, in a position befitting the sins of which he or she repented. Thus Edwin J. Henri, in his treatise on corporal punishment titled **The Kiss of the Whip,** tells us that the perjuror would lie on his side, the adulteress face downwards, the murderer prone on his back. Then amidst the singing of psalms, a priest or sometimes a city official would send his whip singing through the air to sting the exposed flesh of the penitents, and fill the ether with the sound of lamentations.

The penitents established a kind of brotherhood, swearing life-
long fealty to one another with the promise of fraternal violence in
the community. There was no doubt a sado-masochistic hysteria in
all their proceedings. Many there were who looked sternly at these
gruesome spectacles of flagellation and strove to have them abolished.
In Tarragona, Narbonne, and Toulouse, they were forbidden, while
Uberto Pallavicini of Milan is described by Henri as having had three
gibbets erected by the roadside to await the bodies of those who dared
to attempt to spread their masochistic cult in the neighbourhood.

The attitude of the Church towards these practices was ambivalent
and altered from time to time. Benedict XII ordered that absences
from monasteries should, on the return of the absentees, be punished
with a beating with the *ferula*. To mitigate the severity of the penalty,
it was ordered that the instrument of chastisement should not be
handled by a young man, and that during the administration of such
a punishment on a brother, the others should sit with heads bowed and
eyes covered.   Gradually the Church began to find that the self-
imposed penances were a threat to its own authoritarianism.   Hence
in 1350, Pope Clement VI ordered the churches in every country to
stamp out such practices.

Restrictive codes do not always achieve the end at which they
aim.   For at least another couple of centuries, despite the measures
taken by the Church, the orders of flagellants continued along their
dolorous way.   The last mass wave of flagellomania appeared in
France in the sixteenth century.   But, according to Henri, the public
penances, bringing together as they did men and women, often stark
naked, resulted in sexual orgies on an unprecedented scale.

The Witch Hunt: 'Incubi' and 'Succubi'

The early, almost the middle, centuries of the present Millennium
were literally ' bedevilled ', for the curious superstition arose that the
devil and his evil spirits had decided to indulge in sexual intercourse
with mortals.   As the devil could not transact his business single-
handed, he employed assistants.   A male *incubus* was supposed to visit
a woman by night and perform coitus with her, while the female
succubus would do likewise with a man, though less frequently.   These
incubi and *succubi* were nocturnal visitors from the world of evil
spirits, but the devil also had his assistants among humans who were
called witches.

Though even young women were often accused of witchcraft,
witches were generally old crones.   Fantastic though it may sound
today, belief in the Witches' Sabbath became firm-rooted, and it was
held that they could brew love philtres and magic potions in the
interests of fornication and adultery.   At their harrowing trials the
poor creatures were often threatened with torture when not actually

submitted to it, and browbeaten into making false confessions of intercourse with the devil. Thus we are told, in Richard Lewinsohn's **A History of Sexual Customs,** that in Toulouse, in 1275, "the accused, one Angèle de Labarthe, ' confessed ' that she had had sexual intercourse with the devil in person and had given birth to a monster with a wolf's head and a serpent's tail. Since this monster, her own child, had fed on the flesh of children, she had been forced to kill other children."

From the highly imaginary and forced self-accusations thus obtained, a monstrous composite picture of the devil arose: He was supposed to have an enormous phallus shod with iron or encased in fish-scales and his sperm was freezingly cold. He even had the reputation of being able to have coitus with a virgin and to leave her hymen intact despite his oversized sexual equipment. The strangest legend of all to grow around him was the following as described by Lewinsohn:

" The devil's particular sexual sphere, however, was his hindquarters, in which lustful women took especial delight. Numerous illustrations from the Middle Ages show women kneeling down to peer beneath the devil's tail. If they succeeding in kissing the orifice, mysterious powers were believed to be conferred upon them. If anyone wanted more of the devil, it was necessary to conclude a pact with him. This was not always so formal as in Goethe's ' Faust '. Often it was enough if would-be witches gave the devil four hairs as pledges for their souls. Blood-pacts with the devil were not always necessary, although it was, of course, more convincing to have something put down in red and white. Documents of this kind were at times produced in evidence at witch trials."

The acute consciousness of the existence of the devil derived from older religions, particularly from Mithraism and Zoroastrianism which prevailed in ancient Persia. Zoroaster, the Persian Prophet, had preached a dualism in which Ahura Mazda, the power of Good and Light, was opposed by Ahrimaan devan, the power of evil, in other words, the devil. Even men such as Thomas Aquinas and Albert Magnus, theologians of the thirteenth century, firmly believed in witches.

Witch-trials originated in Southern France, and just as the craze was beginning to die out, there were fresh outbreaks of witch-hunts in the fourteenth and fifteenth centuries, which swept across France, Germany, and Italy, and spread to other countries of Europe. Often the accusation of witchcraft was used merely for States to rid themselves of persons they considered undesirable, either politically or otherwise. The outstanding example of such injustice was that of the simple French peasant girl, Joan of Arc, who, though she had led the French to victory against the English, was eventually burnt at the stake, under the pretext that the voices she claimed to have heard had been those of the devil's advocates.

Pope Innocent VIII, no model of virtue himself, issued a Bull in 1484 expressing fear of people consorting with *incubi* and *succubi*. He enrolled the services of two notorious witch-hunters, Jakob Sprenger and Heinrich Institoris, who carried on their diabolical brand of activities in Germany, the former in the North, the latter in the South, and jointly these sadists produced the *Witches' Hammer* narrating the supposed doings of witches. In the third part of their work of mischief, they indicated the means of trapping witches through legal procedure. Thus if an accused denied belief in witches, she was accused of heresy, and if she admitted such belief she was accused of dabbling in the black arts. " If she tried to deny her guilt.", Lewinsohn tells us, " she was to be put to the torture, and other witches, especially those hostile to her, called in evidence against her. If there was still any doubt of her guilt, a judgment of God, similar to the old Babylonian ordeal by water against adulteresses, was to be invoked. She was bound hand and foot, and cast into the water. If she sank, she was a witch; if she floated, this was proof that the water rejected her baptism, so she was still a witch. A woman was thus drowned for a witch on the Hela Peninsula, near Danzig, as late as 1836."

Even the matristic Popes of the Renaissance such as Leo X, Alexander VI, and Julius II, endorsed the Witches' Hammer. The Roman Catholic Church was not alone in its persecution of witches. The poor creatures were also the bait of Protestants, and, according to Lewinsohn, " In England witch-hunts reached their climax under Queen Elizabeth ".

The 'Holy' Inquisition

In the first Millennium after Christ, the Christian Church was fairly tolerant towards heretics who did not accept the orthodox teachings of the Church. Under Constantine, the Edict of Milan displayed the Church's tolerance in this matter. The few cases of execution of heretics prior to 1000 A.D., were imposed by lay authorities. However, the majority of heretics were punished by banishment, sometimes scourging, and deprivation of the posts they held. In 1049, at Rheims, the Church Council declared that only excommunication was to be the lot of the heretics, and this ruling was accepted with but slight alterations by the Council at Toulouse in 1119, and twenty years later by the Lateran Council.

On the head of Innocent III must rest the responsibility for making the Church a party to the punishment of heretics. He declared heresy to be as treacherous a revolt against God as treason was against the State, and called upon the rulers of Europe to suppress heresy. Though the Church thenceforth took a hand in persecuting heretics, sentences against them were still inflicted by lay authorities. It was Pope Gregory IX who introduced inquisition of heretics by monks, particularly the Dominicans, in 1231. Thus it was the thirteenth century which saw the start of the 'Holy' Inquisition with its subsequent tortures and malpractices that were veritable orgies of sadism.

The trials of the 'Holy' Inquisition were travesties of justice. The victims were arrested secretly, generally by dead of night, and tried secretly too. The charges against them were revealed to them, but they were not told who their accusers were. If a witness refused to give evidence, he was charged with heresy himself. In 1252, Pope Innocent IV introduced a Bull permitting the torture of the accused whose only defence was the making of a statement when first examined. Only by denouncing other heretics and renouncing his own heresy, could an accused person win his freedom. The penalties were varied, ranging from imprisonment, scourging, and penances, to burning and the payment of fines. Imprisonment was of two varieties, the severer one being in a dungeon to which the prisoner was fettered.

The fate of heretics whose heresy was considered to merit the capital penalty, is well described by John Swain in **The Pleasures of the Torture Chamber**: " The victims liable to capital punishment were handed over to the secular arm to be dealt with, and at the same time the inquisitors made an earnest and touching supplication to the secular authorities to be merciful. If this exhortation was taken literally the secular authorities were guilty of heresy ! "

Before the thirteenth century, there were but few trials for heresy, the most conspicuous being Henry II's condemnation of some heretics in the second half of the previous century. In the first quarter of the fourteenth century, the Templars were arrested by Edward II, but due to the hostility displayed towards the inquisitors by the populace, the Pope wisely forbade the use of torture. In the seventeenth century, Charles II curtailed the power of the ecclesiastical courts, depriving them of unlimited authority to excommunicate those who were found guilty of heresy or atheism.

In Bavaria, an ecclesiastical court was set up in every important town, as Duke Albert wished to restore the kingdom to Catholicism. Ironically enough, Nuremberg, the scene of Nazi trials in our own time, had such a court and instruments of torture of great refinement. In Spain, the Inquisition introduced by Pope Gregory IX around 1238, continued to be treated with hostility by the people for over two centuries, till King Ferdinand and Queen Isabella gave it a national flavour in 1480. Thus was born the loathsome Spanish Inquisition which revelled in its orgies of false indictments and brutality till suppressed by Napoleon in 1808, only to be revived by Ferdinand VII about six years later. Its popularity fluctuated thereafter, till it eventually vanished in 1834. Not till 1816 was torture done away with by the offices of the Inquisition all over Europe.

Swain provides us with some gruesome examples of the orgies of torture perpetrated by the Spanish Inquisition: We are told that lay officers who collaborated with the Holy Office, would arrest heretics by night. Resistance resulted in the victim being gagged, his mouth being blocked with a pear-shaped instrument. The trial took place before three inquisitors and the secretary, the Sheriff, other secular officers, and priests. The hall was draped in black, the only light entering in through the door. A crucifix was hung under a black velvet canopy, and three or six candles burned on the Altar.

Swain goes on to give us some instances of the nature of trials and the punishments awarded: For talking derisively of the Pope, a woman was so severely whipped that she died six days later. For sodomy between a friar and a boy of fourteen, the former was awarded one year's confinement in his own convent; but the poor boy of tender years was whipped through the streets of the town and made to wear a mitre into which feathers had been stuck. The lad succumbed the next day to his injuries. A priest, one Father Pueyo, fornicated with no less than five nuns and was brought before the inquisitors. He explained that as they had, when appointing him Confessor to the nuns, beseeched him to take good care of them, he had done so in every respect possible. For this " impious jest ", the accused was freed even from his own penance ! The partiality shown to the clergy betrays the mock justice of those who sat to judge others in the name of God, for offences against that God.

The Inquisition's Orgies of
Torture and Brutality

Tortures were divided into five degrees: The first degree was merely the threat of torture. The second degree was being taken to the scene of the torture. The third degree consisted of the victim being stripped and bound, and the fourth was being hoisted on the rack. The last and fifth degree was ' squassation ' in which the victim's hands were bound behind him and his feet tied with heavy weights. He was then lifted till his head was in level with a pulley, and kept hanging for a time so that the weights at his feet would stretch his limbs and joints. Then, all of a sudden, the rope would be slackened and he would be let down to almost but not quite floor level, the jerks causing his limbs to become disjointed, and the weights round his feet causing him excruciating agony.

Sometimes the victim's feet were greased with lard and then placed near an iron chafindish filled with lighted coals. Then there was the 'Wooden Horse', hollow like a trough, with a bar in the centre. On this the victim was stretched out, his head buried in the contraption lower than his feet, his weight on the iron bar. Cords of strings, drawn by screws at regular distances, cut into the flesh of the thighs and arms and bruised the shins. His mouth and nostrils were coverd with a thin cloth to make it difficult for him to breathe, while a trickle of water, faint but continuous, would be made to descend on the cloth and into the victim's mouth making it practically impossible for him to breathe, his mouth being choked with water and his nostrils with the cloth which would be withdrawn after a time, being covered with blood.

All the instruments of torture that human ingenuity could devise were utilised by the 'Holy' Inquisition. Perhaps the best known was the 'Iron Mother', a statue of the Virgin Mary, a description of which is quoted by Swain from 'The Percy Anecdotes': "'In a subterraneous vault, adjoining the secret audience chamber, stood in a recess in the wall a wooden statue made by the hands of monks, representing the Virgin Mary. A gilded glory beamed round her head, and she held a standard in her right hand. It immediately struck the spectator, notwithstanding the ample folds of the silk garment which fell from the shoulders on both sides, that she wore a breastplate. Upon a closer examination it appeared that the whole front of the body was covered with extremely sharp nails, and small daggers or blades of knives with the points projecting outwards. The arms and hands had joints, and their motions were directed by machinery placed behind the partition . . . " The arms would extend and the victim would be thrust into the embrace of the Iron Virgin whose arms would clasp him, the daggers and blades piercing his flesh, as she drew him nearer and nearer in a grip of vice.

After the trial of a victim with its manifold tortures, the last phase was the handing over of the victim to the secular authority for the purpose of execution: the *auto-da-fé*. This was always held on a Sunday, and preferably on a day of festivity. Dominican friars would lead a procession of penitents wearing sleeveless black coats, with unshod feet and with candles in their hands. Penitents who had narrowly escaped penalty by burning wore black coats painted with flames whose points ran downwards, followed by those about to be burned with similar coats but with the flames pointing upwards. Last of all came those whose doctrines clashed strongly with the Church's and these had devils, serpents, and curs, painted on their breasts. Jesuits marched alongside them entreating them to abjure. Inquisitors on mules and the Inquisitor General, astride a white horse, brought up the rear of the ghoulish processions. After reading of the sentence of death a priest would hand over the condemned to the secular authorities, who would lead them in chains to the gaol, after which the civil judge would try them. Those of them who chose to die in the Roman Catholic faith, would first be strangled and then burnt; those who, like the Jews or Freemasons, clung to beliefs other than those of the Catholic Church, would be burnt alive in the name of the Saviour who died on a Cross to redeem mankind. Truly the 'Holy' Inquisitors knew not what they did.

One stake per each condemned person would be ready at the place of execution, and after those who were about to die had mounted the stakes, the cry would go forth: "Let the dogs' beards be made". This would be done, as Swain tells us, " . . . by thrusting flaming bunches of furze, fastened to long poles, against their beards, till their faces are burnt black, the surrounding populace rending the air with

the loudest acclamations of joy. At last fire is set to the furze at the
bottom of the stake, over which the victims are chained, so high that
the flame seldom reaches higher than the seat they sit on, and thus
they are rather roasted than burnt. Although there cannot be a more
lamentable spectacle and the sufferers continually cry out as long as
they are able, 'Pity for the love of God ! ' yet it is beheld by persons
of all ages and both sexes with transports of joy and satisfaction."

That these barbarian inquisitors of the Dark Ages should have
dared to pluck the mote from the eye of the pagans of classical times
boggles the imagination, and one cannot but compare these 'stalwart'
Roman Catholics and their sadistic, brutal orgies to the spectacle, if
such can be imagined, of Satan casting out the devil. Each flame that
burnt a heretic, each screw and mechanical device that scourged human
flesh, was surely a fresh nail driven into the flesh of the crucified
Christ, and every 'Christian' inquisitor a Judas betraying his Master's
command to love his neighbour as himself.

To such inhuman inquisitors, Oscar Wilde might well have
dedicated these lines from his **Ballad of Reading Gaol :**

> " *This too I know—and wise it were*
> *If each could know the same—*
> *That every prison that men build*
> *Is built with bricks of shame,*
> *And bound with bars lest Christ should see*
> *How men their brothers maim.*

> " *With bars they blur the gracious moon,*
> *And blind the goodly sun :*
> *And they do well to hide their Hell,*
> *For in it things are done*
> *That Son of God nor son of Man*
> *Ever should look upon !* "

And for every victim of these sadistic, brutal torturers who dared
to call themselves Christians, Wilde might justly have written this
epitaph :

> " *And he of the swollen purple throat,*
> *And the stark and staring eyes,*
> *Waits for the holy hands that took*
> *The thief to Paradise;*
> *And a broken and a contrite heart*
> *The Lord will not despise.*"

The Feast of Fools, May Games, and Choreomania

Many Christian festivities were extensions of old Pagan revelries.
The Feast of Fools and the May Games were not of a truly religious
character but rather cathartic. Celebration of the former was mostly

by the lower ranks of the clergy who parodied the religion to which they belonged.   It was a French festival full of horseplay.   Thus whoever celebrated mass, would bray three times like an ass instead of using the appropriate religious phrase.   The priests donned grotesque masks and often wore women's costumes thus adding a touch of transvestitism to the custom.   As the Feast of Fools corresponded with the Feast of the Circumcision, Partridge observes: "Transvestitism was a universal feature of this debauch, which, if one remembers that circumcision is a vestigal form of castration, is not surprising."

A 'Lord of Misrule' was elected to preside over the antics and the gaily decked transvestite throng wended its way to the church performing there a parody of the usual mass, after which they would caper round the church and then camp in the churchyard.   Denunciations of the feast were plentiful, and in 1445 bishops received a strongly worded one from the Faculty of Theology in the University of Paris. However, the Church had to tolerate it willy-nilly, and it continued till the seventeenth century.   The burlesquing of religious customs in the church and its precincts was often followed by the beating of men and women in the streets, all, of course, in a spirit of tomfoolery.   In Bohemia a clerk would be dressed as a bishop and led to the church sitting on a donkey, facing its tail.   Torches were substituted for candles and priests wore their habits inside out.

The complaint made by the Faculty of Theology, refuted the argument that the Feast of Fools was of a cathartic nature   Yet the custom survived, and when it finally declined in France, it was succeeded by a similar festivity called the *Mère Folle*, the title role of course being played by a man in feminine garb.   It was Louis XIII who suppressed the society in the opening years of the seventeenth century.   In England, its equivalent had vanished in the previous century, in the reign of Queen Elizabeth, but its substitute, the 'Abbot of Misrule', survived.

Another relic of Pagan times was the Worship of the Horned God resembling the *Dionysia* and the *Priapeia*.   Women dressed as witches arrived and bestowed on the posterior of the man dressed as the devil, the Obscene Kiss, sometimes a mask being tied to his buttocks so that it lightened the witches' task.   On the other hand, he could order them to kiss him on any region of his body where he might desire such a token of affection.   It has been recorded that the feast of the Horned Deity was accompanied by dancing and copulation which was promiscuous.

Dancing was greatly frowned upon by the mediæval Church. Calvin described it as 'the mischief of mischiefs', that it was conducive to lust, and that those who indulged in the pastime were mad.   It is likely that nudity accompanied dancing at the time.   The dancers were referred to as 'choreomaniacs' and accused of gross immorality, and of demoniac possession resulting through coitus with *incubi* and *succubi*.

The May Games, like Easter and Christmas, were survivals of fertility rites. Families repaired to the woods to bring back the gaily decked ox and the maypole as described elsewhere in this work. Promiscuous eroticism prevailed a great deal among the young men and women on these jaunts, helped by the general merriment and the dancing and drinking.

Masques and Carnivals

In the opening years of the sixteenth century, Pope Alexander VI, father of Lucrezia and Cesare Borgia, witnessed a masque in St. Peter's Square in which false noses shaped like phalli of extraordinary proportions were worn by many of the revellers, some of whom were mounted on little donkeys. In England, by the next century, masquerades attained great popularity, and the elite of society appeared decked out in fancy dress, some as gypsies, some as priests, gnomes, and gods of antiquity. In the eighteenth century, masques, or fancy-dress balls, as they came to be called, won a reputation for spreading vice and immorality.

Roman carnivals presented the singular spectacle of Christian festivities through which ran a strong undercurrent of paganism. The Forum in Rome was the scene of the sacrifice of a bull during the papacy of Leo X. Fancy dress was assumed by many who participated in the carnival, and prostitutes joined the revels so that the celebrations achieved an orgiastic character. Faces were disguised by masks which further promoted sexual abandon. Lawlessness reigned for the three or four days that such carnivals lasted, and even vendettas were carried out under the protection of the masks. In Florence the Carnival attained a high peak of licentiousness.

A Victorian Orgy :
Jack the Ripper

Both permissive and repressive periods have their quota of orgies. On the whole, the former tend to breed group or mass orgies, while the latter often give rise to individual orgies. We shall deal with one such individual orgy in the restrictive period of the Victorian era—the murders of Jack the Ripper which remain unsolved in the annals of Scotland Yard:

In the year 1888, a crime wave had swept through the East End of London, in such districts as Whitechapel, Stepney, and Spitalfields. On the night of Monday, August 6th, of the same year, East Enders were returning from their Bank Holiday jaunts to Hackney Fields or Epping Forest, many congregating in the public houses for a last drink before closing time which was 1 a.m. at the time. In the ' Angel and Crown ', near Whitechapel Church, a soldier from the garrison at the Tower of London, was drinking with a local prostitute separated from her husband. She was Martha Turner, alias Martha Tabram, about thirty-five years old according to police records, who lived at No. 4, Star Place, off Commercial Road. Also drinking in the same public house were Mr. and Mrs. Mahoney who had returned from a trip to Epping Forest.

When they returned home to No. 47, George Yard Buildings, just after two o'clock, they detected nothing strange or peculiar as they went up the stone stairway. But about an hour and a half later, a cab driver named Albert Crow who lived at No. 35 in the same block of buildings, noticed a body sprawled out on the first landing. Believing it to be someone in a drunken fit, he paid no attention to it. Two doors away from Crow, one John Reeves got up early in the morning with the intention of going to the markets in quest of a job. It was 5 a.m., and as he descended the stairs, he noticed a woman's body in a pool of blood. It was the body of the prostitute Martha Turner. She had apparently been murdered between just past 2 a.m., when the Mahoneys arrived home, and 3.30 a.m., when Crow took the sprawling body on the landing to be that of a drunkard.

Murders not being uncommon in the area, not much notice would have been taken of this one, but for the fact that Dr. Timothy Keleene who examined the dead prostitute's body made an amazing discovery when carrying out the post-mortem: The poor woman had suffered thirteen stab-wounds in the abdomen, nine in the throat, and seventeen near the breasts, thirty-nine wounds in all. An ordinary murderer would scarcely stop to inflict so many wounds. This was the work of a blood-thirsty sadist. The soldier who had been seen with the victim in the ' Angel and Crown ', the previous night, had a perfect alibi— he was able to prove that he had joined his mates by 1.30 a.m.

Dr. Keleene came to the conclusion that the wounds on Martha Turner's body had been inflicted by two weapons, one of them being a knife with a long blade, and the other a surgical instrument. He therefore contended that the murderer had at least a basic grounding in surgery.

Thrawl Street in the East End of London housed many ' sluts ', some of them very young and forced by circumstances to take to the streets. At No. 18, lived Mary Nicholls whose pet name was Polly. She was a woman of forty-two and with not a foe in the world, having a nature that made friends easily. A married woman with five children, her main failing, drink, had been the cause of her separating from her machinist husband.

On the night of Friday, August 31st, about twenty-five days after the murder of Martha Turner, a friend of Polly's, one Emily Holland, encountered her at 2.30 a.m. where Whitechapel Road met Osborne Street, Polly's excuse for being out being that she had no rent money. At 3.15 a.m., a carter called William Cross, walking down Bucks Row in Whitechapel, saw what appeared to him like a tarpaulin lying on the other side of the street. He crossed over, and discovered the object to be a drunken street-walker as he thought. As he looked down on her, another passer-by, John Paul, joined him. Together they lifted the woman in the half-darkness of the early hour. As they did so, Cross cried out that she was bleeding from the throat, and Paul, taking a closer look, exclaimed that she was dead. On the street was a pool of blood where her neck had lain. They quickly fetched the police.

Dr. Lllewellyn, who examined the body, declared that the woman had not been dead for more than half an hour. Yet three police constables and the two discoverers of the body had all passed that way within twenty minutes of the actual killing without seeing or hearing anything. Perhaps the murderer used smelling salts or chloroform before his butchery? Three night watchmen, too, had been in the vicinity, yet had heard no sound.

The body was taken to the old Montagu Street Workhouse and the mortuary attendant actually handled the corpse before the post-mortem, a major blunder. To make matters worse, the pool of blood on the spot where the dead woman had been found was washed away before the Chief Inspector of Scotland Yard arrived ! On lifting the clothes of the murdered victim, a policeman discovered that she had been disembowelled, " ripped from the throat to her belly."

The murdered woman was identified as the popular Polly, or Mary Nicholls, to give her her proper name—yet another prostitute murdered within three hundred yards of Martha Turner's murder less than a month before. Whether one and the same person had committed both murders was a moot point. Both Chief Inspector Abberline and Sir Robert Anderson, Assistant Commissioner of the Metropolitan Police, felt that it was the same killer who was now referred to as the ' Ripper '.

On the other hand, Sir Melville Macnaughten who joined the Criminal Investigation Department as Assistant Chief Constable one year after the Ripper's gruesome activities had ceased, later opined that Polly had been the first of the Ripper's victims. Donald McCormick, author of **The Identity of Jack the Ripper,** quotes Sir Melville as having written: " ' At one time or another fourteen murders were attributed to Jack the Ripper—some before and some after 1888. Suffice it to say that the Whitechapel murderer committed *five* murders and no more.' "

Bucks Row where Polly's body had been found, was often jestingly referred to as ' Killer's Row '; the agitation of the local residents resulted in its being changed to Durward Street.

' Leather Apron ' Ripper

The Whitechapel murders were reported by **The Times** with many a gory detail. Polly's death was attributed to the killer using a shoemaker's knife, and as shoemakers wore leather aprons, Jack the Ripper was often referred to as ' Leather Apron ', and an assortment of women came forth to claim that they had been raped or assaulted by leather-aproned men !

Only about a week after Polly's murder, a little after 6 a.m. on Saturday, September 8th, 1888, Inspector Joseph Chandler was urged by several agitated men who rushed to him as he was strolling near Spitalfields Market, to go with them to the scene of a crime in the small backyard of No. 29, Hanbury Street. The victim, a woman, lay on her back, savagely stabbed with her head almost severed from her body and her clothes in a state of complete disarray. Near the corpse's feet, two farthings, two brass rings, and some pennies and farthings, had been neatly and deliberately laid out. Not far away was a water-soaked leather apron.

On Monday, **The Times** reported that a handkerchief had been found wrapped round the victim's neck as if the murderer had thought he had cut her head loose from her body and had wished the handkerchief to hold it close to the body, which was identified as being that of 'Dark Annie' or Annie Sievey, her real name being Annie Chapman. She was forty-seven, and the widow of an army pensioner who had been a veterinary surgeon, and later a coachman.

Dr. Bagster Phillips who carried out the post-mortem, complained that the body had been stripped and washed before the post-mortem. From his findings, there was no doubt that the same murderer had perpetrated this third crime, but with each murder his brutality had increased. In the case of Martha Turner, the throat had not been cut but the incisions had been made from left to right as if by a left-handed man. Polly's neck had been cut from left to right and ear to ear, while in the latest case it had almost been severed. Another coincidence was that, as in Polly's case, two front teeth were found missing from Annie Chapman's corpse. Incisions in the throat, back, and spine, had all been made from left to right. Two incisions, parallel to each other on the left side of the spine, and but half an inch apart, indicated that the murderer had removed a kidney.

The murderer had apparently stifled his victim's cries because bruises were found on the chin and the jaws, and the tongue was swollen. The killer had employed a sharp knife with a very thin blade at least six or eight inches long, most probably a surgical instrument. Annie Chapman, like the two other victims, had also been a prostitute.

Sensation and controversy raged in the Press. The killer might be a homicidal maniac, a member of the upper classes, or a working man. Even George Bernard Shaw took the opportunity to air his witty views on Capital and Authority in a letter to the **Star,** in which he complained of the callous attitude of the magistrates and judges who in 1886, during the Dock Strike, displayed " . . . open class bias . . . (and) zealously did their worst in the criminal proceedings which followed, behaving, in short, as the propertied class always does behave when the workers throw it into a frenzy of terror by venturing to show their teeth."

At Annie Chapman's inquest, the coroner insisted on Dr. Phillips giving more medical evidence, in the course of which the doctor emphasised, as McCormick reports, "'the deliberate, successful and apparently scientific manner in which the poor woman was mutilated. The murderer showed great anatomical knowledge. I myself could not have performed such surgery, even working at top speed, in under a quarter of an hour. If I had acted deliberately and with the greatest care in removing the organ from the body, it would have taken me the best part of an hour.'"

The coroner's report stated at the end: "The conclusion that the desire was to possess the missing abdominal organ seems overwhelming."

The Autumn of 1888 was one of terror for Londoners. The public houses lost a lot of customers in Whitechapel. Even West End squares were deserted at night. Yet the East End prostitutes who were apparently the killer's marked victims, continued to ply their wares in dark alleys and streets, probably because necessity compelled them to do so.

In the early hours of September 30th, 1888, twenty-two days after Dark Annie's murder, the Ripper struck again—and struck twice within three-quarters of an hour. The first crime was committed in a small court in a quiet thoroughfare in Berner Street which ran from Commercial Road down to the London, Tilbury, and Southend Railway. In the vicinity of the court was a club which was "an offshoot of the Socialist League and a rendezvous of Russians, Poles, and Jews." One of the members, Louis Diemschutz, was in his pony cart on his way home to Berner Street at about 1 a.m. As his pony would not budge at the entrance to the court, Diemschutz dismounted and near the right-hand wall of the court, discovered the murdered body of a woman.

Three doctors examined the corpse. This time, though the throat had been cut, and the incisions revealed the Ripper's scientific touch, the body had been unmutilated. This was probably due to his being disturbed in his nefarious deed by the arrival of Diemschutz. Again nobody in the neighbourhood had heard a cry or an untoward sound.

Within an hour, the Ripper had struck again. Major Smith, Assistant Commissioner of the City of London Police (later, Lieutenant-Colonel Sir Henry Smith who wrote 'From Constable to Commissioner') hurried to Mitre Square, the scene of this latest crime, within the City of London itself. The victim was Catherine Eddowes, a prostitute who had been, but a few hours earlier, under arrest at Bishopsgate Police Station; indeed Major Smith is reported by McCormick as having gone on record as saying that only twenty minutes before being killed, the woman had been under arrest, which was roughly the time it would take to walk down from the Bishopsgate Police Station to Mitre Square. At 1 a.m. she had been released, and at 1.45 a.m. her body was discovered.

Catherine had been living with a labourer named John Kelly and they had both returned from hop-picking in Kent only a few days before her death. Unfortunately, when she parted from Kelly to go to the casual ward while she sent him back to the lodging-house, Major Smith's instructions that every prostitute, in view of the Ripper scare, should be shadowed in dark passages, was not observed by the police. It was Police Constable Watkins who had found her body in Mitre Square at 1.45 a.m.; yet only about a quarter of an hour earlier, he had, he avowed, been in the square.

The killer was clearly a pathological case. He had torn part of Catherine Eddowes's dress before leaving the scene of the crime, and had washed his blood-stained hands in a close off Dorset Street, for Major Smith had actually noticed the blood-stained water while wandering around till six o'clock. The Ripper had wiped his hands on the torn part of Catherine's ' apron ' as McCormick calls it, and had thrown it away probably because he had been disturbed while rinsing his hands.

The apron was " found at 2.55 a.m. in the doorway of a house in Goulstone Street, parallel to Commercial Street, about a third of a mile from Mitre Square and not far from Petticoat Lane. Police Constable Alfred Long who discovered the apron, noticed on the wall of the passage inside the doorway the words: " The Jewes (sic) are not the men to be blamed for nothing."

The writing had not been on the wall till midnight, it was ascertained; therefore it could have been written by the Ripper, particularly as it is recorded that some of the words were a little blood-stained. The Police were convinced that the Ripper had been the scribbler. But Sir Charles Warren, the Commissioner of Police, fearing anti-Semitic riots if the police find got highlighted, had the words rubbed off, or as Major Smith surmised, wiped them off himself, thus destroying what might have been a useful clue.

To return to the first murder of that night in Berner Street, the victim was identified as Elizabeth Stride aged forty-five whose nickname was ' Long Liz '. She had lived in Flower and Dean Street, a hotbed of prostitution, and had herself belonged to the profession like all the murderer's victims. One Mrs. Mary Malcolm, the wife of a tailor in Red Lion Square, claimed that the murdered woman was her sister, Elizabeth Watts, the wife of a wine merchant.

Before Elizabeth's body was discovered by Diemschutz at 1 a.m., a labourer, William Marshall, had seen her being kissed by a man about fifteen minutes earlier. A police constable also maintained having seen the couple. Their descriptions of the man tallied more or less. He was about twenty-eight to thirty years old, about 5 ft. 5 ins. or 8 ins. tall, with a small moustache either brown or dark, with a dark jacket and trousers, and a black cap with a peak. One of them also said that he had carried a parcel with a newspaper wrapping. Other somewhat similar descriptions were provided, and several of them

spoke of the man carrying a black bag. One police constable even
arrested a man carrying such a bag, only to discover at the police
station that he was a respectable doctor living in Brixton.

The murder in Berner Street had obviously been disturbed, for
the Ripper had not mutilated Elizabeth's body as was his wont. But
the lobe of her left ear had been torn. Similarly, the lobe of Catherine
Eddowes's right ear had been cut slantwise, and Dr. F. G. Brown who
carried out the post-mortem on Catherine's body, discovered that the
left kidney and entrails had been removed.

Jack the Ripper chooses
his own Nickname

As a pathological murderer, Jack the Ripper is a highly interesting
case; it is this side of him, with its orgiastic outbursts of murderous
frenzy and mutilation during a repressive era of extreme prudery,
with which we are here concerned, rather than the trails of detection
or his identity which latter still remains a matter of conjecture.

After the murder of Elizabeth Stride and Catherine Eddowes, a
letter signed 'Jack the Ripper' was received by the Editor of the
Central News Agency. This is how the murderer came to be called
by the name that has gone down into the annals of crime history. The
letter is in a vein of flippancy. Towards the end of it, the Ripper
promised that he would clip off the next victim's ears and send them
to the police. One sentence in the letter reveals that he probably had
a grudge against prostitutes, for he says: " I am down on whores and
I shan't quit ripping them till I do get buckled . . . " That is
probably how the theory arose that he, or someone dear to him, had
caught venereal disease from a prostitute and he had taken to assault-
ing members of that profession by way of revenge.

A builder, one George Lark, who was a prominent member of
the Vigilance Committee, received a cardboard with an object that
was supposed to be a kidney, and a note we reproduce from
McCormick's work on the Ripper : " ' From Hell, Mr. Lark, sir, I
send you half the *kidne* I took from one woman, *prasarved* it to you,
tother piece I fried and ate it; it was very nice.' "

When the kidney was examined, the pathological curator of the
London Hospital Museum declared it to be part of the kidney of a
person addicted to drinking, probably a woman of forty-five, and
removed from her body not more than two weeks earlier.

Some of the letters were hoaxes and two of the letters of the
Ripper, which were preserved in the Black Museum of New Scotland
Yard, written in red ink, were eventually removed, and the official
police view was that the correspondence was indeed a hoax. However,
McCormick declares: " I find the hoax theory unsatisfactory. It is
far too glib a method on the part of officials to explain away something for which they had no solution . . . "

Verses also emerged from the killer's pen, of which we quote three samples from McCormick:

> " ' *I'm not a butcher,*
> *I'm not a Yid,*
> *Nor yet a foreign skipper,*
> *But I'm your own light-hearted friend,*
> *Yours truly, Jack the Ripper.*' "

> " ' *Up and down the goddam town*
> *Policemen try to find me.*
> *But I ain't a chap yet to drown*
> *In drink, or Thames or sea.*' "

> " ' *I've no time now to tell you how*
> *I came to be a killer.*
> *But you should know, as time will show,*
> *That I'm society's pillar.*' "

Whether the letters were genuinely the Ripper's penmanship or hoaxes, will always remain a mystery. Over the years, it has been estimated that at least a couple of thousand such letters were received by newspapers and the police, and even ' confessions ' from people claiming to be Jack the Ripper. The last line of the last verse in which he claims to be ' society's pillar ', led to the theory, especially strongly put forward by one Mr. Forbes Winslow who was given to making a scientific study of such letters, being a specialist of mental and nervous diseases, that " the killer was a homicidal maniac of religious views who believed he had a divine mission to fulfil in killing as many whores as possible."

On October 19th, Jack the Ripper again wrote, this time prophesying that on November 9th he would carry out his next killing. Winslow, the specialist, asserted that it was in the same handwriting as that on the wall of the doorway of the house in Goulstone Street after the murder in Mitre Square. Though this had been wiped away, McCormick suggests that Winslow might have read it before it was effaced, as the specialist was in the habit of dashing to the scene and area of the crime. The fact remains that the prophecy in the latest letter came true, and on November 9th the Ripper executed his butchery anew.

Mary Kelly hacked by Ripper's Butchery

Various trails were followed up by the police, but to no avail. Even Queen Victoria wrote to the Home Secretary expressing doubts as to the absolute efficiency of the detective department, and suggesting that more detectives be concentrated in the small area where the crimes recurred.

Only two hundred yards from Hanbury Street where Annie Chapman had been murdered, lay Dorset Street in the parish of Spitalfields. No. 26 in the street was a lodging house for the poor, owned by one John McCarthy. Room No. 13 in the house was occupied by a twenty-five year old girl, Mary Anne, sometimes called Mary Jane, and sometimes Marie Jeannette Kelly. She was both attractive and vivacious and well known in the neighbourhood. Like most prostitutes, she was given to drinking heavily when she could afford it, and this was the reason she seemed to fall out with all the men with whom she lived from time to time. When not living in this manner, she took to the streets.

Mary Kelly, the Irish Catholic whore from Limerick, fell out with her latest paramour, Joseph Barnett, a labourer, because she took another whore to share Room 13 the entrance to which was not in Dorset Street but through Miller's Court, in a dark and dismal side street or lane. On the night of November 8th, which was a Thursday, Mary parted from Barnett who had dropped in on her, at about 7.30 p.m. Later, several people saw Mary in Commercial Street, a bit on the tipsy side. At about 11.45, a neighbour, Mrs. Cox, saw her with a shabbily turned out man who was short and stout. A few minutes later, she heard the girl singing, and saw a light in her room, as she herself went out. The light was no longer there when she returned at approximately 3.10 a.m. At 6 a.m., she heard a man leave Mary Kelly's room.

Later evidence revealed that after Mrs. Cox had gone out at about 12.30 a.m., Mary had also left her room, and had met George Hutchinson, an out-of-work labourer. In the early hours of the morning of Friday, November 9th, Hutchinson who had nowhere to sleep, and was still on the streets, noticed a man at the corner of Commercial Street and Whitechapel Road. He then saw Mary Kelly approaching and hoped she would take him home with her. Instead she asked him for sixpence, and since he could not oblige her, she went her way saying she would have to get the money elsewhere. Hutchinson saw her stop and talk to the man he had already spotted in the corner. He stood watching the two of them, hoping, perhaps, that when she had finished with the customer and earned some money, she might take him into her room for the remaining hours till dawn. But for poor Mary Kelly there was to be no dawn.

As she and her customer came in line with him on the way to Mary's room, Hutchinson was surprised to note that her escort was a man too well dressed for this part of the East End. The stranger was about 5 ft. 6 ins. tall, wore a man's felt hat, was dark and had bushy eyebrows, as well as a thick moustache with curled ends. To Hutchinson, he seemed a foreigner. He was wearing a dark coat with astrakhan trimmings, spats over his boots, and Hutchinson even noticed his tie-pin shaped like a horse-shoe. He carried a long, thin parcel wrapped in a dark-coloured cloth and tied with a string, in his left hand, while in the right he held brown kid gloves. When their eyes met, the man seemed displeased, and turned away as he made his way alongside Mary Kelly.

With time on his hands, Hutchinson followed the couple at a distance till they vanished into the court. He waited for forty-five minutes, then as there was no sign of the stranger leaving Mary's room, presumed that he would be there for the night and so departed to tramp the streets once more, the clock striking three as he left Dorset Street.

The next morning, Mary Kelly's landlord, McCarthy, looking through his books, found that Mary Kelly owed him thirty-five shillings by way of rent. He decided to take the matter up with her and sent to Room 13, his assistant, Bowyer. At 10.45 a.m., Bowyer knocked on Mary's door. As there was no response, he knocked a second time, then decided that she was deliberately taking no notice, so tried the door handle but found the door locked. He peeped through the keyhole, and noticed that there was no key in it. He then observed that a pane of glass in the window of the room that looked out on the court, was broken, and so he thrust his hand in and drew the curtain. The sight that met his eyes filled him with horror:

Mary Kelly, the pretty, lively girl was not in bed; in her place lay a body with limbs and a trunk, absolutely naked and lying in a thick pool of blood. McCormick's description makes one's flesh creep and one's blood curdle: " Lying on the bed was an obscene parody of a woman. But for the fact that she obviously had a trunk, arms and legs, Bowyer might have been forgiven for mistaking her for the carcass of a butchered beast. Her throat was cut from ear to ear right down to the spinal column. The ears and nose had been severed from her head, the stomach and abdomen ripped open. Her clothes lay in a neat pile at the foot of the bed . . . On a table placed beside the bed was the final and most awful horror. There, symmetrically arranged, were what appeared at first to be piles of flesh. Then, slowly, it dawned on Bowyer what had happened. The maniacal killer had cut off the woman's breasts and set them on the table. Alongside them were her heart and kidneys. Other parts of her body were hanging on picture-frame nails."

When Superintendent Arnold went with Bowyer from Commercial Street Police Station to Number 13 in Miller's Court, the ghastly sight that met his eyes made him exclaim that it was the foulest crime " this madman has committed yet." The four doctors who, after assembling all the separated parts of Mary Kelly's body, examined it, a task that together took them no less than six and a half hours, commented that it was the most brutal butchery the Ripper had yet carried out.

Stark fear held the people in its grip those sooty, foggy nights in the winter of 1888. Many a false alarm that Jack the Ripper had been seen, reached the police. Several suspects were caught by crowds who manhandled them mercilessly, one of the cases of mistaken identity being that of a policeman in plain clothes who was almost lynched on a lamp post by a hysterical mob before being saved in the nick of time by a colleague who chanced on the spot. McCormick tells us: " A popular fallacy of the day was that, when anyone died, the reflection of the person he or she last looked upon was retained photographically and indelibly on the retinæ . . . " To test this theory, the Police Commissioner, Sir Charles Warren, had Mary Kelly's eyes photographed. " This was carried out ", we are informed by McCormick, " and, as far as is known, was the first recorded instance of disproving this fable. Yet the superstition lived on for many years, even until the 'twenties of the present century when a man shot a policeman in each eye, convinced that he was removing incriminating evidence."

Jack or ' Jill '
the Ripper ?

The doctors who examined Mary Kelly's butchered body asserted that she had been dead at least five or six hours before her corpse was found. Yet two women who had known her well, swore they had seen her the next morning and they had even greeted one another. So the theory developed that Jack the Ripper was either ' Jill the Ripper ', a woman, or at best a transvestite male dressed in women's clothes, which could account for his being undetected after every murder, as those searching the killer would be looking for a man. According to this theory, Mary Kelly's murderer had dressed in her clothes and had thus been mistaken by her two acquaintances for the girl herself. But what of the moustache that Hutchinson had noticed the previous night ? Had it been shaved off ?

Opinions continued to differ, even among police officers, as to how many victims the Ripper's butchery had claimed, and also as to which of the women found murdered at the time, were his actual prey. For seven months after the case of Mary Kelly, the crimes suddenly stopped. Then in June 1889, portions of a female body were found near the Thames, one of them being wrapped in a white cloth such as medicos use when engaged in certain studies. Though Munro, the Police Commissioner who had succeeded Sir Charles Warren when the latter resigned, was convinced that the crime was the work of the Ripper, particularly as one of his letters had arrived to say he would " resume operations " in July, this particular murder was not positively linked with the jesting killer.

About a year and a half later, on a windy night on February 13th, 1891, two policemen found the body of a dead woman, presumably in her twenties, near a railway arch running from Royal Mint Street to Chambers Street in Whitechapel. Her throat had been cut, and it looked as if the butchery had occurred only a minute or two before one of the policemen, who was later stabbed to death in a coffee-house, had discovered the dying woman. In spite of the weather, large numbers of police and civilians went on a mass hunt of the murderer. The dock area was cordoned off and the members of boat crews were all interviewed before the boats were allowed to sail away. But the intensive search was in vain.

A new crepe-hat that had been found in a gutter near the dead body, led the police to the shop in Spitalfields where it had been bought. The woman was identified as Frances Coles, a prostitute known as 'Carroty Nell'. The shopkeeper had seen her join a man outside the shop after she had purchased the hat. This same man, who was described as wearing a pointed beard and a peaked cap, had called at the lodging-house in White's Row where Nell would take her customers, at about 3 a.m. The keeper of the lodging-house, who had seen the man with Nell the previous night when he had stayed till 1 a.m. with the girl, having come with a bleeding hand because he claimed he had been waylaid by hooligans, noticed that the man was bleeding again and on being questioned once more gave the excuse that he had been beaten up. He asked for a room at the house, but the lodging-house keeper, not trusting him, refused to give him one and advised him to go to the London Hospital, where, the police discovered, a man with a pointed beard had indeed called and had an injury to his eye, which bled profusely, attended to, the night of Nell's murder.

A man with a beard, whose wife in Kent claimed that he had black moods and was highly destructive when under their spell, and had deserted her, was arrested. Mr. Harry Wilson carefully studied the allegations against him and defended him so well that he was able to prove him innocent of the latest Ripper crime. Some nights later, McCormick tells us, Wilson was going along Bow Street after leaving his office, when he was startled to see a thickset man carrying a large black bag and dressed in black with the brim of his hat pulled well down over his eyes, treading noiselessly down the street. Wilson asked the man who he was. The odd-looking stranger claimed he was Jack the Ripper in a whisper, and then jestingly said that soon perhaps there would be more work for Wilson to do. With that, he vanished, and Wilson, uncannily, found himself alone.

McCormick, whose book, **The Identity of Jack the Ripper,** traces in detail the foregoing cases, declares: " No murder—in Britain, at least—within a period of twenty years after the death of Frances Coles can be compared, even remotely, with the ' Ripper ' crimes . . . I have aimed to give in some detail all possible cases of murder which *might* be attributed to the ' Ripper '. I must stress the word *might*. There is insufficient evidence to link the deaths of Martha Turner, Mary Nicholls, Annie Chapman, Catherine Eddowes, Elizabeth Stride, Mary Kelly . . . and Frances Coles positively with one and the same killer . . . " He adds that it may just be possible that one man butchered the lot of them.

McCormick goes on in his work tracing various clues as to the identity of the murderer. He cites Leonard Matters, an expert in calligraphy who had examined letters purported to have been written

by the Ripper, as forming the theory that the murderer had been looking for one particular prostitute and that he had eventually found her
in the person of Mary Kelly, he being a reputable West End surgeon
whose son had died of venereal disease contracted through Mary Kelly.
As to why the Ripper had murdered the other women, Matters's
theory was that he had used them to try to find Mary Kelly, and
fearing that if they lived Mary Kelly would discover he was hot on her
trail, he had preferred disposing of them summarily to prevent such
an eventuality, he being determined to avenge his son's untimely death.

The theory that the Ripper might have been a woman, is also
examined thoroughly by McCormick who must be complimented on
the exhaustive research he seems to have done. He then continues to
put forward his own theory that an ambidextrous Polish barber from
Warsaw, skilled in elemental surgery, had actually committed the
Ripper crimes, or a junior Russian surgeon, either being skilled in
female disguises. We are not here concerned with detective work, or
with finding out the identity of the Ripper. To those interested in this
absorbing aspect the present writer would strongly recommend
McCormick's classic work. Our own concern here has been to show,
by unfolding the gruesome events of the Autumn and Winter of 1888,
that even so prudish and repressive a period as the latter Victorian
Age, could produce the horrors of an individual orgy on a truly Grand
Guignol scale.

CHAPTER 14

PARTING NOT ALWAYS 'SWEET SORROW'

Sexual Disharmony Cause for Divorce—Semitic Divorce Customs—Hebrew Divorce Laws—Islam and Divorce—Did Christ sanction Divorce?—Three Kinds of Muslim Divorce—Ancient Babylonian Divorce Customs—Divorce in Classical Civilisations—Purely Procreative Role of Marriage among Early Greeks—Marriage a Sacrament among Aryan Hindus—Ancient Rome and Divorce—'Confarreatio' Marriage Indissoluble—Wife's Father could exercise 'Pater Potestas' to free Daughter from Husband—Liberal Divorce Laws of Pagan Britain and Ireland—Modern Primitives and their Divorce Habits—Ramifications of Divorce under Christianity—Roman Catholic Marriage Sacramental—Varieties of Roman Catholic States—Divorce in Protestant Countries—Henry VIII's Antics to obtain Divorce—Why Clement VII withheld Annulment of Henry's Marriage—Whirlgig of Divorce—Divorce Laws in the U.S.A. and the U.S.S.R.

L IKE marriage, customs of divorce vary among different races and nations. Marital ties are usually formed with a permanent relationship in mind, though one is inclined to be sceptical of this when one is confronted by the repeated divorce and remarriage capers of film stars, society gauds, and playboys. In the average marriage of the humdrum world, a break-up is usually caused by neglect, incompatibility of temperament, or adultery, probably as a result of the desire to escape the tedium of married life. Sexual disharmony may often be the basic reason for marriages falling apart, due mostly to either or both partners being ignorant of sexual technique that makes of sex an art and rescues it from monotony.

All but the orthodox will agree that when there is irreparable discord between husband and wife, to continue to make each other unhappy for the sake of appearances is rather an unwise policy. Sexual maladjustment and frustration leave the door wide open for extra-marital relations. Separation or divorce are, of course, not the best of events for the children of a marriage; nor, on the other hand, is an atmosphere of tension and constant friction between parents. Of the two evils, parting seems to be the lesser one. Separation does not leave either party free to remarry, and divorce appears to be a far better choice as the freedom to pursue a new path to happiness with a fresh partner lies open to both.

Grounds for divorce vary everywhere according to a nation's or race's code of morality. A lightning historical survey of divorce makes an interesting study of various sexual mores and of the values attached to them. Vice in one community may become virtue in another; what is deemed of high moral worth in one age, may appear scandalous in another.

The origin of divorce is lost in the mists of antiquity. Before the evolution of marriage rites and civil ceremonies, couples probably cohabited when they pleased and parted if they felt like it. Unbelievable though it may sound, there are communities, even among primitives, in which divorce is unknown, but they are few and far between. Prominent among the few are the Veddas of Ceylon among whom death alone can sever the marriage bond. The wife is jealously guarded and infidelity can result in murder.

Among the Moriori of Chatham Island in the Pacific, and certain Amazonian tribes, a wife who has lost favour with her husband is neglected and must suffer, but the man can always take a new wife, these primitives being polygamous. The Wintuns of California would also not dream of setting aside wives who displeased them, but would find others, or kill in a fit of passion the ones that had fallen out of favour. Likewise the Navajos resorted to killing rather than permit a wife to desert her husband, divorce among them being permitted, but generally prevented by this violent means. Since the Catholic Church made marriage sacerdotal, it has forbidden divorce except by dispensation from the Pope for very special reasons. We shall deal with the indissolubility of a Catholic marriage when covering the Christian faith in general in regard to its incidence of divorce.

Semitic Divorce Customs

HEBREW DIVORCE CUSTOMS: Till about the eleventh century of the present Millennium, the Hebrew wife could never divorce her husband, but he could divorce her " if it come to pass that she find no favour in his eyes, because he hath found some uncleanness in her: then let him write her a bill of divorcement, and give it in her hand, and send her out of his house " (Deuteronomy, 24: 1). However, the law was not entirely merciless to the woman, as it is specified: " And when she is departed out of his house, she may go and be another man's wife " (Deuteronomy, 24: 2). However, if the second husband died or divorced her, the first husband could not take her back, " . . . for that is abomination before the Lord . . . " (Deuteronomy, 24: 4).

The interpretation of the word 'uncleanness' in the first paragraph, caused the Jews to be split into two factions, one of which claimed that the word was meant to be confined to adultery, while the other maintained that 'uncleanness' in that context could apply to anything the husband found displeasing in the woman. The second opinion won the day, and thenceforth, a Hebrew could set aside his wife for reasons other than adultery, though there was a proviso that if the reasons were too trivial the wife's consent would first have to be obtained.

The wife was her husband's chattel, and to protect man's property rights, there were severe penalties for rape, adultery, and prostitution. However, the wife had no escape from even a cruel and merciless husband. Barrenness in a woman was abhorred, and was a common cause of a husband setting aside his wife. The interest in the woman was centred on her fertility, and for this reason wifehood and motherhood were valued. Woman was, to the early Hebrew, not an individual entity, but rather a sexual being. This was what made the Jews polygamous.

The bill of divorcement was not just written out by the husband; he had first to go before a public official and unfold his reasons for wanting a divorce, which prevented hasty decisions; only after this procedure had been followed, could he make out an official document and hand it to his wife. As William Graham Cole points out in his **Sex and Love in the Bible,** interpreters differed greatly as to what were sufficient causes for divorce. "The school of Hillel", explains Cole, " . . . said that a wife's burning her husband's bread constituted good reasons for divorce."

Though the initiative for divorce was solely the husband's, there were a few restrictions imposed on him too. If a man had married his wife because he had taken her first by rape while she was yet a virgin, and had entered into wedlock with her as an amends for his crime, after giving her father fifty *shekels* of silver, he could never put her away. If he had violated her outside the city in a lonely spot, he alone was punished with death if he refused to marry the girl.

The Hebrew god, Yahweh, detests divorce: "For the Lord, the God of Israel, saith that he hateth putting away: for one covereth violence with his garment, saith the Lord of hosts: therefore take heed to your spirit, that ye deal not treacherously " (**Malachi,** 2: 16).

The Hebrew woman's position altered after the eleventh century, and the *Mishnah* gave even her the right to divorce her spouse on grounds acceptible to the court which decided the case. If the husband was found guilty, he had to give her back her dowry, but if he divorced her because of her guilt, the dowry remained with him. In the matter of children, the old Mosaic law had always allowed the mother their custody even when she was the guilty party, but the reformed Hebrew law gave the father the right to keep a son over six years old. Still later reforms left it to the court to exercise its discretion.

ISLAM AND DIVORCE: Another Semitic race, the Arabs, had divorce laws similar to those of the Jews, prior to their becoming Mohammedans. The Arab could put aside his wife at will under a custom called *talaq* which Mohammed condemned and yet sanctioned. Different Muslim sects differ on the procedure to be adopted, the number of witnesses essential, and whether divorce should be verbal or in writing. However, the Koran, the sacred book of the Muslims, lays down certain basic principles: If the husband has, before witnesses, repudiated his wife three times, uttering a particular one of three formulæ, he cannot take her back; but, unlike the old Jewish law, if she marries another and is divorced from him, later, or widowed, she can return to her first husband and be accepted as a wife.

The wife's dowry must be returned to her when divorce breaks up the marriage. However, if a wife, lacking the power of repudiation, wishes her husband to divorce her, she may persuade him to do so provided she relinquishes the right to part, or whole, of the dowry she had brought him. The husband has the right to revise his decision within four months of repudiation if the formula has not been repeated more than twice. Should the wife be weaning a child at the time of the divorce, under Islamic law, the husband, or his heir in the event of his sudden death, must provide for the divorced wife for a period of two years which is taken to be the full suckling period. A divorced wife may not marry till three menstrual periods have passed after the divorce, *i.e.*, about three months, roughly the time allowed the husband to retract his decision to divorce her.

Talaq takes three forms which differ as to the effects of the divorce: In the first, the husband merely says, " I repudiate you ", or " Depart ". If he has not repeated it more than twice, he can alter his decision and take her back. The second formula makes him declare her dead to him or compare her to swine whose flesh Muslims never touch or eat. This repudiation makes it impossible for him to take her back unless, as explained before, she remarries and is later either widowed or divorced. The third and final formula makes the decision irrevocable, for it orders the wife to turn her back to her husband as if it were his own mother's back, which brings her under the incest prohibition.

DIVORCE IN ANCIENT BABYLONIA: Yet another Semitic race were the people of Babylon with whom hedonism reached a remarkable peak as they believed that humans were created to afford pleasure to the gods which, naturally, they could not do if they were sad or miserable. Babylon was, no doubt, a patriarchate with remnants of matriarchy clinging to it. While, therefore, the laws were partial to man, the woman was not reduced to the inferior position as among the Jews and the Arabs, but treated almost as man's equal.

The laws of Babylonia were well codified by King Hammurabi two millenniums before Christ: The husband could unilaterally divorce his wife for her childlessness, or bad health, or even if she turned out to be a poor housekeeper. Her marriage portion was given back to her, and the children's upkeep had to be paid for by the husband. The wife could, if the judge permitted, stay on in the husband's home, reduced to the position of a slave.

If a husband deserted his wife or remained away from her for an inordinately long period, she had the right to conduct a liaison wtih another man without giving up the first marriage with the absent spouse. With the consent of the court, the wife could, on occasion, seek a divorce from her husband for negligence of his marital duties or for conducting himself improperly. If she won her case, he was liable to pay her compensation and to return her dowry to her. She could marry again.

In the matter of adultery, the law was unfair, for the wife had no redress apart from abandoning her adulterous spouse; whereas if he caught her in a compromising position with a lover, they could be bound together and drowned. If there were a doubt as to the guilt, they were still cast into the water, but without being bound. A Babylonian husband could obtain credit by leaving his wife and children as collateral with whoever lent him the money, but the law was modified so as to permit the human security to remain in the hands of the creditor for no more than three years. This prevented a man from misusing the pledge system as a substitute for divorce.

Divorce in Classical Civilisations

THE GREEKS: Women in the Arab and Jewish communities occupy a somewhat inferior status. Similarly, the position of the wife among the Greeks of classical time, was far from enviable. Hence Greek divorce customs treated her with scant respect. The husband alone had the right of repudiation, and he could set her aside without even the presence of witnesses being essential. Her dowry, though, remained inviolate and had to be returned with her to her parental home, or, in lieu of it, interest on it had to be paid.

Among the Greeks, marriage was a duty to society; they, therefore, did not relish childlessness, and a woman's barrenness was enough cause for setting her aside. Men had so high a status in ancient Greece that even when the father was the guilty party, the children were invariably entrusted to his care. Be it said to the honour of Classical Greece, that despite the ease with which a man could repuliate his wife, divorce was infrequent.

For the Greeks of antiquity the chief object of marriage was to raise a legitimate family; therefore it can be easily understood that if a wife proved barren, it was a reason for divorce. The wife's adultery was yet another reason, though the husband himself could have extramarital relations with hetæræ or meretrices, or boys, and it was not considered at all immoral as they understood man's polyerotic nature and allowed it free rein; being patrists, of course, they confined this freedom to their own sex and to those women who had not become members of the institution of marriage. If a daughter lost her virginity and was discovered, her father could sell her into slavery. Little wonder that Aristophanes in his play, the comedy ' Lysistrata ', advised the women to go on a love-strike in order to win equality with men. As can be imagined, it was not taken seriously.

THE ARYAN HINDUS: Classical India's attitude to divorce was unequivocal: Marriage was a sacrament and whom the gods had joined together no man could put asunder. But, as in the Roman Catholic Church, on certain very serious grounds, such as adultery, a wife could be put aside without being sent away from the household where her position became that of a virtual slave. This constituted a judicial separation, which, for the woman, was disadvantageous, as it did not leave her free to marry again. The man could marry as many wives as he wished, the Hindus having been polygamous up to recent times when monogamy has been made the only legal marriage.

The Laws of Manu of ancient India did not, as many writers seem to think, sanction divorce, but rather the separation already referred to. They gave the exclusive right of instituting such proceedings to the husband, the Hindu wife being a mere chattel, as Hindu society was, and still remains, strongly patriarchal. A wife could be judicially separated if in ten years of marriage she had failed to produce male issue; if she remained barren for eight years; if she had the misfortune to lose all her children in death by the tenth year of marriage.

In a society in which a man had to have a male heir to mourn him after death, these reasons are understandable, but frivolous reasons for separation such as a wife's arrogance, her extravagance, her addiction to drink, or her developing, by some misfortune, an incurable disease, seem to be harsh measures, and only go to prove how callously these highly civilised people treated their women folk, and what an inferior position the generally loyal, noble Hindu wife, occupied in society. The poor woman could sometimes be turned out of the husband's house deprived of the dowry she had brought with her, and with nothing but the clothes she stood in.

As a woman put aside was merely separated, since divorce did not exist, there was no hope of any other man marrying her, and to make it difficult for women like her, the Code of Manu enjoined men to marry only virgins even when they already had a number of wives. Except among the Brahmins, the priestly and highest caste among the Hindus, the code was not as rigidly adhered to as one imagines, and practice served to modify it. In the modern India, divorce is permitted even among Hindus, and both divorced men and women may remarry. What is more, monogamy has come to stay.

Among the Buddhists of Burma, marriage is not looked upon as a sacrament but has the status of being a civil contract pure and simple. Hence divorce is easy, particularly when adultery or desertion is involved. Buddhism is, essentially, a philosophy, a way of life, and is, therefore, very practical.

ANCIENT ROME AND DIVORCE: In the Rome of antiquity, divorce depended on the form of marriage contracted. The most sacred type of marriage was the *confarreatio* confined to patricians, and in early Rome it could not be dissolved. While divorce was possible in later years, with a rite called *diffarreatio,* it was a most difficult procedure, and the incidence of divorce was very low, perhaps because, apart from the difficulty involved, the marriage contract itself was considered to be too solemn and binding.

The next type of marriage, which surrendered the wife into the *manus* or power of her husband, could be dissolved on the husband's initiative and his alone, whenever he pleased. However, the wife was protected from his abuse of power by the magistrates, backed by public opinion, exercising control over his authority.

Under the Roman law of Romulus's time, we are told by Plutarch that the husband could exercise his right of repudiation "in case of her poisoning his children, or counterfeiting his keys, or committing adultery, and if on any other account he put her away she was to have one moiety of his goods, and the other was to be consecrated to Ceres." Ancient Roman law made the woman forfeit her dowry if the reason for divorce was a crime committed by her. For adultery, a sixth of her dowry was held back, and for lesser crimes, an eighth. The divorce system developed quickly among the early Romans.

The easiest form of marriage, from the point of view of dissolution, was the one in which the wife had not passed into the control of her husband, and the majority of marriages were of this nature. Divorce was effected by either or both partners issuing simple declarations. The divorced wife could, of course, take her dowry back with her, particularly as many fathers, at the time of such marriages, not only settled the dower on their daughters themselves, but also took the precaution of reserving their *patria potestas* or patriarchal authority over them in case of just this kind of emergency. What is more, the father himself could force a divorce by demanding the return of his daughter at any time and the husband's remonstrances were of no avail. However, in later times, legislation modified this rule and forbade the father from attempting to dissolve a happy marital union.

When past the age of sixty, the once-lecherous Emperor Augustus introduced fresh legislation aimed at protecting the family unit. Under this, divorce was made a far from easy procedure, and no less than seven witnesses had to testify at the proceedings. Freed slave girls could not divorce the masters they had married and thus achieve their freedom. However, under the later Emperors, divorce was simplified. Thus it can be seen that, except in the case of the solemn *confarreatio* marriage, ancient Rome shed no tears over a marriage that was on the rocks. After the second Punic War, divorce became farcically easy.

If campaigns took a husband away from his wife too long, she could claim a divorce and remarry. At a still later stage, the mere conscription of a husband for military service, was sufficient grounds for dissolution of a marriage.

Infidelity and childlessness constituted good excuses for divorce. Societies of antiquity looked upon marriage as a social obligation in the interest of reproduction and it was a man's right, more, his duty, to set aside a wife who could not bear him children. If, however, it could be proved that he was the sterile party, then the wife had an equal right to claim a divorce.

PAGAN BRITAIN AND IRELAND: The divorce laws of Wales and Ireland in the pre-Christian era, seem to be models of enlightenment and point to those countries being matriarchates, for women appear to have been placed on a footing of equality with the men. Thus in Wales, if a husband divorced his wife because of her adultery or improper behaviour, he had the right to her property, but she, too, could divorce him for impotency or even halitosis, and retain her possessions.

Ireland appears to have been even more generous to her women folk. The Brehon Tracts emphasise the woman's right to compatibility, and furnish her with many reasons for divorce from her spouse: for inflicting physical injuries on her; for blackening her character and spreading false rumours about her; for making her the laughing-stock of her neighbours; for denying her her conjugal rights because " . . . her husband prefers to lie with servant boys when it is not necessary for him." This last provision suggests the existence of homosexuality even in those remote times—a tendency that persists to a remarkable degree among the Irish even today, particularly among the lower classes.

In old England, divorce was permitted either by mutual agreement, or due to one party desiring it, even if no particular reason were advanced. A wife's adultery had to be brought to light though, if it were the ground for divorce. The woman, on the other hand, could not ask for divorce because of her husband's adultery as it was not considered a crime committed against her. He could, however, be punished for having impinged on the cuckolded husband's property.

MODERN PRIMITIVES: On some of the Solomon Islands, there is an astonishing equality between men and women relating to divorce which becomes understandable when it is realised that many of these are matrilineal societies though with patrilocal customs. If a husband sends his wife away because of her misconduct or any genuine grievance against her, he can claim from her the bride-price paid to her family. If she forsakes him, then there is no compulsion for such a return though it is normally done for her family's honour. The children always remain with the wife as is to be expected in a matrilineal community. Should the woman marry again, the responsibility for the children's upkeep rests on the new spouse.

Among the Sudanese Nuba tribe, the practical husband will decide to divorce his wife only if he is sure of getting back the bride-price. A very sensible attitude, as the bride's family may already have spent the money, or if paid in heads of cattle, may be reluctant to split their herd. Better, then, to lose the herd than lose a wife into the bargain. Among non-Christian Abyssinians, marriage is a free partnership and dissolution by mutual accord. No stigma of illegitimacy prevails, and the parted couple can come together without much ado. When the parents decide to part, the mother takes the sons with her, the father keeps the daughters. Similarly, the Polynesians part by mutual consent.

Ramifications of Divorce under Christianity

When we come to Christian divorce, the important and interesting question arises as to whether Christ forbade marriage *unequivocally,* or whether he considered it permissible in certain cases. According to **Matthew,** 19: 3, 9, when asked by the Pharisees whether it was lawful for a man to put away his wife, he answered: " . . . Whosoever shall put away his wife, *except for fornication,* commiteth adultery: and whoso marrieth her which is put away doth commit adultery."

Note the italics—ours. Surely that one phrase, ' except it be for fornication ', clearly implies that Christ made fornication the one exception when divorce is allowable, even if **Mark,** 10: 11, Paul (**Corinthians,** 7: 10, 11), and **Luke,** 16: 18, chose to omit the phrase —probably because, in their individual opinion, they themselves disapproved of divorce ? Roman Catholics, well versed in quibbling, bring forth the theory that ' to put away a wife ' is to be interpreted as separation and not divorce, to which one can only reply that the phrase translated into English as ' putting away ' was clearly used by the Jews of Christ's time as applying to divorce.

Again, in Matthew's account of the Sermon on the Mount, Christ includes the same exception in a slightly different phraseology from the one already quoted: " But I say unto you, that whosoever shall put away his wife, *save for the cause of fornication,* causeth her to commit adultery: and whosoever shall marry her that is divorced commiteth adultery " (**Matthew,** 5: 32).

Theological controversies have been raised over this question, yet it seems crystal clear, according to both texts, that the man who sets aside his wife because of her fornication is *not* committing adultery even if he takes a new wife, nor causing her to commit adultery. Despite this, however, though the early Christian Church recognised divorce on a few grounds such as childlessness, adultery, fornication, and even incompatibility, the sado-masochistic code of mediæval times would grant only annulment if the marriage could be proved to have been invalid, or separation for cruelty, adultery, or heresy, the bugbear of the times. Separation excluded the liberty to marry again, whereas annulment, if it could be obtained, would leave the way open to marriage.

As a result, many abuses crept in, as C. Rattray Taylor affirms in his **Sex in History,** for the Church " for a sufficient consideration . . . could be induced to find a reason for permitting an annulment —the only drawback being that an annulment made any children of the marriage bastards. This power of granting annulments became a major source of revenue to the Church and a source of great scandal."

As till then marriage had been a private contract, annulment could be got by proving that there had been a previous marriage. For this reason, sacerdotal marriage was eventually introduced, and it was to take place in the presence of witnesses and an officiating priest as well, so that if, perchance, the former were given monetary inducements to keep their knowledge to themselves, at least the priest, considered to be above such inducements, could testify to the marriage having taken place. Banns were later introduced for the same reason. While the Church insisted on sacerdotal marriage, it was not in a position to declare private marriage invalid, and in England it was left, by a strange irony, to the Tudor monarchs to introduce compulsory church weddings even after Henry VIII had opened the way to the Reformation in England.

The dogma of the indissolubility of marriage, asserted after the Council of Trent in 1563, was reaffirmed in the nineteenth century by Pope Leo XIII. Once consummated, the marriage, under this doctrine, becomes as sacred as the link between the Church and Christ. Without consummation, the marriage is not a sacrament and can be annulled. Likewise, if it has infringed prohibitions relating to consanguineity, or if undue pressure has been brought on either party to contract the marriage.

Some Roman Catholic countries are in absolute accord with the Church, in both religious and secular affairs. It is normally in such countries that one finds an excess of bigotry, and often considerable interference by the Church in political and secular matters. Typical examples are Southern Ireland and Spain, both backward European countries with a vast illiterate or semi-literate peasantry whose minds have been conditioned by religious superstition.

As an instance of the Church's meddlesome ways, freedom of political thought is not permitted in Ireland, and Irishmen will frankly admit that the Church would not permit the existence of a political body such as the Communist party. As a matter of fact, most ' religious ' Irishmen are aghast at the very thought of such an eventuality. Another example is the deprivation of freedom of worship in theocratic Spain which insists on Roman Catholic worship alone; no other Christian church, and much less a mosque or temple, is allowed to function openly, or even secretly, for if the latter clandestine form of worship were discovered it would carry a heavy penalty. In Spain,

Ireland, and the South American states of Columbia, Chile, and Brazil, all Roman Catholic countries, divorce is non-existent.

In contrast to such countries are Roman Catholic nations that owe religious allegiance to the Church of Rome, but diverge from it in secular matters. Thus in France, after the Revolution, civil marriage was made compulsory in September, 1792, and became " the only legally valid form of marriage ", as Fernando Henriques tells us in his **Love in Action,** going on to add: " At the same time divorce was legalised . . . Then, France at once went far beyond the Protestant countries, in which the right to divorce had existed since the Reformation but in practice had been made very difficult to exercise . . . The new French legislation made things easier for couples who did not wish to go on living together. They had only to hand in a joint declaration that they wished their marriage to be dissolved: they had not even to tell the authorities their reason." This was done, as the preamble to the Divorce Act of 1792 explained, in pursuance of the individual's right of freedom.

Though the Napoleonic Wars were not religious wars, the Bourbon Government which followed in France, abolished divorce, and in the middle of the second decade of the last century, divorced persons were not permitted to remarry. Only separation was allowed, and this, too, for grave reasons only, such as the wife's, though not the husband's, adultery, unless he went so far as to make his mistress a member of his married household. These severe measures remained in force all through the Restoration period, *i.e.*, during the reign of Louis Philippe, on through the Second Empire and the Third Republic, till at last in 1884, divorce was again permitted.

Even Portugal, from the end of the first decade of the present century, permits divorce though its incidence is said to be comparatively low. In areas of Germany which are predominently Catholic, divorce may be obtained even by a Catholic, under the secular law, but, one would imagine, in defiance of the Church which would probably excommunicate the erring member, the Bishop of the diocese refusing such a one admission to all the sacraments—confession, communion, and even the last rites. The states of Salvador and Costa Rica in Central America, as well as Mexico, permit divorce, the two former ones since the last decade of the nineteenth century, and Mexico from the commencement of the present century.

Eastern Europe had her own Orthodox Church in the Slav countries, except in Poland. Such an Orthodox Church flourishes in Greece, and still exists even in Russia and some other Communist countries, contrary to the popular misconception that their political ideology does not allow freedom of religious worship. As mentioned earlier in this work, the Catholic Church did allow divorce for special reasons, such as adultery and barrenness, in the earlier times of of Christianity, and the Orthodox Church has never revised its view in this respect. Moreover, where it exists in non-Communist countries —the Orthodox Church is allowed in Communist countries but obviously exercises no influence in secular matters—it is closely identified with the secular state, as in Greece. Hence divorce has existed in Slav countries for very many centuries with the full sanction of the Orthodox Church.

Divorce in Protestant Countries

In Western Europe, Protestant reformers such as Martin Luther, Calvin, and Melanchthon, asserted that marriage was not a sacrament but a private contract, and could, accordingly, be dissolved. Luther was eager to remove marriage entirely from the authority of the Church; but while marriage under the Reformation lost its religious meaning, it still remained wedded to the religious ceremony and in England the Tudors made such a ceremony compulsory. In modern Protestant countries, both civil and ecclesiastical marriages are valid in law.

If one may digress for a moment, the leaders of the Reformation feared that the celibacy enjoined on the Roman Catholic clergy was an evil eating at the roots of the Church and encouraging concubinage even among the religious orders. It was a young man of twenty-six, Phillipp Melanchthon, who first raised the question. His cry was echoed by a secular priest, Ulrich Zwingli, at Zürich. Zwingli went farther, and demanded that the rule of celibacy be abolished unconditionally. Suiting action to words, he married a judge's widow. In his wake, in 1525, Martin Luther, a monk who had been excommunicated, married a nun, Katherine von Bora, who had deserted a convent after reading his works. Thus by their own example, both Zwingli and Luther were instrumental in putting celibacy to flight within a large section of Christendom in the space of a generation. Many monks threw off their cowls, and nuns their habits, and the Protestant person's right to marriage and divorce, even if he happens to be a Minister of the Church, has existed ever since. In Holland, the highly respected Erasmus fumed at these goings-on rather in vain as future ages have proved.

Luther was not against divorce as is evidenced by the fact that, as we learn from Lewinsohn, " when his fellow-Protestant, the Landgraf Philip of Hesse, wanted to put away his wife, Christine of Saxony, and marry another, Luther gave his permission . . . " Fielding tells us in his **Strange Customs of Courtship and Marriage** that " Luther maintained that the *cause* of divorce itself effected divorce without the necessity of any judicial decree, although a magisterial order was required for a remarriage." Many pioneers of the Reformation thus adopted the practice of self-divorce as prevalent among the Semitic races such as Jews and Arabs.

DIVORCE IN ENGLAND: As a result of the Reformation, many sensible reforms were introduced in the secular life of Europe, particularly the legislation of divorce. In England, however, divorce was the main reason for ushering in the new movement against the Catholic Church. The Pope held in his hand the prerogative of granting 'divorce' which was by declaring a marriage null and void and thus enabling the parties, or one of them, to remarry.

Henry VIII of England, enamoured of one of his consort's ladies-in-waiting, Anne Boleyn, desired to have his marriage with Catherine of Aragon annulled. Till then, he was one of the stoutest props of the Catholic Church, and had even written a book attacking Luther's doctrines. However, he had been married to Catherine in a *mariage de convenance*, for almost two decades, and she had borne him no less than six children, of whom only one daughter, the future 'Bloody Mary', had survived. One would imagine that the Pope, Clement VII, a solemn man, would find it a gargantuan task, apart even from matters of conscience, to find a good reason to declare the marriage invalid. The absence of a male heir could not, of course, be sufficient excuse, even though, no doubt, Henry, having a bastard son by Elizabeth Blount—who being illegitimate, could not succeed to the throne—was chafing to have a son born within wedlock.

Henry VIII was considered a devout son of the Church, but the lack of genuine grounds for invalidating the marriage, and the fact that the Pope, in wielding his prerogative, had always to exercise political discretion, weighed against the English monarch—for, alas, Catherine of Aragon was the daughter of the mighty Ferdinand of Aragon and his Queen Isabella of Castille, as well as an aunt of the Emperor Charles V, whom Pope Clement VII needed in his struggle against the forces of the Reformation. Accordingly, the Pope refused to annul the marriage.

Henry VIII marshalled the lawyers of Europe to come to his aid. A reason for invalidating the marriage was found: When Henry married Catherine, six years his senior, she was the widow of his elder brother. It was contended that though the Levirate of the Old Testament enjoined the marriage of a man with his brother's widow, there was another rule forbidding marriage with an in-law of the first degree. But Pope Clement VII, a Medici, depended on the Emperor Charles V to reinstate the Medicis on the Florentine throne which had been lost to them, and could not afford to offend this regal nephew of Catherine of Aragon.

For the second time, the Pope declared Henry's marriage with Catherine to be perfectly valid, as indeed it was, Henry having obtained a special dispensation from Rome to marry her in the first place.

Clement VII's refusal to annul the marriage, riled Henry, and to save face before his subjects, he broke away from the Roman Catholic Church, had himself declared Head of the Church of England, and had Catherine's marriage invalidated by a group of theologians. The way was now clear for Henry to marry Anne Boleyn, who, shrewdly, had refused to give herself to him out of wedlock. Thus was formed the union that was to give England one of her most brilliant monarchs,

Elizabeth I, in whose reign there was a flowering of English literature, the acquisition of fresh colonies, increased trade particularly with India, doubled piracy on the high seas, and a glittering court studded with intrigues. With Henry's future marital escapades—four more of them—we are not here concerned. It is, however, a strange irony that though Henry VIII became a Protestant to facilitate his divorce from Catherine, and established the precedent that every English monarch must be head of the Church of England, a future king, Edward VIII, had to renounce his throne because—or so we were officially told—he had chosen to fall in love with a *divorcée*. Or could it be that, while this served as the ostensible reason, the real causes, even in a widely-trumpeted democracy, were social snobbery and xenophobia, the lady in question being both a commoner and a foreigner ?

England is, essentially, a conservative nation. Even the lecherous Henry VIII, after breaking away from Rome, still insisted on celibacy for his clergy, the abolition of which even the Catholic Charles V had advocated in Europe ! The reform element on the Continent had been a liberal one, but the pioneers of the Church of England, who formulated the new laws for marriage and divorce, were extremely conservative in keeping with the English character. However, the reformers in the short reign of Henry's son, Edward VI, showed more liberalism and were getting ready to relax the laws of marriage and divorce, when, alas, the boy king died. His sister Mary, daughter of Catherine of Aragon, bore allegiance to Rome and on coming to the throne plunged England into a blood bath in the name of the Roman Catholic faith winning for herself the appellation ' Bloody Mary '.

Elizabeth I, daughter of Anne Boleyn, restored the balance and gave to England the golden epoch of the first Elizabethan Age. But the real reform of the laws on marriage and divorce, did not come till the Marriage Reform Acts (1644 and 1653) following the Civil Wars and the triumph of the Puritans. Marriage was then unequivocally declared to be " . . . no sacrament, nor peculiar to the Church of God, but common to mankind, and of public interest to every Commonwealth." These acts rescued marriage from the clutches of the Church and made it an entirely secular affair as Luther had long ago advocated.

The whirlgig of history discarded the reforms in the Restoration period, and brought back the old mumbo-jumbo of Canon Law. Humorously, Fielding comments: " Once more English marriage became what A. P. Herbert called ' Holy Deadlock '." It was not until almost the end of the sixth decade of the last century that the Civil divorce law came into force in England, and made divorce once again possible, but only for the adultery of the wife, or some grave offence.

Rattray Taylor sums up English mores in these words: " . . . it will now be clear . . . how muddled and arbitrary our system of sexual morality is. In fact, it is not in any consistent ethical sense a morality at all. It is essentially a hodge-podge of attitudes derived from the past, upon which is erected a shaky and inconsistent system of laws and social prohibitions. Some of these fragments from the past date from before the introduction of Christianity; some are magical in origin, others are based on faulty science; yet others have grown up by reinterpretation of old laws, originally passed with quite a different purpose. That we have retained these ancient regulations is due to the fact that they effectively express the prejudices of the dominant group. For the great majority of the prohibitions which regulate our sexual conduct are, or were, taboos—that is, prohibitions introduced to relieve unconscious, irrational anxieties. (This is not the less true just because they have been supported from time to time by a great parade of scholarly justification.) "

Under prevailing English law, a marriage may be annulled if one party refuses to consummate it or if the husband is found to be impotent. If, on the other hand, the marriage has once been consummated, consistent refusal on the part of one partner to allow coitus is not grounds for divorce though the other partner can live apart and not be liable to be sued for desertion so long as he or she is willing to return if the other party decides to permit coitus. Such a law, as can be plainly seen, encourages fornication by throwing the frustrated party into the arms of the first male or female, as the case may be, ready to enter such a liaison.

Childlessness was, at one time, sufficient grounds for divorce, even among Catholics in the early centuries of Christianity, but today, as far as the law is concerned, neither annulment nor divorce is possible if one of the parties is sterile or uses contraceptives against the other's wish, or if the man indulges in *coitus interruptus* or interrupted sexual intercourse, as a measure of birth-control. This is under a new ruling of the House of Lords given in 1947.

Insanity, desertion for a minimum period of three years, and recurring physical cruelty, are recognised as reasons for divorce, but not incompatibility, which last was sufficient cause even in Pagan Ireland. At one time, only a wife's adultery was grounds for divorce, but since 1923, the wife may also sue for divorce for the husband's adultery. Anal intercourse against the wish of one of the partners (mostly the woman, though the latter, by pestering the man for such an act, could, perhaps, lay herself open to such a charge) is also a valid reason for claiming divorce.

Though divorce carries with it no social stigma, except in court circles, and there, too, the odium seems to be dwindling, the Church of England still assumes an ambivalent attitude towards it. There is no clear declaration embodied in a Canon. Individual bishops express personal views, now and again, which are conflicting. Whether a guilty party in a divorce can be remarried in a church or not, is still a puzzle; sometimes even an innocent party may be prevented from doing so. However, while on this question, the Anglican Church seems incapable of coming to a joint decision, from a practical point of view the position is not so bad, because somewhere in the country is always to be found an unorthodox Anglican padre who will consent to preside at the marriage of a divorcee in his church.

Whirlgig of Divorce

The United States of America present a bewildering picture of varying divorce laws in the different States, but no doubt the laws are far more liberal, generally speaking, than in Western Europe. Cruelty, for instance, is recognised as a ground for divorce in all the forty-eight Federal States, except three; even mental cruelty is included in this kind of case.

South Carolina, with the smallest Roman Catholic population in the entire country, did not permit divorce till 1948. New York, closest to Europe, has inherited divorce laws that depict many Old World prejudices. Adultery alone is considered a suitable ground for divorce, and couples are often compelled to resort to the use of professional co-respondents. Agencies are said to run even businesses along these lines.

In the gay 'Twenties, wealthy Americans sought Mexican divorces and enterprising lawyers flourished, for a while, arranging for their clients divorces that did not even necessitate their landing from the ship. However, the American authorities soon clamped down on this practice and a Mexican divorce does not count any longer in the U.S.A.

But where there is a demand, there will always be a supply if the business brain can figure out a profitable way. So Nevada became a factory for churning out divorces. Only six weeks' residence, contrasted with the one or two years that other States require, can win you back your sexual freedom until the next plunge. The mountain resort of Reno in Nevada was for long the stamping ground of those about to be divorced. But its neighbour, Las Vegas, is beginning to steal its thunder.

Even the Supreme Court set its seal of approval on the Nevada divorce when, in 1942, it upheld the validity of its divorce laws. Lewinsohn comments amusingly: " This decision was one of great importance, especially for the sex-life of Hollywood, whose inhabitants are among Nevada's regular visitors . . . " To show the diversity of American divorce laws, the State of Maryland is the only one which accepts a bride's lack of chastity before marriage as ground for divorce.

Lewinsohn declares: " Today, half of all American women, and at least two-thirds of all European, have been deflowered before marriage. The bridal night has lost its mystique for both parties. Others besides the romantics may deplore this, but it undoubtedly has its good side. The dread of the unknown, the inhibitions centring round ' deflowering to order ', which often led to physical disorders (*vaginism*) are gone; women who enter on marriage with knowledge behind them are partners from the first, sexually as otherwise, and not subjects. What has been realised here is a part of the emancipation of women, and not the least important part."

Dissolution or annulment of a marriage is allowed in the United States and in several Continental countries, if it is discovered that, without the husband's previous knowledge, his wife has been carrying another man's child at the time of marriage. This, of course, amounts to fraud and nobody could blame a husband who seeks a divorce on this ground. In France, however, the husband cannot divorce a wife who has cheated him, but to repudiate paternity of the child, a special procedure has to be adopted.

Revolution generally brings about reforms in marriage and divorce laws as we saw in the case of the French Revolution. With the victory of the Bolsheviks, church marriage was abolished in Russia, in December, 1917, civil registration becoming compulsory. A simple application to the Registrar procured a divorce, when it was desired mutually by both partners. However, the courts had to intervene and make a decision should one partner be unwilling to part. In the first score of years of the new Soviet regime, the nation's economic life was scrupulously planned, but sex-life was left unhampered as far as possible.

The Russian divorce law sought a higher status for the woman than she had previously enjoyed in Capitalist countries. Efforts were made to eliminate the commercial factor from the sexual field so that women could be rescued from the humiliations of prostitution and marriage for the sake of 'making a good match'. In this, they were following the doctrines of Engels who, in his 'Origin of the Family', had expressed the view that if these economic conditions that made women tolerate marital infidelity, were to disappear, then marriage would become increasingly monogamous and be based on sexual attraction and love, and on no ulterior considerations such as influence marriage in bourgeois society. However, even Engels expressed a doubt as to man's monoerotic stability, and so the Bolsheviks made divorce convenient for those who could not find happiness in the marital state, and also in order to prevent adulterous liaisons such as prohibition of divorce would tend to encourage.

Engels was in favour of monogamy, but he was realistic enough to realise that a marriage may be founded on love to begin with, but the love may not last. Lenin, after the matter had been argued for quite a number of years, decided in favour of monogamy. But following his death in 1924, the opposite view gained favour. Collectivisation and industrialisation had parted many married couples owing to each taking a job in a different place. This resulted in extra-marital alliances being formed, and marriage itself was thus imperilled.

In 1927, divorce laws became laxer. Cohabitation was raised to the level of marriage. A husband had no longer to implore his wife to agree to a divorce, for by merely cohabiting with another woman and informing the registrar officially, his previous marriage was dissolved and the cohabitation became a lawful marriage. Women enjoyed the same rights as men, and a woman could similarly cohabit with another man and apply to the registrar for a divorce from her husband.

The lax divorce laws were, in actuality, a licence for free love, the aim presumably being increase of birth rate. But the Kremlin's wish was not fulfilled, and as the State needed more hands, it was decided that marriage, after all, was the best means of ensuring large families. Hence the divorce laws were tightened up in 1936. A divorce could no longer be registered without the mutual consent of both husband and wife, and it was even taxed. The first divorce cost only 50 *roubles*, the second 150 *roubles*, but each subsequent one cost double the amount of the second, *viz*, 300 *roubles*, which most workers could barely afford.

Towards the mid-forties, as the second World War was at its tail end, there was further tightening up of the divorce laws of the Soviet Union. The People's Court would first hear a divorce petition and attempt to reconcile the pair. If the efforts of the Court were not successful, divorce would be granted. To prevent recurring divorces among habitual ' offenders ', the cost was sent soaring to a couple of thousand *roubles*. Thus divorce became a luxury in which not too many Soviet citizens could revel. In this way, the Union of the Soviet Socialist Republic seems to have come as near as possible to Lenin's idea of a family revolving round a monogamous marriage.

Marriage and divorce laws vary from nation to nation, and race to race, as we have seen. Perpetuation of the human species is still the primary concern of the world, and family life is at the very core of human existence. However, most societies today realise that marriage is not merely an institution for breeding fresh generations, but also a sexual partnership. Neither should be subservient to the other, but both the procreative and sexual urges should blend, one with the other, to produce harmony in family life—and, dare we hope, harmony among the different races of the world ?

London, 15th July, 1962.

BIBLIOGRAPHY

ÆSCHULUS, The *Oresteia,* and *Danaides.*
ALLEN, FREDERICK LEWIS, Only Yesterday.
ALLGROVE, GEORGE, Love in the East.
ARNOLD, SIR EDWIN, The Light of Asia.

BANCROFT, H. H., The Native Races of the Pacific States of
    North America.
BEAUVOIR, SIMON de, A History of Sex.
BENEDICT, RUTH, Patterns of Culture.
BERRILL, N. I., Sex and the Nature of Things .
BLOCH, DR. IWAN (or IVAN), Sexual Life in England, Past
    and Present.

CARPENTER, EDWARD, Love's Coming of Age.
CHATTERJEE, SANTOSH, Devadasi.
COLE, WILLIAM GRAHAM, Sex and Love in the Bible.
CORYATE, T., Coryat's Crudities.

DADACHANJI, SEROZH, and GOPAL, RAM, Indian Dancing.
DANIELSSON, BENGT, Love in the South Seas.
DUBOIS, Abbé J. A., Hindu Manners, Customs and Ceremonies.
DUTT, ROMESH C., The ,Ramayana (English Translation).

ELLIS, HAVELOCK, Sex in Relation to Society.

FIELDING, WILLIAM J., Strange Customs of Courtship and
    Marriage.
FIRDAUSSI, The *Shah Namah* or Book of Kings.
FRAZER, J. G., Totemism and Exogamy.
FREUD, SIGMUND, Totem and Taboo.

GUTHRIE, W. K. C., The Greeks and their Gods.

HARDING, M. E., Women's Mysteries.
HENRI, EDWARD J., The Kiss of the Whip.
HENRIQUES, FERNANDO, Love in Action.
HERODOTUS, *Historiæ.*
HINDU EPICS, The *Mahabharata* and The *Ramayana.*
HOLY BIBLE, The

JEAFFRESON, J. C., Brides and Bridals.
JOHNSON, DR. SAMUEL, Lives of the Poets.

KIEFER, OTTO, Sexual Life in Ancient Rome.
KNIGHT, R. PAYNE, Remains of the Worship of Priapus.

LEA, H. C., History of Sacerdotal Celibacy.
LEWINSOHN, RICHARD, A History of Sexual Customs.
LICHT, HANS, Sexual Life in Ancient Greece.
LINTON, R., The Study of Man.

MACAULAY, LORD, History of England, Vol. II.
MALINOWSKI, BRONISLAW, The Natives of Mailu, and
　　　　　　　　　　　　　　Sex and Repression in Savage
　　　　　　　　　　　　　　Society.
McCORMICK, DONALD, The Identity of Jack the Ripper.
MEAD, MARGARET, Sex and Temperament.
MOLMENTI, P. G., Venice.
MORGAN, LEWIS N., The League of the Iroquois.

NADEL, S. F., The Nuba.

OVID, Ars Amatoria.

QUINLAN, M. J., Victorian Prelude.

RIVERS, W. H. R., The Todas.
ROUSSEAU, JEAN JACQUES, Confessions.
'SARDI', The Symphony of Sex.
SELIGMAN, C. G., The Melanesians of British Guiana.
SHAKESPEARE, WILLIAM, Romeo and Juliet, and
　　　　　　　　　　　　　Julius Cæsar.
SMITH, W. ROBERTSON, Kinship and Marriage in Early
　　　　　　　　　　　　Arabia.
STENDHAL, De L'Amour.
SWAIN, JOHN, The Pleasures of the Torture Chamber.
SWINBURNE, ALGERNON, Poems and Ballads.

TAYLOR, G. RATTRAY, Sex in History.
THACKERAY, WILLIAM M., The Four Georges.
THURSTON, E., Notes on Southern India.

VALMIKI, Original sage-composer of The Ramayana.

WESTERMARCK, EDWARD, The History of Human Marriage.
WHITING, J. A., Becoming a Kwoma.
WILDE, OSCAR, The Ballad of Reading Gaol.
WILSON, C. T., and FELKEN, R. W., Uganda and the Egyptian
　　　　　　　　　　　　　　　　　Sudan, Vol. II.

INDEX

(descriptive)

and

GLOSSARY

ABBERLINE, Chief Inspector of Police, Victorian England, 224
' ABBOT OF MISRULE ', 180, 221
ABEL, son of Adam and Eve, husband of his step-sister Sarah, 88
ABELARD, Pierre, scholar and lover of Héloise, *q.v.*, 43 *et seq.;* castration of, 44; founded school, 44 *et seq.*
ABRAHAM, 88
ADAM, 87, 89
ADAMITES, nudist community, 28
ADULTERY: in Classical Greece, 112; in Rome, 114; in the Middle Ages, 116-118; in 19th Century Europe, 144; punishment of, 149-152, 241; artificial insemination, adultery ?, 152; ritualistic and orgiastic, 153-154; in the Dark Ages, 212 *et seq.*
ÆBUTIUS, exposed Roman Bacchanalian orgies, 204
ÆGISTHOS, lover of Clytæmnestra, slayer of her own husband, 112
ÆSCHYLUS, Greek dramatist: *Oresteia*, 112; *Danaïdes*, 197
ÆSCULAPIUS, Greek god of medicine, plate 3
AGAMEMNON, husband of Clytæmnestra, *q.v.*, and father of Electra, *q.v.*, and Orestes, *q.v.*, slain by his own wife, 112
AGAPEMONITES, 55 *et seq.;* 56
AGONES, Greek gymnastic contests, 202
AGRIPPA, second husband of the elder Julia, *q.v.*, 114, *et seq.*
AGRIPPINA II, mother of the Roman Emperor, Nero, 115, 116 *et seq.*
AHMED-AL-BEDAWI, Feast of, 159
AHRIMAN DEVAN, Power of Evil in the Zoroastrian faith, *q.v.*, 215
AHURA MAZDA, Power of Good or Light in the Zoroastrian faith, *q.v.*, 215
AKAMBAS of E. Africa, the, 25
ALBA, Duchess of, sister of Empress Eugénie, *q.v.*, 147

ALBANI, Franciso, Italian painter, 120
ALBERT, Duke, Bavarian champion of Catholicism, 217
ALBERT, Prince, consort of Queen Victoria of England, 140, 193
ALCIBIADES, bisexual Greek, 112 *et seq.*, 113
ALEXANDER VI, incestuous and licentious Pope, 43, 89, 119, 169, 212, 222
ALEXANDER the Great, 163, 164 *et seq.*, 166
ALFRED, King, 72 *et seq.*
ALLAH, Muslim name for God, 149 *et seq.*
ALLEN, Frederick Lewis, writer: ' Only Yesterday ', 194
ALLGROVE, George, writer: ' Love in the East ', 149
AMBULATRICES, Roman prostitutes who walked the streets, 167
ANAITIS, Persian Mother- goddess, 162, 165
ANDERSON, Sir Robert, Assistant Commissioner of the Metropolitan Police, 224
ANGEL DANCERS, 55
ANGEL RAPHAEL, the, 105
ANGLO-SAXON Synod, 84
ANNE, Lady Castlehaven, victim of husband's lechery, 182
ANTHESTERIA, the, Greek wine festival, 199
ANTONIA I, daughter of Mark Antony, 115
ANTONY, Mark, 88, 114, 115, 210
ANU, a Japanese tribe, 72
APELLES, painter: ' Aphrodite rising from the Sea ', 164
APHRODITE, Greek goddess of love, 4, 112, 158, 159, 160 *et seq.;* as Porne, 162, 163, 196; as Peribaso, 162; as Trymalitis, 162; foals of, 162; corsairs of, 165; at Paphos, 197-198; as Kalliypgos, 198; as Venus in Rome, 203
APHRODISIA, the, 196-198
APOLLO GARDENS of Victorian times, 142

WHARE TAPERE, Polynesian pleasure-houses, 48
WHARTON, Duke of, Georgian Buck, 184
WHITING, J. A., writer: 'Becoming a Kwoma', 50
WIFE-LENDING, 108
WILDE, Oscar, dramatist and poet: 'The Ballad of Reading Gaol', 220
WILKES, John, author of 'Essay on Woman', 136
WILLIAM IV, King of England, 139, 140
WILLOUGHBY, Agnes, courtesan, 192
WILSON, Mary, brothel-keeper, 187
WILSON, Mr. Harry, lawyer, 233
WINCHESTER, Bishop of, owner of brothels, 169
WINCHESTER GEESE, nick-name of English prostitutes, 169
WINSLOW, Mr. Forbes, calligraphist, 229 *et seq.*
WITCHES' HAMMER, the, work by German witch-hunters, Jakob Sprenger, *q.v.*, and Heinrich Institoris, *q.v.*, 216
WITCHES' SABBATH, the, 214
WITCH Trials, 215
WIVES for Sale, 75
WOLFENDEN COMMITTEE on Homosexuality, 130; on Prostitution, 189
WORLD WAR I: 1914-1918, 193 *et seq.*

XENOCRATES, Greek philosopher, 164
XENOPHON of Corinth, double victor at the Olympiad of 464 B.C., 163, 196
XERXES, ancient Persian monarch, conqueror of part of Greece and plunderer of the Athenian Acropolis, 164

YACATAN Indians, 72
YAHAVEH, Hebrew name for God, 87, 151, 237
YAKUTS, the, a tribe of Siberia, 70, 90
YONI, Hindu term for vagina, 156

ZEPHYRUS, Greek god of the wind, 200
ZEUS, Father of the Greek gods, 8, 76
ZOROASTER, prophet of ancient Persia, 24, 88, 215
ZOROASTRIANISM, religion founded by Zoroaster, *q.v.*, and followed today by the Parsis of India, 88, 93, 215
ZOROASTRIANS, followers of Zoroaster, *q.v.*, 24
ZULU tribes, the, 84
ZUNI tribe, the, 8, 23
ZWINGLI, Ulrich, Swiss priest at Zürich who spoke out against the enforced celibacy of the priesthood, 246 *et seq.*